T0279398

# RHYTHMS OF RESISTANCE AND RESILIENCE

# RHYTHMS

## OF

# RESISTANCE

## AND

# RESILIENCE

How Black Washingtonians Used
Music and Sports
in the Fight for Equality

Maurice Jackson

GEORGETOWN UNIVERSITY PRESS / WASHINGTON, DC

The publisher is not responsible for third-party websites or their content. URL links were active at time of publication.

Library of Congress Cataloging-in-Publication Data

Library of Congress Cataloging-in-Publication Data

Names: Jackson, Maurice, 1950- author.
Title: Rhythms of resistance and resilience : how Black Washingtonians used
    music and sports in the fight for equality / Maurice Jackson.
Description: Washington, DC : Georgetown University Press, 2024. | Includes
    bibliographical references and index.
Identifiers: LCCN 2024019178 (print) | LCCN 2024019179 (ebook) | ISBN
    9781647125219 (hardcover) | ISBN 9781647125226 (ebook)
Subjects: LCSH: African Americans--Washington (D.C.)—Music—History
    and criticism. | Music—Washington (D.C.)—History and criticism. | Jazz—
    Washington (D.C.)—History and criticism. | African American musicians—
    Washington (D.C.) | African American singers—Washington (D.C.) | African
    Americans—Sports—Washington (D.C.)—History. | Sports—Washington
    (D.C.)—History. | African American athletes—Washington (D.C.) | African
    Americans—Civil rights—Washington (D.C.)—History. | Washington (D.C.)—
    History. | Washington (D.C.)—Race relations—History.
Classification: LCC ML200.8.W3 J33 2024 (print) | LCC ML200.8.W3 (ebook) |
    DDC 780.9753—dc23/eng/20240429
LC record available at https://lccn.loc.gov/2024019178
LC ebook record available at https://lccn.loc.gov/2024019179

♾ This paper meets the requirements of ANSI/NISO Z39.48-1992 (Permanence of Paper).

26 25      9 8 7 6 5 4 3 2 First printing

Printed in the United States of America

Cover design by Faceout Studio, Amanda Hudson
Interior design by Classic City Composition

To Laura, Lena, Miles, and Rowan, and to Cilaos Pearl Jackson Gerety, who has brought such joy to us all. And to my late friends Charlie and Ruth Haden, Ron Clark, Randy Weston, Hank Jones, and Geri Allen, who have taught me so much and given me even more to think about and to listen to.

# CONTENTS

# FOREWORD

The nation is like our selves, together
seen in our various scenes, sets where ever we are
what ever we are doing, is what the nation
is
doing or
not doing
is what the nation
is
being or
not being.

—Amiri Baraka

The history of Washington, DC, is also a history of sound. The sound of Black music, or maybe even the birth of sound, when one acknowledges the nation's capital as being the birthplace of Duke Ellington—the pianist, the composer, the conductor, and the lover of baseball. Is it possible baseball was his mistress, and not jazz?

Historian Maurice Jackson has written a fascinating book that flows better than the Potomac River. Here are the well-known as well the lesser-known, individuals who shaped African American culture in music and sports. Jackson writes as a fan of both. He writes about Charles Douglass (the son of the famous abolitionist), who organized two baseball teams in the city where his father resided. Here we find Jackson providing us with the narrative of another Douglass.

*Rhythms of Resistance and Resilience* is filled with many facts that tend to glitter and together create a necklace of extremely useful information. The book is a brief encyclopedia, a handbook of and guide into Washington history. It reads like something produced back in the 1930s by the Works Progress Administration: essential as well as interesting, nuanced and analytical.

Jackson writes about music and sports while holding up a canvas that captures the colorful motion of history. People and events are placed against the backdrop of world wars and the movement of people amid the Great Migration. Jackson tells the tales of Black achievers like Will Marion Cook and James Reese Europe. Space in this book is given to basketball coach John Thompson as well as Lulu Vere Childress, the music director at Howard University for many years.

Washington was a very segregated city. A color line existed outside the White House and beyond the shadow of the Capitol. Jackson highlights the contributions of Ahmet and Nesuhi Ertegun, who opened the Turkish Embassy to jazz, documenting the cracks that would break down the walls of separation.

This is a book to dance with. Jackson writes from his heart, and the love he has for both music and sports will make one shimmy like a baseball player for the Homestead Grays, rounding the bases and heading home.

—E. Ethelbert Miller

# INTRODUCTION

The ideas for this book were polyrhythmic, describing many circular currents. A few summers ago my family and I were vacationing near Cambridge, Maryland, along the trails where Harriet Tubman had led enslaved Africans to freedom. The winds were blowing slightly, the leaves were crackling, the birds were chirping, the insects were doing their thing, and the creeks were flowing. As I walked, somehow I found myself listening to a conversation with three thoroughly unique human beings: the baseball player Leroy "Satchel" Paige and the musician Louis—or "Satchmo" or "Pops"—Armstrong were whooping it up with Tubman, called the "Moses" of her people. Each of these people were known as griots, as raconteurs, as tellers of truth through the telling of tall tales. I thought of how Tubman had led men, women, and children to freedom along these trails in the pitch of night, with hound dogs and armed vigilantes on her heels. She never lost a soul along the route and always had a story to tell. I thought of how these two Black men, born into poverty, became the best in the world at what they did, and of how, through sports (baseball) and music (jazz), they had done so much to both explore and seek to change the human condition. Music and sports have been vital to Black self-expression and survival. One can be good at them or not so good—but still enjoy both.

When my older brother Akeelee and I lived with our grandmother, Ma Pearl, for a few years in Grove Hill, Alabama (we were born in Newport News, Virginia), in the Piney Woods on the edge of the Blackbelt, where cotton was king and white bigotry and hatred was all around, we would go down to Brother Pace's and Miss Mary's house. Before I had even heard of Harriet Tubman, Satchel, or Pops, there was Brother Pace, who told fantastic tales of hitting the baseball farther than Buck Leonard, or "Hammering" Hank Aaron. He had a "bucket catch" like Willie "the Say Hey Kid" Mays, and could outthrow Satchel Paige. He could outrun the Cleveland Browns' Jim Brown. And he was stronger than the Baltimore Colts' "Big Daddy" Lipscomb. We were Colts fans in the days when the Washington

Redskins refused to integrate. Baltimore had other Black players, like Big Jim Parker, Ordell Brasse, John Mackey, and the great Lenny Moore. Brother Pace could out rebound the Boston Celtics' Bill Russell and outscore the Philadelphia 76ers' Wilt Chamberlain. Because the Celtics had African American players like Russell, Sam Jones, K. C. Jones, and Satch Sanders, they were our team.

Brother Pace also said he had played guitar with Pops and King Oliver and sang with Vera Middleton and Louis Jordan. He said he had played music on a Mississippi steamboat, where he was also the ship's captain, taking the blues from the Deep South to Chicago. He told jokes that referenced comedians Pigmeat Markham and Moms Mabley. It was from Brother Pace that I learned the fine art of meaningful storytelling.

Ma Pearl had an old Victrola with a bad needle in her tool shed, and a bunch of 78 RPM records that I still have. We would go and play the records after a Bro Pace story. There was Count Basie, Paul Whiteman, Jack Teagarden, Louis Armstrong, and Miss Peggy Lee. There was the Golden Gate Bridge Quartet singing wonderful versions of the Negro spirituals. Ma Pearl would listen to the *Texaco Hour*'s classical music and the old-time *Gospel Hour* on her radio.

Musically, it was my stepdad, Pete Ballard, and mother, Zeola (Zee), who gave me jazz. He was a member of the old US Army Air Force Band during the Second World War. After he mustered out, he played with Dinah Washington, Earl Grant, Lloyd Price, and Ruth Brown. Whenever the legends—Nat King Cole, Wes Montgomery, Brown, and Jimmy Smith, Grant, and Price—came to town, some would stop by our little shotgun house at 1231 31st Street in Newport News, Virginia, or our folks would see them at performances. They knew Ella Fitzgerald and Pearl Bailey, both of whom were born in Newport News. My brothers, Akeelee and Daryl, and I loved to ride in Pete's milk truck turned band-wagon, often loaded with their instruments and a sign on the side: *The Mellow Tones*. Pete and Zee helped form the Los Aficionados Society, which often met at the Dochiki Civic and Social Club, the sister club of the Left Bank Jazz Society of Baltimore. The building where they met still sits in the east end of Newport News.

In 1968, the inaugural year of the Hampton Jazz Festival, the events were held at Armstrong Stadium and football field at the Hampton Normal and Industrial Institute (now Hampton University). The stadium is named after the school's founder, Samuel Chapman Armstrong, who had commanded regiments of the US Colored Troops during the Civil War and later worked with the Freedmen's Bureau under Reconstruction. That first festival featured artists Cannonball Adderley, the Count Basie Orchestra, Gary Burton, the Dizzy Gillespie Quintet, Earl "Fatha" Hines, Skip James, Ramsey Lewis, the Herbie Mann Quintet, the Thelonious Monk Quartet, Mongo Santamaria, the Archie Shepp Quintet, the

Nina Simone Trio, Willie "the Lion" Smith, Dionne Warwick, Muddy Waters and his Blues Band, and the Original Tuxedo Jazz Band. Cars and busloads came down from DC. The second year, 1969, brought such notables as Cannonball Adderley, Booker T & the MGs, the George Benson Quarter, the Dave Brubeck Trio with Gerry Mulligan, Ray Charles, Miles Davis, the Duke Ellington Orchestra, Herbie Hancock, the Roland Kirk Sextet, Nina Simone and Quarter, Sly and the Family Stone, Sun Ra and Solar Arkestra, Young-Holt Unlimited, and the United House of Prayer Choir. Consuela Lee, the pianist, arranger, and aunt of filmmaker Spike Lee (and who was assistant music director on Lee's second film, *School Daze*), taught music theory at Hampton and also performed at the festivals.

Around that time Julius Erving, Rick Barry, and George Gervin, the Hall of Fame hoopsters, were playing for the Virginia Squires as part of the old American Basketball Association. The Squires also had crowd favorite Fat Taylor. Based in Norfolk, the team sometimes played games in Richmond, Roanoke, and Hampton. The Central Intercollegiate Athletic Association (CIAA), a division of Black colleges that included Virginia Union, Howard University, and North Carolina A&T, held special interest. Earl "the Pearl" Monroe, from Philadelphia, played at Winston-Salem State under legendary coach Clarence "Big House" Gaines. Before playing for the New York Knicks, the Pearl was a Washington favorite as a player for the Baltimore Bullets, before the team moved to DC. One main attraction was Norfolk State, where we went to see the New York playground legend Richard "Pee Wee" Kirkland. At the time, *Sports Illustrated* called Kirkland "maybe the fastest man in college basketball"—years before Georgetown's Allen Iverson claimed that mantle.[1]

At Norfolk State, Pee Wee teamed with future Washington Bullets Hall of Famer Bobby Dandridge. Kirkland had been scouted by both Red Auerbach of the Boston Celtics and Red Holzman of the New York Knicks, and ultimately was drafted by the Chicago Bulls. Instead, he chose the street life and ended up in federal prison, where he again set the concrete court ablaze. In his book *The Reckoning*, Randall Robinson, the founder of Washington-based TransAfrica, the organization that played a leading role in the United States in the struggle against South African apartheid and for the freedom of Nelson Mandela , wrote about Kirkland's path from basketball savant to street hustler to community organizer.[2] Robinson had attended Virginia Union, where another CIAA Legend, Henry Boyd Hucles, Sr., coached football, basketball, swimming, and tennis.

When I came to Washington in the 1970s, the jazz clubs I visited were: the One Step Down; Harrold's Rouge & Jar; the Childe Harold, where I saw Roy Haynes; and Woodies Hilltop Lounge, where I saw the DC-born Charley Rouse. I also went to Howard University's Cramton Auditorium, where I saw Lee Morgan and

Donald Byrd. Later I checked out DC Space, where the Avant Garde played. I saw Sam Rivers and Marion Brown. When I could afford it I went to Blues Alley, where Dizzy Gillespie once invited me to his dressing room and signed my copy of his book, *To Be or Not to Bop*. One night decades ago at the One Step Down changed my life musically. Prior to seeing Charlie Haden and JoAnne Brackeen there, I had bought many of Ornette Coleman's records, with Charlie on bass, at the DuPont Circle Record Store. That same DuPont Circle office building housed the Washington office of the Southern Christian Leadership Conference (SCLC), where I once worked, and the National Sharecroppers Fund. At the store I bought Charlie's first Liberation Music Orchestra album. In those days you could spend hours in any record store, reading liner notes on the backs of the albums and learning music history. The night I met Charlie we spoke of politics—of the Spanish Civil War, of his arrest in Portugal for supporting the People's Movement for the Liberation of Angola, of the Front for the Liberation of Mozambique, and of the African Party for the Independence of Guinea and Cape Verde and their fight for independence against Portuguese colonialism. Over the next three decades, whenever he was in the United States, Charlie would call me, saying, "Hey, man." I would speak with him perhaps once a week. Our conversations were mostly politics—but also music, especially his love of Bach. In several of those calls we spoke of Chile, of the US-supported 1973 coup, of her people's struggles against the regime of Augusto Pinochet, and of the song of the resistance, "The People United Shall Never Be Defeated." We also spoke of the anthem of the African National Congress, "NKosi Sikeleli Afric," and the South African peoples resistance to apartheid. I encouraged Charlie to record both, and to my surprise and delight he did. Charlie asked me to write the liner notes to two of his and Hank Jones's CDs, *Steal Away: Spirituals, Folksongs and Hymns* and *Come Sunday*. When he first asked, I suggested he instead ask a famous, now infamous comedian and jazz lover to do it. I am glad that Charlie ignored my suggestions and insisted that I write the notes. This collaboration gave me a new understanding of the power that music and lyrics have for understanding and analyzing society. Sometimes when Charlie came to town he brought two special musicians with him—the singer Bill Henderson and the drummer Lawrence Marable. They both were great storytellers, making Brother Pace's colorful tales about sports and music come back to me.

When I came to DC, the "Commanders" (the one-time segregated "Redskins") were the team. Their games against the Dallas Cowboys were legendary, and on any given Sunday, people from all over the city donned Washington's burgundy and gold or Dallas's blue and white, bantering before, during, and after the game days and the next days at work or school. I did not attend many games, but a few times, John Wilson—who became the Ward 2 councilman and later chair of the DC Council—or David A. Clarke—who had been my boss at the Washington office of the SCLC and who became Ward 1 council chair and later the chair of the DC Council—or Anne Forester Holloway, the SCLC policy director and later US Ambassador to Mali—would give me a free ticket. The old RFK Stadium literally rocked back and forth. In those days people in the stands were not bifurcated or separated by race and economic status. The rich and the not so well off, Black and white, sat together.

In the late 1970s I worked at the United Planning Organization (UPO) as a self-taught demographer and analyst. I mapped the economic plight of inner-city Washington Black and Latinx people. At one UPO center my boss was the iconic Jerry "the Bama" Washington (a.k.a. "Wash"). Wash was a US Air Force veteran who had retired after twenty-three years with his pension and his UPO job; he knew several of the players on the Washington Bullets, including Elvin "the Big E" Hayes, Bobby Dandridge, and Phil Chenier, and he would take me to games. He had attended Morehouse College with Martin Luther King Jr. A political conservative compared to me, Wash was a friend of Ronald Reagan's advisor Lee Atwater, a blues lover. Nonetheless, we bonded during hours listening to James Moody and John Coltrane in his crowded UPO office, plus works by Charlie Parker, June Cristy, and Billy Eckstine. We listened to Dinah Washington, and he told me stories about her and her onetime husband, the Hall of Fame Detroit Lions linebacker Dick "Night Train" Lane. I went with Wash to guitarist Bill Harris's Pigfoot restaurant and nightclub, where he was as well-known as the musicians, and this was before he began his WPFW radio programs. On Saturdays Wash hosted *The Bama Hour*, which featured blues, and on Sundays he had *The Other Side of The Bama*, featuring jazz. He once told the *Washington Post*, "the Saturday show is bib overalls and work clothes; Sunday is sharkskin suit, what you'd wear to church."[3]

In Washington, DC, the nation's capital, music and sports have always played a central role in the lives of African Americans and served as a barometer of wider social conflict and social progress everywhere. Sports clubs and ball games, jam sessions and concerts, have served to entertain and to enlighten, to encourage and at times to offer a means of escape from the harsh realities of everyday life. Along the way many Blacks have used their skills and their determination to learn and develop their crafts in music and sports and to develop meaningful careers. Using their creative genius, some have improved their lot and found ways to cope with day-to-day racism, to be a credit to their communities, and to bring joy to those who watched them perform their craft.

Because so many Black people came to Washington from the Deeper South, the music of the Negro spirituals, the blues, and jazz found their voices in the city. Will Marion Cook and James Reese Europe were among the city's first musical progenitors. Cook, born in Washington, and Europe, born in Mobile, Alabama, but raised in the capital city, were creative innovators, moving from one genre of music to the next. Cook, a friend of Frederick Douglass, trained at the Oberlin Conservatory and moved with ease between classical music and working with poet Paul Laurence Dunbar. In Europe's case, he moved from performing marches to writing his own symphonies to forming the Clef Club, one of the first musicians' unions, as well as leading a band in wartime and at the same time performing heroically on the battlefield as a member of the famed Harlem Hellfighters.[4]

Washington became an international focal point in the Black struggle for equality in the 1930s, when, for one of the first times in modern history, large numbers of Black and white people, including First Lady Eleanor Roosevelt, bonded in mass protest after the Daughters of the American Revolution denied the world-famous opera singer Marian Anderson the right to perform at Constitution Hall. Although Anderson did not win that battle, a more important victory eventually came when, on Easter Sunday 1939, over seventy-five thousand people gathered at the Lincoln Memorial to see her perform. Millions more worldwide heard this call for equality on their radios. With that concert the Lincoln Memorial became a gathering place of protest for democracy. This was most clearly evident when Martin Luther King Jr. led the March on Washington in 1963.

Duke Ellington, Washington's greatest musical ambassador and one of the greatest in world history, was born and came to prominence here. In 1917 he formed The Duke's Serenaders, and the rest, as they say, is history. His more than one thousand compositions, from "Take the A Train" to "Mood Indigo," still enthrall and give proof to the creative genius of Black people.

Jazz has become the world's music, and among its greatest adherents were the Turkish brothers Ahmet and Nesuhi Ertegun, whose father was the Turkish ambassador to the United States in the 1930s. The two men organized one of the first pubic integrated events in the city at the Jewish Community Center at 1529 16th Street NW (16th and Q). The event was historic in itself: two foreign-born Muslim men presenting African American music at a Jewish Community Center. In a real way it paved the way for interracial cooperation that often seems missing today.

Early jazz musicians like Jelly Roll Morton once called the city home. Lead Belly, born Huddie William Ledbetter, recorded "The Bourgeois Blues" in the city in 1937, as a protest to the rigid class and color lines that whites and even well-off African Americans had erected. Some of the words have stood the test of time in a city where caste discrimination has been as rigid as color and class discrimination:

Me and my wife run all over town
And everywhere we go, the people would turn us down
It's a bourgeois town
I got the bourgeois blues
Gonna spread the news all around.

Black women blues performers like Elizabeth Cotton, who recorded "Freight Train" (first recorded in 1958), were examples of how music portrayed the moment. They played a central role that led to events like the Smithsonian Institution's Folklife Festival, held annually around July Fourth.

Much like music, sports can unify people or it can bring out the worst in them. When Frederick Douglass's youngest son, Charles, joined the 54th Massachusetts Regiment, he became one of the first Black men to enlist in the Union Army during the Civil War. Charles, also one of the first African American clerks in the Freedman's Bureau in 1867, helped organize two Black baseball teams in Washington. While neither Black nor white teams were integrated, they did play each other at a field called the White Lot, located near where African Americans lived in Foggy Bottom and not far from the White House. Presidents Andrew Johnson and Ulysses S. Grant were known to stop by to catch a few innings at the field, where the American Cricket Clubs also played. Unfortunately, by 1873, under the guise of security concerns for the president, Blacks were denied access to the fields and told to apply for permission to play, a permission never granted. While the field had no "Colored only" signs, as with the rest of official Washington, African Americans confronted a whites-only mentality and a whites-only reality.

When professional baseball came to the city, the Washington Senators played their home games at the Old Olympic Grounds at 7th and Florida Avenue NW, near Howard University. Blacks who wanted to attend games could sit only in the section behind right field. It did not matter much, because African Americans went to the games of their favorite team, the Homestead Grays of the Negro Leagues. The Grays split their home games between Washington and Pittsburgh but could use the stadium, renamed Griffith Field after its owner, Calvin Griffith, only when the white team was away. The irony of the segregationist policies was that the Black team sold more tickets and generated more revenue than the white team did. Griffith was also the owner most steadfast against the integration of baseball.

Football was no different. When George Preston Marshall bought the Boston Redskins in 1937 and brought the team to Washington, it became the first professional football team based below the Mason-Dixon Line. It became known as "the Team of the South." The team never allowed Black players during the twenty-four years it played at Griffith Stadium. The owner was so racially backward and so against change or progress that he long resisted updating the lines of the team song. It originally went:

> Hail to the Redskins,
> Hail victory,
> Braves on the warpath,
> Fight for old Dixie.

The last lines were eventually changed to "Fight for old DC." At games the fight song was fired up right after the team played the segregationist song "Dixie." If any ticketholders protested the melodies, their protests were not registered nor heard. Over time sportswriters like Sam Lacy, an African American, and Shirley Povich, a Jewish American, joined with the National Association for the Advancement of Colored People (NAACP) to pressure the team and the federal government for a policy change. Finally, in 1962 the first African American, future Hall of Famer Bobby Mitchell, was added to the team.

Individual African American men and women made momentous contributions to sports and to society. E. B. Henderson, a graduate of Dunbar High School, spent two summers at Harvard College, studying sports and physical training.[5] While in New England he learned the game of basketball from lessons imparted by the game's creator, James Naismith.[6] He also gained a working knowledge of soccer and rugby. He did not just teach sports—he used sports to "promote the well-being of Blacks."

John R. Thompson Jr., coach of the Georgetown University Basketball Team, was a product of segregated Washington. I attended my first Georgetown basketball game before starting graduate school, in the company of three Georgetown history professors—Marcus Rediker, Jim Collins, and the late Hisham Sharabi—at the old Cap Centre in Landover, Maryland. I once wrote an article in the *Washington Afro-American* about Coach Thompson long before I studied with these scholars. Thompson used sports as vehicle of change and a maker of men. When the Georgetown Hoyas defeated the University of Houston for the NCAA Championship on April 2, 1984, he was asked about being the first Black coach to win the title. He was forceful in his response: "I'm not interested in being the first or only black coach to do anything, because that implies that I'm also the first with the ability."[7]

When the Washington football team won Super Bowl XVII in 1983, the *Washington Post* headline read "City's Soul on a Roll," as the team had defeated the Miami Dolphins 27–17 in Pasadena, California.[8] Tens of thousands celebrated, jumping on cars and blocking intersections. One Pepco worker summed it all up: "This town has never been this way before ... the team has brought us so close together. Never mind everybody's everyday problems."[9]

A few years later Doug Williams, a graduate of the HBCU Grambling State University, led the team to victory over the Denver Broncos in Super Bowl XXII. He had one of the best performances of a quarterback in NFL history and was named the game's MVP, the first African American quarterback to start and win a Super Bowl game. As Thompson would agree, he was not the first Black quarterback with the ability, just the first to be given the opportunity. He said: "I knew it was history-making. I'm just glad to be a part of Martin Luther King's dream."[10]

That team endeared itself to many because, in a season where a players' strike began after the second game, it was the only team with no players crossing the picket line. Labor and community groups showed support with solidarity rallies in the RFK Stadium parking lot. Those victory celebrations for the Washington football team and the Georgetown Hoyas to this day stand as among the most racially, socially, and economically diverse gatherings the city has ever seen.

The ideas for this book are also rooted in the life of a racially mixed family from Washington, DC. In our home, as my wife, Laura, and I raised our now-grown children, Lena and Miles, we insisted, with little resistance, that their schoolwork had to be balanced with music and sports. We saw how both outlets enhanced their lives and how they enhanced ours too. Both children played basketball and soccer at Jelleff Community Center Boys & Girls Club, which to my mind is one of the most integrated and diverse places in DC, bringing kids from all over the city to one of the most segregated parts of town, Georgetown.[11]

Both kids also played in the DC Youth Orchestra and the National Cathedral Orchestra. Like Jelleff's, the DCYO was an integrated place. The DCYO and Jelleff's were far more racially diverse than their own school or any schools in the city, both in the young people who were in the orchestra or on the teams and in the families who came out to hear or watch them play.

Amiri and Amina Baraka came down to Washington from Newark, New Jersey, a few times to watch the Super Bowl at our house. I often invited him to my classes at Georgetown. Few leaders in American letters possessed a fuller knowledge of the literature of the world, from Langston Hughes to Maya Angelou, from Aimee Cesare to Nazim Hikmet, from Pablo Neruda to Jacques Romain to Maxim Gorky to Nicolas Guillen to Washington's own Sterling Brown and Georgia Douglass Johnson. The man knew his letters and he knew his jazz. And he knew sports. Along with a few jazz buddies from the Listening Group, at halftime we would talk music and sports. They went hand in hand. Baraka had attended Howard University, and we both knew that it was not coincidental that around the same time in the early 1970s that Donald Byrd was creating the Jazz

Studies Program at Howard, the Howard Soccer Team came to the attention of the city, the nation, and the broader African and Caribbean world, less than two decades after many of her nations won independence. This book seeks to make those connections.

The people, the organizations, the moments, and the movements recorded in this book are part of Doug Williams's and my own dream: for equality and social progress. Music and sports will not in of itself bring forth that dream. But they can help bring people together, with rhythm and in harmony.

**Notes**

1. Quoted in Vincent M. Mallozzi, "The Legend of Pee Wee Kirkland Grows," *New York Times,* January 12, 1997.

2. Robinson, *The Reckoning.*

3. Bart Barnes, "Disc Jockey Jerry 'The Bama' Washington Dies," *Washington Post,* October 4, 1994.

4. Miller, *Union Divided,* 41.

5. Henderson, *The Grandfather of Black Basketball.*

6. Henderson, 61.

7. Ken Denlinger, "Thompson Wants to Divvy Up the Pride," *Washington Post,* April 3, 1984, D1. In 1982, when asked how he felt about being the first Black coach to reach the Final Four, Thompson answered, "I resent the hell out of that question; it implies that I'm the first Black coach *capable* of making the Final Four. That's not close to true. I'm just the first one who was given the opportunity to get here" (italics in original). See John Feinstein, "Thompson and I Argued Plenty of Times," *Washington Post,* September 1, 2020, D1.

8. Christian Williams, "A City's Soul on a Roll," *Washington Post,* January 31, 1983, D1.

9. Blaine Harden, "Touchdown Gallop Sparks Jubilation in Washington," *Washington Post,* January 31, 1983. Laura and I were among the celebrators in Adams Morgan that day.

10. Liz Clarke, "For Black Quarterbacks, Williams Indeed Was the MVP," *Washington Post,* January 31, 1988.

11. Tracy L. Scott, "An American Ideal: Diversity Makes Club a Melting Pot," *Washington Post,* September 30, 1999.

# PART I

# Music

## Music Is the Message

We who believe in freedom will not rest.
—From "Ella's Song" by Sweet Honey in
the Rock. Dedicated to Ella Baker.

# 1

# THE EARLY YEARS

## From Slavery to Freedom

Washington is the home to two of the founders of "Great Black Music," Will Marion Cook and James Reese Europe.[1] A concert violinist, Cook received excellent classical training in both the United States and Europe; as an adult he found inspiration in traditional African American folk tunes and spirituals, incorporating them into his compositions. Bandleader and composer Europe was outspoken in his belief that "we colored people have our own music that is part of us. It's the product of our souls; it's been created by the sufferings and miseries of our race."[2] Both men lived in Washington when they were young, and their outlooks on life were inevitably shaped by DC's social landscape.

Between 1890 and 1918 the African American population in Washington grew dramatically. Blacks moved to the city in large numbers to flee the lynch mobs, political and economic oppression, and the poverty of the South. The prospect of steady employment for the federal government provided unique opportunities for African Americans and accounted in part for this migration. These federal jobs also contributed to the emergence of a Black middle class, who generally lived near Howard University. Poet Paul Laurence Dunbar wrote in 1901, "Here comes together the flower of colored citizenship from all over the country . . . the breeziness of the West here meets the refinement of the East, the warmth and grace of the South, the culture and fine reserve of the North."[3]

Within this milieu Washington native Cook emerged as one of the founders of Great Black Music. Born in 1869, Cook was the son of John Harwell Cook, dean of Howard University Law School. At age fifteen Will began violin studies and composition at Oberlin Conservatory at Oberlin College in Ohio.[4] Frederick Douglass and members of DC's First Congregational Church, where Douglass had organized a recital, raised money for Cook to attend the Hochschule für Musik in Berlin, Germany, from 1887 to 1889.[5] The *Indianapolis Freeman,* an early African American newspaper, noted "the formation of a new Washington, D.C. orchestra with Frederick Douglass as President and Willie Cook as director."[6]

Will Marion Cook, a native of Washington, DC, was the son of John Hartwell Cook, one of the first to graduate from Howard University Law School and one of the school's first deans. Trained as a concert violinist at the National Conservatory in New York, Will Marion was a composer, conductor, and choir and orchestra director. Like one of his teachers, Antonín Dvořák, Cook believed that African Americans ought to use their own folk traditions to compose their music and guide their performances. Cook taught and greatly influenced Duke Ellington and composed music to the lyrics of Paul Laurence Dunbar. Flickr, courtesy University of Illinois Urbana-Champaign.

The orchestra held its first concert on September 26, 1890, at the Grand Army Hall. *New York Age* wrote that "Mr. Cook plays so well and throws so much work that the rest of the orchestra cannot but partake largely of his enthusiasm and strive go do good work."[7] According to James Reese Europe's biographer Reid Badger, the orchestra "failed to last a year—despite the backing of Frederick Douglass and the leaders of Washington's Black society—in part because it followed too closely the European 'high culture' model."[8]

Cook then attended the National Conservatory of Music of America in New York City, studying under the Czech-born composer and conductor Antonín Dvořák. Dvořák had been recruited to the Conservatory in 1892; in 1893, not many months after his arrival, he composed the symphony *From the New World*

Piano sheet music of Will Marion Cook and Frank Clifford Harris's "My Lady, Nicotine (Smoke! Smoke!)," ca. 1910. H. von Tilzer Music Pub., New York, courtesy Library of Congress Music Division, call no. M1508.

(no. 9 in E minor), which incorporates American folk tunes. Dvořák's association at the Conservatory with African American composer Harry Burleigh inspired him to write "Goin' Home."[9] In an interview published in the *New York Tribune* on May 21, 1893, Dvořák said, "I am now satisfied that the future of this music must be founded upon what are called Negro melodies. This must be the real foundation of any serious and original school of composition to be developed in the United States. . . . These are the folk songs of America, and your composers must turn to them. All of the great musicians have borrowed from the songs of the common people." Dvořák also said, "In the Negro melodies of America I discover all that is needed for a great and noble school of music."[10]

A few days later the *Tribune* editorialized that "Dr. Dvořák's explicit announcement that his newly completed symphony reflects the Negro melodies, upon which . . . the coming American school must be based . . . will be a surprise to the world."[11] For three consecutive days, May 26–28 of that same week, the *Paris Herald* carried frontpage critiques of Dvořák's ideas and theories as expressed by Anton Bruckner, the Viennese organist and composer, and Anton Rubinstein, the composer and pianist and founder of the Saint Petersburg Conservatory. Interviews were also conducted with the noted violinist and teacher Joseph Joachim, "a distinguished violinist and pedagogue who may have already been exposed to American Negro music through his student, Will Marion Cook."[12]

James M. Trotter, the father of famed abolitionist William Monroe Trotter, was born in Mississippi in 1842. He was freed along with his mother and sisters by his white father and sent to Cincinnati. The elder Trotter first studied music at the Gilmore School founded by Hiram S. Gilmore, a Methodist minister. At the school, "black students were taught in the same intense Protestant ethic, and classical tradition of the best New England colleges."[13] He passed to his son the most important lessons he had gained from the school: "An unwillingness to be intimidated by powerful white men, and a healthy skepticism of anybody, black or white, who criticized former slaves' academic ambition."[14] While teaching at a colored school in Ohio, Trotter journeyed to Boston, where he joined the Massachusetts 55th Regiment. In 1863 he became only the second Black man to rise to the rank of lieutenant. After being mustered out, Trotter was one of the first Black men to work in what is now the United States Post Office.

In 1878 James Trotter wrote *Music and Some Highly Musical People*, a volume said to be one of the first comprehensive study of any form of music written in the United States and "the first book-length study of African American music history."[15] Dvořák appears to have been familiar with this volume. As music and jazz historian Burton W. Peretti has written, "the first part of the book" barely mentions African Americans but "explores the beauty of music," while the second part "chronicles the activities of black concert singers, bandleaders, pianists, choruses, opera companies, and pedagogues."[16] Trotter did write about "color-prejudice, the extent of whose terrible, blighting power none can ever imagine that do not actually meet it."[17]

The world-renowned Fisk Jubilee Singers came to town in early 1882.[18] They were told that all hotels were full. Jeremiah Rankin, the pastor of First Congregational Church and a noted abolitionist and temperance leader, was among those who sprang into action, but hotel after hotel purported to have no vacancies. One owner said he would not rent his rooms to Blacks no matter how celebrated—not even "for five hundred dollars each." Every hotel violated the Civil Rights Act of 1875. The Jubilee Singers stayed in "Colored only" rooming houses and later moved into the St. James Hotel. Despite their ordeal, the group triumphed in an appearance in the Blue Room at the White House. Pres. Chester A. Arthur wept after they sang "Steal Away," telling Rankin, "I have never in my life been so much moved."[19]

In 1887 Democratic president Grover Cleveland appointed the senior Trotter as the US recorder of deeds, then the highest-paying position an African American could hold in the US government. It was a "post that made up in cash what it lacked in political influence."[20] Frederick Douglass had held that post before Trotter, and former US senator Blanche K. Bruce held it after him.

W. E. B. Du Bois, in his classic essay "The Sorrow Song," from *The Souls of Black Folk,* wrote about the music of Black people "The Negro folk song—the rhythm cry of slavery—stands today not simply as the sole American music, but as the most beautiful expression of human experience born this side of the seas. It has been neglected, it has been persistently mistaken and misunderstood; but not-withstanding, it still remains as the singular spiritual heritage of the nation and the greatest gifts of the Negro people."[21] Frederick Douglass, the former enslaved man, had himself written of the songs Black people sang under slavery, the Negro spirituals. "I have been utterly astonished, since I came to the north, to find a per-son who could speak of singing, among slaves, as evidence of their contentment and happiness. It is impossible to conceive of a greater mistake. Slaves sing most when they are unhappy. The songs of the slaves represent the sorrows of the heart; and he is relieved by them, only as an aching heart is relieved by its tears." He adds "I have often sung to drown my sorrow, but seldom to express my happiness."[22] To many, the music that is most commonly called jazz is one of America's most unique and greatest gifts to the nation and world as it expresses both the joy and happiness and the struggles and sorrows of Black people in America.

In 1898, in collaboration with Dunbar, Cook composed the musical *Clorindy; or, The Origin of the Cakewalk.* Cook wrote that he had borrowed ten dollars and went to Washington to find Dunbar. They "got together in the basement of my brother John's rented house on Sixth Street, just below Howard University, one night at about eight o'clock . . . where without a piano or anything but the kitchen table, we finished all the songs and all the libretto and all but a few bars of the ensemble by four o'clock the next morning."[23] Drawing on African American lan-guage and melody, the one-act musical opened that year in July, the first all-Black cast to appear on Broadway in New York. After the success of *Clorindy,* accord-ing to musicologist Eileen Southern, Cook "became a conductor of syncopated orchestras and a composer of art music . . . [and] 'composer in chief' for a steady stream of musicals, most of which featured the celebrated vaudeville team of Bert Williams and George Walker."[24] Like Dvořák, Cook began to incorporate folk music into his compositions. In 1912 he published *A Collection of Negro Songs.*

Cook was extremely important to the early development of another Washington native, Duke Ellington, both in the District of Columbia and after Ellington moved to New York. In his autobiography, *Music Is My Mistress,* Ellington writes:

> Will Marion Cook, His Majesty the King of Consonance. . . . I can see him now with that beautiful mane of white hair flowing in the breeze as he and I rode uptown through Central Park. . . . It was always when I was browsing around Broadway, trying to make contacts with my music, that I would run into Dad Cook. . . . Several times, after I had played some tune I had written but not really completed, I would say, "Now, Dad, what is the logical way to develop this theme? What direction should I take?" . . . He would answer. . . . "First you find the logical way, and when you find it, avoid it, and let your inner self break through and guide you. Don't try to be anybody but yourself." That time with him was one of the best semesters I ever had in music.[25]

For the first time, in 1838, about three years after opening, the National Theatre refused to seat African Americans in the main gallery, forcing them to sit in the balcony only. In 1873 the theater refused them entry altogether. Blacks then found their own performance spaces, and from the 1870s on, African Americans attended classical, folk, church, and choral music concerts at the Lincoln Memorial Congregational Church, the Asbury United Methodist Church, the Nineteenth Street Baptist Church, and the Fifteenth Street Presbyterian Church. John Esputa founded the short-lived Colored American Opera Company in Washington, which presented its first performance of *The Doctors of Alcantara* on February 3 and 4, 1873.[26]

Henry J. Lewis organized the Amphion Glee Club in 1892. It found success performing all over the city and was active well into the 1930s. In 1902 the Samuel Coleridge-Taylor Society was formed with John Turner Layton as the musical director.[27] The next year, Harriet Gibbs Marshall (1869–1941) founded the Washington Conservatory of Music to provide young African Americans with classical musical training. She had been the first Black woman to receive a diploma in music from Oberlin College and later studied in Boston, Chicago, and eventually France before returning to DC and teaching in its public schools.[28]

A few years after Trotter's book was published, the Treble Clef Club was founded in 1897 by elite African American female musicians and music aficionados in Washington, including Marshall, Mamie F. Hilyer, and Gregoria Goins. The club followed in the tradition of other elite Black clubs formed in the 1880s and 1890s, like the Aeolian Mandolin Club, the Careno Club, and the Guitar Club.[29] Their concerts received broad support from the Washington "Upper Tens" and their out-of-town guests.[30] Goins, who was also on the Howard University music faculty, described it as "an organization of professional female musicians and music teachers [who] promote[d] concerts in Washington that emphasized the music of black composers and the history of black performers."[31] The ladies hosted salon-style discussions and presented performances, billing themselves as providing "the only high class musical entertainment that was given free in the city of Washington at that time."[32] In a city with long-simmering class and color differences among Blacks, "high class" meant the elite—and jazz was not the music at Howard University or in Black elite society. One of the Treble Clef's founders wrote:

> Jazz at that time was unknown and so determined were we that there should be no jazz on our program, we did everything we could to preserve good music. But alas, the Lafayette Players came to Howard Theater, and . . . Clarence Muse. . . . And imagine the disgust of one of our members . . . who went there and heard Muse singing "Yacky Hacky Hoolah." She was so incensed . . . she said that "the more I heard him sing it, the more I wanted to get under the seat. But imagine my surprise, next morning every house in town was playing "Yacky Hacky Hoolah."[33]

The Treble Clef Club played a major role, at Mamie F. Hyler's suggestion, in organizing a musical group to perform works composed by Samuel Coleridge-Taylor.[34] Some years later James Europe founded the Clef Club to organize and energize Black jazz musicians. With a name like the Clef Club, it would be hard to imagine that he had not heard of the Treble Clef Club.

Lulu Vere Childress, who served as the music director at Howard from 1905 until 1942, also became a mover and shaker on the cultural front.[35] Over the years, "while enriching the curriculum Lulu V. Childers also assembled an able and progressive faculty," but steered Howard away from anything that could be remotely associated with jazz.[36] She also served as the director of the Howard Choral Society, whose concerts and lecture series, as Lauren Sinclair has written, "drew big names, such as opera star Marian Anderson, a close friend" who "attracted racially mixed audiences, a Washington rarity" in this segregated city.[37]

Years later, Doris Evans McGinty, a Howard music graduate, would become a faculty member for forty-three years, serve as Music Department chair for eight, and bridge the gap between classical and jazz music. Born just a few blocks from the university's campus, McGinty was one of the first American women to earn a doctorate in musicology from Oxford University in England.[38]

In 1905 Roy Wilfred Tibbs, an Oberlin-trained pianist, also joined the Howard faculty and directed the Howard University Men's Glee Club. Tibbs later married Washington-born Lillian Evanti, the first African American known to sing with an opera company in Europe. In 1934 Evanti was also the "first African American

Portrait of Madame Lillian
Evanti made in Buenos Aires,
Argentina (undated). Courtesy
Anacostia Community
Museum of the Smithsonian
Institution, ACMA.06-016, item
PH2003.7063.045.

opera singer invited to the White House since 1882, when soprano Mathilda
Joyner sang for President Harrison," when she sang for Eleanor Roosevelt, "followed by a state luncheon."[39] Although she sang all over Europe in Italian, English,
German, and French, her 1943 performance of Verdi's *La Traviata* with the
National Negro Opera Company, founded in 1941 in Pittsburgh, Pennsylvania,
stood out to the thousands of Washingtonians, Black and white. The opera was
performed by an all-Black cast at the Watergate Theater barge that was docked
in the Potomac; the audience would sit on the steps near the Lincoln Memorial.
There, "sunset symphonies" were held from about 1935 to the mid 1960s, when
the jet noise from National Airport effectively ended the concerts.

Joseph Douglass, a grandson of Frederick Douglass, also joined the Howard
faculty, among the many who taught and performed with dignity in an often
unkind world.[40] A violinist, Douglass followed in the tracks of his grandfather
and his father, Charles, both amateur violin players. Joseph was acclaimed as "the
most talented violinist of the race," the first Black violinist to make a transcon-
tinental tour and the first violinist of any race to record with the Victor Talking
Machine Company.[41] In addition to being a tenured member of the Howard faculty, he taught at the Colored Music Settlement School in New York, which gave

him a special insight into the power of music and its effect on social conscious-ness. Leaders of the Settlement House movement, such as Jane Addams at Hull House in Chicago and Lillian Wald at the Henry Street Settlement House in New York, had come to prominence, but Blacks also played a role in the movement's rise, within organizations like the New York Colored Mission, which had been founded in 1865 by the Society of Friends, the Quakers, as the African Sabbath School Association and where Quakers and Black ministers conducted religious classes. Because the Music Settlement School in New York would not accept Blacks, violist David Mannes founded the Colored Musical Settlement School, so that, "for the first time in the history of the nation," there would be "the oppor-tunity for talented black youngsters to obtain excellent musical training at nom-inal fees."[42]

Joseph was the apple of his grandfather's eye. A picture taken in 1894 in New Bedford, Massachusetts, not long before Frederick died, shows the elder watch-ing intently as Joseph performs. Just three weeks before his death, some of the elder Douglass's lifelong friends, including Francis James Grimké, gathered at the Douglass home in Cedar Hills, in the Anacostia section of Washington, for dinner. Grimké wrote that as the meal came to an end, "all repaired to the sitting room," where Douglass commanded all to sing as he "took the lead" in singing "In Thy Cleft, O Rock of Ages" and "grandson Joseph took the lead on the violin and someone else played the piano."[43]

James Europe's youngest sister, Mary Loraine Europe, linked music programs at Howard and at Dunbar and Armstrong High Schools. A Howard graduate, she taught music at Dunbar from 1916 to 1944, while also serving as director of the choir at Lincoln Temple Congregational Church, where she said that the "high point of her life" took place when Coleridge-Taylor asked her to perform with him in 1906 "and he was "unstinting in his praise of the young pianist."[44]

The Samuel Coleridge-Taylor Society was named after the Afro-British com-poser, who became known for his trilogy of cantatas, *Hiawatha's Wedding Feast* (1898), *The Death of Minnehaha* (1899), and *Hiawatha's Departure* (1900). The society brought Coleridge-Taylor to Washington in 1904 and 1906 as part of his US tour, performing at Metropolitan African Methodist Episcopal Church.[45] In addition to the *Washington Bee,* city publications that covered local produc-tions of Great Black Music included *The Music Master, The Negro Musician,* and the official organ of the Washington Conservatory of Music, *The Negro Journal of Music.*

Coleridge-Taylor came to the United States in 1910 as the guest of the Litchfield (Connecticut) Choral Union Festival. An early pan-Africanist, he had seen the Fisk Jubilee Singers perform in England in 1899, which sparked his interest in

Frederick Douglass
(*seated*) as his grandson
Joseph plays the violin, in
1894. Courtesy Library
of Congress Prints and
Photographs Division,
LC-USZ62-51527.

Negro spirituals and folk songs. Influenced by Paul Laurence Dunbar, whom
he also met in London, he made an arrangement of many of these songs in his
*Twenty-Four Negro Melodies Transcribed for the Piano* in 1905. Coleridge-Taylor
also set some of Dunbar's poems to music, including the finale of his *African Suite*
(composed in 1898), which shares its title, "Danse Negre," with Dunbar's poem.[46]

Du Bois met Coleridge-Taylor at the First Pan-African Conference convened
in the summer of 1900. Of their first meeting Du Bois wrote, "I remember the
Englishmen, like the Colensos, who sat and counseled with us; but above all
I remember Coleridge-Taylor."[47] Coleridge-Taylor's music inspired Du Bois to
write a pageant, *A Star of Ethiopia*. First drafted in 1911, the work became what
Du Bois biographer David Levering Lewis calls "a three-hour extravaganza in six
episodes, featuring a thousand creamy complexioned young women and tawny,
well-built men and flocks of school children marching through history."[48] The

work was intended as a history of the struggles and achievements of the African American people. With the exception of two compositions from Verdi's *Aida,* all the music was composed by Blacks, including J. Rosamond Johnson (brother of James Weldon Johnson) and Coleridge-Taylor. It was first performed in 1913 at the 12th Regiment Armory in New York as part of the celebrations surrounding the fiftieth anniversary of the Emancipation Proclamation. Du Bois wrote that at least thirty thousand people attended the premier.

In October 1915 it premiered in Washington. Du Bois wrote that "we used the great ball field of the American League," officially called the American League Ball Park, where "a committee of the most distinguished colored citizens of Washington co-operated with me . . . and fourteen thousand saw the pageant."[49] He eloquently describes his own feelings: "Wonderfully, irresistibly, the dream comes true. You feel no exaltation, you feel no personal merit. It is not yours. It is its own. You have simply called it and it comes."[50] The guide program for the pageant said "The Story of the Pageant covers 10,000 years of the history of the Negro race and its work and suffering and triumphs in the world. The pageant combines historic accuracy and symbolic truth. All the costumes of the thousand actors, the temples, the weapons, etc., have been copied from accurate models."[51] The *Washington Bee* called the event "electrical, spiritual."[52]

James Reese Europe, his biographer Reid Badger notes, "was born on February 22, 1880, in Mobile, Alabama. Fifteen years after the end of the Civil War, seven years after the birth of W. C. Handy, and one year before Booker T. Washington began his work at Tuskegee."[53] Europe was almost ten when he arrived in the city with his family. They settled at 308 B Street SE, not far from where his father worked at the Post Office, first as a clerk and later as a supervisor. By coincidence, John Philip Sousa, the famed musician and director of the US Marine Corps Band, and his family moved in a few doors down the street, at 318 B Street. Badger notes that "the Marine Band itself had a long-standing relationship with the African American community in Washington" and "regularly took part in such important events in the black community as Howard University's commencement ceremonies, and band members often provided musical instruction to promising Black children. One of these young men was Jim Europe," who took lessons in piano and violin from the assistant bandmaster of the US Marine Corps.[54] March music, performed with precision by military bands and in parades, had long played a role in New Orleans, where it combined with African and Creole rhythms. Marches were also a big part of the annual DC Emancipation Day parades, so it was not unusual for youngsters to hear and enjoy it. Years later W. E. B. Du Bois would write appreciatively in *The Crisis* magazine (the voice of the NAACP) that Europe had a "genius for organization" and that his marches "all in all . . . are worthy of the pen of Sousa."[55]

For two years Europe attended M Street High School, founded in 1870 as the Preparatory High School for Colored Youth, the first public high school for Blacks in the country. Europe was soon recruited to the school's new cadet corps, started by Major Christian A. Fleetwood, a recipient of the Medal of Honor for his Civil War service. Over the years the cadet corps attracted many other outstanding students, including historian Rayford L. Logan, poet Sterling Brown, scholar and diplomat Mercer Cook (son of Will Marion Cook), US Army lieutenant colonel West Hamilton, federal judge William H. Hastie, and blood-plasma researcher Charles H. Drew; Europe also joined Captain Joseph Montgomery's prized drill company and served as color sergeant for the corps.[56] Both of these experiences served him well, as Badger notes: "His cadet training would later prove useful when he sought to organize black musicians of New York; it was undoubtedly helpful to him as an officer in the 15th New York Infantry Regiment in World War I."[57] In 1916, M Street High School was renamed Paul Laurence Dunbar High School and, as Mary Gibson Hundley writes, it had "a remarkable history which chronicles the achievements of an underprivileged people."[58]

After his father died in 1899, Europe dropped out of M Street School and in 1904 headed to New York City. Europe set his sights on New York both to escape Washington's crippling discrimination and to make his name in music. At the time many artists preferred Harlem, where, as Langston Hughes wrote, "people are not so ostentatiously proud of themselves, and where one's family background is not much of a concern," as he believed was the case with the Black elite of Washington.[59]

Europe quickly became part of the New York Black theater and musical scene, writing songs, composing, and directing stage shows, while always employing the African American idiom. In 1910 he founded the Clef Club, "a combination musicians' hangout, labor exchange, fraternity club, and concert hall," while also serving as a contracting agency for Black musicians.[60] At the time, Du Bois noted the significance of the Clef Club: "Before [Black musicians] were prey to scheming head waiters and booking agents, now they are performers whose salaries and hours are fixed by contracts."[61] Europe then formed the Clef Club Symphony Orchestra and on May 2, 1912, the 125 musicians performed a concert of early jazz music, all by Black composers, titled "A Concert of Negro Music" at Carnegie Hall, "the first performance ever given by a black orchestra at the famous bastion of white musical establishment."[62] The *New York Evening Post* called the collection of musicians "one of the most remarkable orchestras in the world."[63]

On November 21, 1913, at the Metropolitan AME Church, James Reese Europe's Afro-American Folk Singers and his National Negro Symphony Orchestra presented the works of Coleridge-Taylor, Cook, Harry Burleigh, and

J. Rosamond Johnson. They also performed folk songs and arrangements by Dvořák, Tchaikovsky, and Mendelssohn. Burleigh, Johnson, and Abbie Mitchell were the vocal soloists.[64]

In 1913 Europe began performing with the famed white dancers Irene and Vernon Castle, serving as their bandleader, with Ford Dabney as the arranger. The Castles developed the foxtrot "from steps Europe had learned from W.C. Handy, and a score thrown off from Europe."[65] Although some saw such collaboration of white and Black music and dancing as "the devil's work," eventually even the *Ladies Home Journal* wrote approvingly of the Castles and their dancing. Europe also saw the link between Black classical music and his own, adding that "Will Marion Cook, William Tires [Tyers]. Even Harry Burleigh and Coleridge-Taylor are [only] truly themselves in the music which expresses their race."[66]

Ford Dabney was a lesser-known early Washington musician who, with Cook and Europe, made up "three composers and bandleaders who moved to New York City from Washington, D.C. to make their fortune."[67] Born in Washington in 1883, Dabney showed such talent that in 1903 he added an international element to Washington jazz circles when he became the "court pianist to Haitian President Noro Alexis, remaining in that post until 1907."[68] He moved to New York in 1913, where he worked with Europe's orchestra and wrote songs for the Castles and for Florenz Ziegfeld at Ziegfeld's New Amsterdam Theater and roof garden.[69]

The progenitors of music in Washington, DC, were well trained, well versed, and well traveled. Will Marion Cook, James Reese Europe, Joseph Douglass, and Ford Dabney, the Amphion Glee Club, the Treble Clef Club (Black Women), Howard University Men's Glee Club, and music at the M Street High School (later Dunbar High School) all played a role in what became "Great Black Music."

## Notes

1. The term "Great Black Music" was coined in the 1960s by members of the Association for the Advancement of Creative Musicians, which was founded by band members of the Art Ensemble of Chicago and others. Musicologist George E. Lewis writes that Great Black Music "could easily encompass nonblack musicians and non jazz music within its purview." See Lewis, *A Power Stronger Than Itself*, 449.

2. Interview of James Reese Europe, *New York Evening Post,* March 15, 1914.

3. Paul Lawrence Dunbar, "Negro Society in Washington," *Saturday Evening Post,* December 14, 1901, 9.

4. Cook's son was named William Mercer Cook, and so indebted was Duke Ellington to Cook, he named his own son Mercer.

5. Carter, *Swing Along,* 17.

6. Quoted in Carter, *Swing Along*, 20.

7. *New York Age*, October 25, 1890.

8. Badger, *A Life in Ragtime*, 56. Badger adds: "It may have been a competent (or even superb) orchestra, but it was not—in instrumentation, performance, or material—an African-American one."

9. Harry Burleigh was accepted to the National Conservatory for vocal training, but he also played the double bass and timpani. He played in one of the orchestras conducted by Dvořák and eventually worked with him as a copyist. Most important, the two musicians spent hours together, when Burleigh sang Negro spirituals and folk songs.

10. *New York Herald Tribune*, May 21, 1893. See also Maurice Jackson's liner notes to both Charlie Haden and Hank Jones, *Come Sunday* (Verve, 2010) and Charlie Haden and Hank Jones, *Steal Away: Spirituals, Hymns, and Folk Songs* (Verve, 1995).

11. *New York Herald Tribune*, May 28, 1893.

12. Peress, *Dvořák to Duke Ellington*, 24.

13. Greenidge, *Black Radical*, 12.

14. Greenidge, 12.

15. Greenidge, 12.

16. Peretti, *Lift Every Voice*, 40.

17. Trotter, *Music and Some Highly Musical People*, 352.

18. For the role played by the Fisk Jubilee Singers, see Maurice Jackson's liner notes to Haden and Jones, *Steal Away*.

19. Luxenberg, *Separate*, 343–44.

20. Greenidge, *Black Radical*, 28. In fact, "Lieutenant Trotter left D.C. in 1890 having earned over $40,000 in less than two years" (28).

21. Du Bois, *The Souls of Black Folk*, 182.

22. Douglass, *Narrative of the Life of Frederick Douglass*.

23. Cook, quoted in Southern, *Readings in Black American Music*, 228.

24. Southern, "Will Marion Cook," 226.

25. Ellington, *Music Is My Mistress*, 95, 97.

26. Lincoln Memorial Congregational Church, established in 1880 by members of the First Congregational Church, later changed its name to the Lincoln Temple United Church of Christ in 2018. Hamil R. Harris, "After 150 Years, Lincoln Temple United Church of Christ Has Held Its Last Service," *Washington City Paper*, September 24, 2018.

27. Southern, *The Music of Black Americans*, 295.

28. Southern, 288.

29. Moore, *Leading the Race*, 64.

30. *Colored American*, January 28, 1899, 6, and April 15, 1899, 4.

31. Howe, *Women Music Educators*, 183.

32. "History of the Treble Clef Club," 2–3.

33. "History of the Treble Clef Club," 2–3.

34. Moore, *Leading the Race*, 64; Gatewood, *Aristocrats of Color*, 217.

35. Music classes were first held at Howard in 1870; a choir was founded in 1874. Holmes, "Sweet Sounds of Success," 14.

36. Dyson, "Howard University," 131–32.

37. Sinclair, "No Church Without a Choir," 131.

38. "Doris Evans McGinty, Music Professor," *Washington Post*, April 8, 2005.

39. Annie Lillian Evans, a graduate of Armstrong High School, changed her name to Lillian Evanti at the suggestion of writer Jesse Fauset. See E. Smith, "Lillian Evanti," 37.

40. Richard Harrington, "The Classical Muse," *Washington Post*, March 1, 2002.

41. Southern, *The Music of Black Americans*. Recorded in 1914, the recordings seemed to have never been released.

42. Elizabeth Walton to W. E. B. Du Bois, February 17, 1915; and W.E.B. Du Bois to Elizabeth Walton, March 2, 1915, with Du Bois's acceptance letter to be on the board of directors of the Music School, both in W. E. B. Du Bois Correspondence Series One, 1877–1965, University of Massachusetts Archives.

43. Frances Grimké, "Frederick Douglass Address," March 10, 1895, quoted in Blight, *Frederick Douglass*, 762.

44. McGinty, "Gifted Minds and Pure Hearts," 269. Webster, like Lulu Vere Childers, was an Oberlin Conservatory graduate. She completed graduate studies at Catholic University, and taught from 1926 to 1957 at Armstrong High School, where she also led the choral programs. She taught for one year, 1958, at Eastern High School, and also taught a few courses at Howard University and at Miner Normal University. She also played a major role in bringing the National Symphony Orchestra to the public school in Washington.

45. See McGinty, "Washington Conservatory of Music"; McGinty, "'That You Came So Far'"; McGinty, "The Black Presence"; Schmalenberger, "The Washington Conservatory."

46. Liner notes to *African Suite* (CBS, Black Composers Series, College Music Society, New York, 1986), 7.

47. Du Bois, *Darkwater*, 193.

48. Lewis, *W. E. B. Du Bois*, 460.

49. Du Bois, *Dusk of Dawn*, 272.

50. Du Bois, 273.

51. Quoted in Tucker, "The Renaissance Education of Duke Ellington," 117–18.

52. "The Great Pageant," *Washington Bee*, October 23, 1915, 1.

53. Badger, *A Life in Ragtime*, 10.

54. Badger, 20.

55. Du Bois, *The Crisis*, June 1912, 66–67, quoted in Badger, *Life of Ragtime*, 69.

56. Tucker, *Ellington*, 7.

57. Badger, *A Life in Ragtime*, 22.

58. Hundley, *The Dunbar Story*, 20. See also Stewart, *First Class*; and Terrell, "History of High School for Negroes," 255.

59. Hughes, "Our Wonderful Society," 226–27.

60. Lewis, *When Harlem Was in Vogue*, 31; Buckley, *American Patriots*, 192.

61. Du Bois, *The Crisis*, June 1912, 66–67.

62. Gates and Higginbotham, *African American Lives*, 350.

63. Quoted in Kimball and Bolcom, *Reminiscing with Sissle and Black*, 59–61. The orchestra had "forty-seven mandolins, twenty-seven harp guitars, eleven banjos, eight violins, eight trombones, thirteen cellos, seven cornets, five trap drums, two double basses, two clarinets, one tuba, one timpani, and ten pianos crowded onto the Carnegie Hall stage and stunning the audience"; they were also accompanied by two church choirs (Lewis, *When Harlem Was in Vogue*, 31).

64. Tucker, "The Renaissance Education of Duke Ellington," 122, 125; Badger, *A Life in Ragtime*, 93; Carter, *Swing Along*, 96.

65. Lewis, *When Harlem Was in Vogue*, 32

66. Europe, "A Negro Explains Jazz," 240–41.

67. James Weldon Johnson, quoted in Peress, *Dvořák to Duke Ellington*, 199.

68. Dabney, "Ford Dabney," 141.

69. Peress, *Dvořák to Duke Ellington*, 24.

# 2

# FROM THE GREAT WAR
# TO POSTWAR WASHINGTON

## A New Era of Racial Solidarity

When the United States entered World War I, brave men like James Reese Europe served among the 325,000 Black soldiers in the segregated US military. Europe saw action with Harlem's famed 369th Regiment and put together an outstanding regimental band, which he led. The 369th was originally the 15th Infantry Regiment of the New York National Guard, which was formed after many African Americans petitioned for its creation in early 1912. New York governor John Dix agreed to form the unit, but nothing was actually done until 1916, when then-governor Charles S. Whitman said, "Either the regiment ought to be built and given a fair chance of proving itself, or the law ought to be repealed."[1] He meant discriminatory provisions against Black enlistment.

Europe did not join the 15th Infantry Regiment simply out of patriotism. When first approached by one of the few Black officers in the national guard, he resisted. But over time he came to believe that such a unit would enhance the status of his race. He told his good friend Noble Sissle, the composer and bandleader who also joined the 15th, that in his sixteen years in New York, "there has never been such an organization of Negro men that will bring together all classes of men for a common good." He added, "Our race will never amount to anything, politically or economically, in New York or anywhere else unless there are strong organizations of men who stand for something in the community."[2] Europe was commissioned as an officer and the leader of the regimental band; Sissle enlisted as a private, played violin, and became the band's drum major.

Of the four Black regiments under the American Expeditionary Force led by Gen. John J. "Black Jack" Pershing, three, including Europe's regiment, were positioned under French command. As Gail Buckley writes, "They weren't really *American,* anyway, so giving them to the French seemed to satisfy both Woodrow Wilson's expressed desire to serve humanity and his racism. They would be adopted with fulsome gratitude by the French Fourth Army."[3]

Although the members of the 15th Infantry Regiment preferred to call themselves "Men of Bronze," they were nicknamed "the Enfant Perdus" (the lost or

29

abandoned children) by the French and were first called "the Hellfighters" by the Germans. The regimental band's performances helped introduce European audiences to African American musicians and to ragtime, blues, and jazz. When they played a snazzy rendition of the "Marseillaise," the French crowd did not at first recognize their national anthem, but then, according to Sissle, "there came over their faces an astonished look, quickly alert, snap-into-attention and salute by every French soldier and sailor present."[4] At performances at an opera house in Nantes to honor Abraham Lincoln's birthday, the band played "The Stars and Stripes Forever" and W. C. Handy's "Memphis Blues." Sissle described "the fireworks" and then a "soul rousing" crash of the drum cymbals and, when "the audience could stand it no longer[,] the 'jazz germ' hit them and it seemed to find the vital spot."[5]

The unit fought with Black African soldiers from Morocco and Senegal, who had distinguished themselves at the First Battle of the Marne in 1914. According to Emmet J. Scott, France declared that "it is because these soldiers are brave and just as devoted as white soldiers that they receive exactly the same treatment, every man being equal before death which all soldiers face."[6] Europe became one of the first African American officers to experience combat, in World War I, on April 20, 1918. Injured during a German poison attack, from his hospital bed he wrote "On Patrol in No Man's Land":

> I recall one event in particular. From February to last August, I had been in the trenches, in command of my machine-gun squad. I had been through the terrific general attack in Champaign when General Gouraud annihilated the enemy by his strategy and finally put an end to their hopes of victory, and I had been through many a smaller engagement. I can tell you that music was the farthest thing from my mind when one day, just before the Allied Conference in Paris, on August 18, Colonel Hayward came to me and said "Lieutenant Europe, I want you to go back to your band and give a single concert in Paris."[7]

After protesting that he "hadn't led a band since February," Europe agreed, and what was supposed to be one concert lasted eight weeks. Quite modestly, he said that he had some anxiety when his band gave a concert in the Theatre des Champs-Elysées but "the audience went wild." He recalled performing in conjunction with

> the greatest bands in the world . . . the British Grenadiers . . . the band of the Garde Republican [sic], and the Royal Italian Band. My band of course could not compare with any of these, yet the crowd was such as I never saw anywhere else in the world, deserted them for us. We played 50,000 people, at least, and had we

James Reese Europe's 369th Infantry Harlem Hellfighters Brass Band in Paris. Smithsonian Institution National Museum of African American History and Culture, 2011.57.39.

wished it, we might be playing yet . . . everywhere we went there was a riot. . . . The Morocco negro bands played music which had an affinity with ours. . . . We won France by playing music which was ours and not a pale mutation of others and if we are to develop in American we must develop along our own lines. . . . Our musicians do their best work when using negro material.[8]

He added: "The music of our race springs from the soul, and this is true today with no other race, except possibly the Russians and it is because of this that I and all my musicians have come to love Russian music. Indeed, as far as I am concerned, it is the only music I care for outside of Negro."[9] Perhaps he was also influenced by authors such as Claude McKay, who took a "magic pilgrimage" to Russia, or others who would visit there after its 1917 revolution.[10] Some noted V. I. Lenin's adaption of Karl Marx's mantle, "Workers of the World Unite," to "Workers of the World and Oppressed Peoples Unite."

Before the war was over the 15th had amassed 191 combat days. For their fighting, without loss of life or an inch of ground, the French government awarded the unit with the Croix de Guerre, the French Army's highest honor. The regiment also won 171 decorations for bravery, the most of any US regiment. On

In the courtyard of a Paris hospital reserved for the American wounded, an American military band led by Lt. James R. Europe entertains the patients with real American jazz. 1918. Photograph by US Army Signal Corps, courtesy Library of Congress Prints and Photographs Division, LC-DIG-ds-09800.

its return on February 17, 1919, the regiment marched up Fifth Avenue in New York City to thunderous applause. However, in DC, racial bigotry by the federal government did not allow returning Black soldiers to march down Pennsylvania Avenue past the White House.

James Reese Europe was knifed in the neck by Herbert Wright, a disgruntled drummer in his band, after a quarrel on May 9, 1919, at Mechanics Hall in Boston.[11] Europe died in the hospital later that night. As his body lay in state at Paris Undertakers on 131st Street in Harlem in New York City, thousands of people viewed his casket. At 11:00 a.m. on May 13 his funeral procession passed through Harlem, and the funeral was held at St. Mark's Episcopal Church. He is buried at Arlington National Cemetery.[12]

W. E. B. Du Bois wrote of Black men's bravery in the war, and of the racism they came home to, in his article, "Returning Soldiers." There he declared:

> We return.
> We return from fighting.
> We return fighting.
> Make way for Democracy! We saved it in France, and by the Great
>      Jehovah, we will save it in the United States of America, or know the
>      reason why.[13]

## Postwar Washington

With the coming of peace, the few advances made by Black Americans during the war became grounds for increasing resentment among some white Americans. Returning white soldiers saw themselves wrongly competing with Blacks for the jobs they had left when they went to war. Black soldiers seldom found the respect and benefits they had been promised, but instead encountered disdain for taking pride in their wartime heroism.[14]

By the summer of 1919, postwar ethnic and economic tensions following demobilization, combined with fear of the Bolshevism that had taken hold in Russia, flared into violence in some northern US cities, including Washington, DC. The "Red Summer" riots of 1919 hit over twenty-five cities; that year there were eighty-three recorded lynchings in the country.[15] White mobs killed hundreds of Blacks, as postwar ethnic and economic tensions flared. During their time in the service, many African Americans like James Reese Europe had experienced a taste of equality and opportunity in Europe, which they were reluctant to relinquish. They had fought with French and African units and came home willing to wage war against inequity at home. Bolshevism and socialism had appealed to some and others were influenced by Pan-Africanism led by W. E. B Du Bois.[16]

James Weldon Johnson notes that "the Negroes saved themselves and saved Washington by their determination not to run, but to fight, fight in defense of their lives and their homes."[17] Shocked by the Blacks who defended themselves and their communities, white mobs dispersed and stopped their attacks.[18] Whites blamed outside agitators and socialist and Bolshevik propaganda.[19] Black DC leaders knew that the root causes were economic, social, and domestic.[20] Although whites had initiated the conflict, in DC merely eight or nine of the nearly one hundred people arrested were white.[21] In Washington, at least four Blacks and three whites died and hundreds were injured.

Over the next decade, Howard University philosopher and scholar Alain Locke advocated the development of the "New Negro" and a new self-awareness and confidence in racial identity. Locke noted "a renewed race-spirit that consciously and proudly sets itself apart," a result of the "ripening forces as culled from the first fruits of the Negro Renaissance."[22] Coming amid what he saw as a new intellectual and cultural self-awareness, Locke believed that the "New Negro is keenly responsive as an augury of a new democracy in American culture" and is "contributing his share to the new social understanding." This concept ignited a Washington renaissance for Blacks, creating new cultural opportunities and in many ways preceding the better-known Harlem Renaissance.[23] Blacks in the nation's capital adopted the words of the poet Claude McKay, who captured their spirit and determination in his poem "If We Must Die": "Like men we'll face the murderous pack, / Pressed to the wall, dying, but fighting back!"[24]

A new intellectual and cultural solidarity that had been promoted by Locke was tested in June 1922, when Robert Russa Moton was roped off from attending the dedication of the Lincoln Memorial. A national outcry gave rise to a new solidarity.[25] A concert by internationally celebrated contralto Marian Anderson in 1939 exposed Washington's segregated society to the rest of the country. For several years the Howard University Music Department had presented an annual concert featuring Anderson, using space at Dunbar High School and local auditoriums. In 1939 Anderson was fresh from a successful European tour and her promoters, along with Howard officials, wanted to move the event to Constitution Hall, which was owned by the Daughters of the American Revolution (DAR), not realizing that the DAR had in its leasing agreements a "white artist only" clause. Unlike the National Theater, which denied admittance to Black audiences but allowed Black performers, Constitution Hall allowed Black patrons to sit in roped-off areas but did not allow African American performers.[26]

When denied the use of Constitution Hall, the newly formed Marian Anderson Citizens Committee (MACC) tried to reserve the whites-only Central High School, but the school board denied the auditorium to any events with either African American performers or audience members.[27] The Black press took up the cause, denouncing both the DAR and Washington's system of segregation. The *New York Amsterdam News* highlighted both in an article captioned "Nazism in D.C.," stating that "the real tragedy, is, however, that democracy and justice are so flaunted so cruelly in the nation's capital," a city claiming to be the capital of democracy.[28] Contradictions abounded, as "Anderson could inhabit a site controlled by the National Park Service, but not the city of Washington, D.C.," which showed "the pervasiveness of segregation in the nation's capital."[29]

The MACC saw the concert as just part of its mission. Howard University professor Doxie Wilkerson, a member of the National Negro Congress, rose to be the leader of the ad hoc committee that challenged the school board's decision to deny Anderson the right to sing at Central High.[30] At a mass meeting on March 26, a few days before the concert had been scheduled, Herbert Marshall, head of the DC branch of the NAACP, declared, "The denial of the use of the Central High School auditorium is the very antithesis of democracy."[31]

Then, with the support of First Lady Eleanor Roosevelt, who resigned her DAR membership over the issue, Secretary of the Interior Harold Ickes arranged for Anderson to perform on the steps of the Lincoln Memorial. On Easter Sunday, April 9, 1939, the concert was held at the Lincoln Memorial with more than seventy-five thousand in attendance. Anderson sang Negro spirituals, such

Marian Anderson performs before thousands at the Lincoln Memorial in April 1939 after being denied the use of DAR Constitution Hall. The concert brought national attention to Washington's pervasive segregation and was hailed by Mary McLeod Bethune as "our triumphant entry into the democratic spirit of American life." Courtesy Scurlock Studio Records Archives Center, Smithsonian Institution National Museum of American History.

as "Nobody Knows the Trouble I've Seen," "My Soul Is Anchored in the Lord," "Gospel Train" (arranged by her old friend Harry Burleigh), Franz Shubert's "Ave Maria," and a moving rendition of "America." The program was broadcast over NBC Radio, meaning millions in America and the world heard it live or rebroadcasted in newsreels at movie houses. Others read about it in newspapers, broadsheets, and magazines.

Mary McLeod Bethune, head of the National Council of Negro Women, an appointee to the National Youth Administration, and a member of President Roosevelt's Black Cabinet, wrote to Charles Hamilton Houston, special litigation counsel of the NAACP and dean of Howard University Law School, that Anderson's performance "cannot be described in words. There is no way. History may well record it, but it will never be able to tell what happened in the hearts of the thousands who stood and listened yesterday . . . through the Marian Anderson Protest Concert we made our triumphant entry into the democratic spirit of American life."[32] Historian Constance McLaughlin Green later wrote that "no one who was present at that moving performance ever forgot it. . . . It was a turning point, one man averred, in Washington Negroes' seventy-year-old fight against discrimination. And it was no longer a local affair only. Race relations in the nation's capital thenceforward were a matter of interest to Americans everywhere."[33]

Historian Raymond Arsenault has noted that though the DAR skirmish had been won, "the battle over racial justice in the nation's capital was just beginning" and "it would be years before black Washingtonians achieved anything approaching fundamental reform in the District's schools."[34] The efforts did have an immediate effect, however, as Ickes ordered the National Park Service to effectively desegregate all government-owned parks in the city. Ickes also desegregated Interior Department offices and other departments did the same. City agencies and facilities nevertheless remained segregated. Still, in many ways the campaign around Marian Anderson paved the way for desegregation in the nation's capital city. As historian Mary Elizabeth Murphy so aptly puts it, "It took a national embarrassment to force the federal government to pursue racial integration" in the seat of power and beyond.[35] It would be some years before integration would come in full. There would be bumps along the road, and humps to jump, but there was no turning around.

A few weeks after the Lincoln Memorial concert, Anderson performed at the White House during a private audience for FDR, Mrs. Roosevelt, and King George VI and Queen Elizabeth of Great Britain. Mrs. Roosevelt's education in civil rights did not end with the DAR event. She later read Countee Cullen's poem "Black Majesty," from his book *The Black Christ,* as well as other poems, which were dedicated to Toussaint L'Ouverture, Jean-Jacques Dessalines, and Henri Christophe. Two lines of "Black Majesty" read, "'Lo, I am dark, but comely,' Sheba sings; / 'And we were black,' three shades reply, 'but kings.'" Mrs. Roosevelt was so moved that years later she wrote in her newspaper column that everyone should be required to read *The Black Christ.*[36] During the 1963 March on Washington, Anderson again sang at the Lincoln Memorial, the cite of her 1939 concert, which in a real sense set the stage for the 1963 march.[37] Scheduled to sing the National Anthem, she was, like many, caught up in a massive traffic jam, but she did arrive in time to sing "He's Got the Whole World in His Hands."

The DAR's bigotry did not stop with African American performers. Michael Terrace (Michael Gutierrez) wrote of being part of Mambo USA, a mixed-race Latino touring company in the summer of 1952. The review was set for its Washington premier. As Terrace describes it:

Constitution Hall was a munificent auditorium, the highest ceiling and plush seats. It made one feel proud to be an American, but it didn't last long. The following day we went to Constitution Hall in Washington, DC, and this time at our rehearsal we met again with a similar confrontation that was belittling, coming from three ladies that claimed to belong to the Daughters of the American Revolution, in their own Southern lady like fashion, that n——rs were not allowed to perform on the stage of Constitution Hall with whites. . . . We were told that we were mix breeds and could not perform on the Constitution Hall stage.[38]

The DAR finally relented after the show was sold out, though at the show, all Blacks and darker skinned peoples were searched and whites were not. At the performance one of its stars, Myrta Silvia, said, "Why should we continue on a stage that only belongs to the supreme whites?"[39] To this the audience stood and cheered "love refrains" until she sang her next song. Feeling victorious, many from the integrated concertgoers went to the local Arthur Murray Dance Studio for a celebration. This was during the time of the early picket lines and protests against segregation, just a few years before the court rulings that desegregated the city.

## Billie Holiday

That same April 1939, when Marian Anderson performed at the Lincoln Memorial, Billie Holiday first performed "Strange Fruit" at New York's Café Society, a midtown club that attracted a varied audience, from Nelson Rockefeller to Lillian Hellman to Langston Hughes. Other performers at the club included such stars as Lena Horne, Sarah Vaughn, and Imogene Coca. According to David Margolick, "It was probably the only place in America where 'Strange Fruit' could have been sung and savored."[40] The song was written by Abel Meeropol, a New York schoolteacher, under the pen name Lewis Allan. He explained, "I wrote 'Strange Fruit' because I hate lynching and I hate injustice and I hate the people who perpetuate it."[41] Holiday told how a hush enveloped the room as she sang the song, then one by one audience members began to applaud as they understood the meaning and the sadness of the song about lynchings in the South. The song was studio-recorded on April 20 and released a few months later. "Strange Fruit" had a riveting effect on jazz and on the struggle against lynching.

Holiday had signed on as vocalist with Artie Shaw, a Jewish clarinetist and bandleader, in 1938. Shaw was the first to hire a Black female singer and the first to tour the segregated South with her. The singer endured Southern bigotry for months, but by the time of her April 1939 club date at Café Society, she "had just quit Artie Shaw's band in part because she had been forced to take the freight elevator during a gig at a New York hotel. And not just any hotel, but one named after Abraham Lincoln."[42] But Holiday respected Shaw: "There aren't many people who fought harder than Artie against the vicious people in the music business or the crummy side of second-class citizenship which eats at the guts of so many musicians. He didn't win. But he didn't lose either."[43] In later years Shaw came to DC with integrated bands and to lobby President Roosevelt for federal support for the arts.

The *Baltimore Afro-American* newspaper reported in March 1940 that "Miss Holiday recently sang ['Strange Fruit'] at the Howard Theatre in Washington" and "speculation became rife as to whether it actually will incite or condemn mob action," but the paper said the song "immediately won praise from both the hot and classical schools."[44] The paper also speculated "that Holiday might have even won the NAACP's prestigious Spingarn Medal, given annually to blacks for special achievements, had the black church not disapproved of entertainers at the time." Even the more moderate National Urban League's Lester Granger praised the song. Holiday continued to sing "Strange Fruit" at progressive and antiracist events, including a benefit concert in 1943 "for Ben Davis Jr., a black man elected as a Communist to the New York City Council (Paul Robeson, Teddy Wilson, Josh White, Ella Fitzgerald and Hazel Scott participated in the same event)."[45]

Holiday performed regularly in Washington and was especially fond of playing at Club Bali at 14th and T Streets NW and staying at the Dunbar Hotel on 15th Street, between U and V Streets. In 1949 she had a three-week engagement there, breaking the club record and ending on April 7, her birthday. Around this time pianist Carl Drinkard, a twenty-year-old Howard University senior, caught her attention while he was playing at a small club called Little Harlem. After hearing him play, Holiday "marched over to the piano and said 'You! You're coming with me!'"[46] He soon joined her at Club Bali and on his first night, one of the greatest piano players, Art Tatum, was in the audience and gave young Drinkard his approval.

Georgianne Williamson of the *Washington Post* wrote in 1949, "There's a singular kind of repose about [Holiday's features]: Billie is earthy, but with complete good grace. More factual than suggestive, still she's got a gallop that has the bar sitters, around her in a semi-circle at her feet, supplying a chorus of adulation."[47]

## Notes

1. Harris, *Harlem's Hell Fighters*, 31.
2. Quote from "Memoirs of Noble Sissle" in Badger, *A Life in Ragtime*, 142.
3. Buckley, *American Patriots*, 165.
4. Badger, 163.

5. Ward and Burns, *Jazz*, 68. Sissle said they played alongside "the greatest concert bands in the world—the British Grenadier's Band, the band of the *Garde Republicain,* and the Royal Italian Band. My band, of course, could not compare with any of these, yet the crowd deserted them for us."

6. Scott, *Official History*, 118. Scott was the principal deputy to Booker T. Washington and the highest-ranking African American in the US military during the war, serving as special advisor for Black affairs to Secretary of War Newton Baker.

7. Europe, "A Negro Explains Jazz." Europe wrote that "the reed players I got from Porto Rico [*sic*], the rest from all over the country. I had only one New York Negro in my band—my solo cornetist."

8. Europe, "A Negro Explains Jazz."

9. Europe, "A Negro Explains Jazz."

10. McKay, "Soviet Russia and the Negro"; Baldwin, *Beyond the Color Line*, 28–32; Williams, *When Harlem Was in Vogue.*

11. "The United States World War One Centennial Commission?," *New York Clipper,* May 1919.

12. Badger, *A Life in Ragtime*, 218.

13. Du Bois, "Returning Soldiers."

14. "The Rights of the Black Man," *Washington Bee*, August 2, 1919.

15. Monroe N. Work, Tuskegee Institute Study data; Kerlin, *The Voice of the Negro,* 100–101; "The Lynching Industry"; Krugler, *1919*, 272; UMKC School of Law, "Lynching Statistics by Year," http://law2.umkc.edu/faculty/projects/ftrials/shipp/lynchingyear.html.

16. Peter Perl, "Race Riot of 1919 Gave Glimpse of Future Struggles," *Washington Post,* March 1, 1999.

17. Johnson, "The Washington Riots."

18. "Race Riots," *New York Times,* July 28, 1919.

19. "Blames Newcomers for Violence," *Washington Post*, July 31, 1919.

20. "Riots Elsewhere, Forecast by Negro," *Washington Post*, July 25, 1919.

21. Green, *The Secret City*, 192.

22. Locke, *The New Negro*, xvii, 9; *Savanah Tribune,* "Racial Clashes," July, 26, 1919.

23. Williams, *When Washington Was in Vogue*; Tucker, *Ellington*; Ruble, *Washington's U Street.*

24. McKay, "If We Must Die," 21.

25. "Colored Folk Defy Jim Crow: Near Riots Marks Enforcement of Segregation by Soldiers with Guns and Bayonets," *Baltimore Afro-American,* June 2, 1922.

26. Hughes, "Trouble with Angels."

27. Central High School, at 13th and Clifton Streets NW, was later renamed Cardozo. Washington writer Edward P. Jones is a 1968 graduate.

28. "Nazism D.C.," *New York Amsterdam News,* April 8, 1939.

29. Murphy, *Jim Crow Capital*, 165.

30. Bruce Lambert, "Doxey Wilkerson Is Dead at 88; Educator and Advocate for Rights," *New York Times*, June 18, 1993; Lyons, "The Making of a Black Community Educator," 29: "On June 19, 1943 Wilkerson announced his official membership in the

CPUSA. Upon this announcement, he resigned from the OPA and Howard and resumed responsibility for leading the Party's education program for Washington, D.C."

31. Arsenault, *The Sound of Freedom*, 174.

32. Arsenault, 163. For more about Houston see Mack, *Representing the Race.*

33. Green, *The Secret City*, 249.

34. Arsenault, *The Sound of Freedom*, 174.

35. Murphy, *Jim Crow Capital*, 165.

36. Ferguson, *Countee Cullen*, 115.

37. Sandage, "A Marble House Divided."

38. Michael Terrace (a.k.a. Michael Gutierrez), "A Mambo Musical Dance Show in the Summer of 1952 that Made History," http://michael terrace.blogspot.com12/31/04. My thanks to WPFW *Latin Flavor* host Jim Byers and the Jim Byers Archive. According to Terrace, this was the same week that several Puerto Rican nationalists were arrested in a shootout on Capitol Hill.

39. Terrace, "A Mambo Musical Dance Show."

40. Margolick, *Strange Fruit*, 42.

41. Margolick, 29. Meeropol, a Jewish American and member of the Communist Party USA , and his wife, Anne, later adopted the children of Ethel and Julius Rosenberg, who were executed in 1953 for providing secrets to the Soviets at the height of the Cold War.

42. Margolick, *Strange Fruit*, 37.

43. Nolan, *Artie Shaw*, 104.

44. Margolick, *Strange Fruit*, 96, 98.

45. Margolick, 98.

46. Blackburn, *With Billie*, 228; Stokes, *Growing Up with Jazz.*

47. De Ferrari, *Historic Restaurants of Washington, D.C.*, 100.

# 3

# THE DUKE, THE SULTAN, AND SATCHMO

## Rhapsodies of Freedom

### Maestro Duke Ellington

Edward Kennedy "Duke" Ellington, composer, bandleader, and pianist, was born on April 29, 1899. Ellington's father, James Edward, was from Lincolnton, North Carolina, and was born in 1879, exactly twenty years before his son. James worked as a driver and later as a butler for the family of Middleton F. Cuthbert, a white physician who both allowed and encouraged the senior Ellington to read works in his extensive library.[1] James later got a job working as a blueprinter in the Navy Yard. Ellington's mother, Daisy, was born in Washington, DC, into a middle-class family the same year as his father. Like so many Black families, they moved often, at least fourteen times, by all accounts mostly in Northwest Washington, but stayed generally among the strivers in the Shaw area. Music scholars like Mark Tucker and John Edward Hasse have documented Ellington's early musical development in the city, from his early gigs on U Street to ones in Georgetown, Foggy Bottom, Anacostia, and Alexandria. What stands out are the early lessons he learned, not just about music but about life, race, and class.

Duke wrote that his father "raised his family as though he were a millionaire . . . the best had to be carefully examined to make sure it was good enough for my mother."[2] White society had its demands, but those of the family came first. Ellington was taught by people like Mrs. Bolton, his eighth grade English teacher, that "everywhere you go, if you were sitting in a theater next to a white lady or something like that or you were on stage representing your race, no matter where you go or what you do, you are representing your race and your responsibility is to command respect for that race. They taught that. I've always had that."[3] In short, the Ellingtons, like so many of their time, practiced the politics of respectability. So did many African Americans of the time, regardless of their social standing, sometimes without realizing it. Any Black of a certain age would have remembered the lessons their parents or grandparents taught them or that were passed down. Lesson One: Always walk like you own the place, although you knew you never would. Lesson Two: Always have on clean underwear, for if you have to go to the hospital, at least whites could not refuse you for not being clean, even though they could refuse you for being Black. Barry Ulanov, one of Ellington's first biographers, saw the same pattern of the politics of respectability— "a Washington pattern"—among other musicians. He notes, "It involved a certain bearing, a respect for education, for the broad principles of the art of music; a desire for order, for design in their professional lives."[4]

Ellington attended Garnett Elementary School and first took piano lessons there. Unlike many of Washington's high-achieving or status-conscious Blacks, he did not attend Dunbar High School, but instead chose Samuel H. Armstrong Technical High School on O Street between 1st and 2nd Streets NW. The school, like Howard University, was named after a Union Army leader.[5] Other Armstrong graduates, who could have been considered "underachievers" by those who attended Dunbar, included the football great Willie Wood, who played college football for the University of Southern California Trojans and was inducted into the NFL Hall of Fame as a stalwart with the Green Bay Packers.. The satin voiced jazz crooner, arranger, and big band leader Billy Eckstine, known as "Mr. B." also attended Armstrong.[6] (After graduation, Eckstine attended St. Paul Normal and Industrial School and then went on to Howard University, but left there in 1933 after winning a talent contest.[7])

Duke's younger sister, Ruth, said that "in our house, while I was growing up, people of all colors were there. More whites than colored. My father was like that. He didn't talk about color. In our house, you didn't talk about color."[8] Ellington himself said, "There was never any talk [at home] about red people, brown people, black people, or yellow people, or about the differences that existed between them."[9] Still, early on he learned the realities of Black life in the city. In his own biography he wrote, "I don't know how many castes of Negroes there were in the city at the that time [sic] but I do know that if you decided to mix carelessly with another you would be told that one just did not do that sort of thing."[10] It is hard to believe that Ellington would see himself beneath any person, white or Black, but it is clear that he saw himself as transcending boundaries. He wrote as much in describing what he learned by hanging around U and 7th Streets, near Frank's Pool Hall, adjacent to the Howard Theatre: "All levels could and should mix."[11] This is where he stood out as a musician and as a human being. This is where he moved "beyond category."

In 1916 Ellington, who studied commercial art at Armstrong High School, won an NAACP poster contest and with it a scholarship to study art at Pratt Institute in Brooklyn.[12] Instead of accepting it, he dropped out of Armstrong in

Duke Ellington with composer, arranger, and lyricist Billy Strayhorn. The two men worked together from 1938 until Strayhorn's death in 1967. Courtesy *Look* magazine photograph collection, Library of Congress Prints and Photographs Division, LC-L9-57-7111-V, no. 7.

early 1917, a few months short of receiving his diploma, and began his life as a full-time working musician. He also worked with partner Ewell Conway, running a business painting signs for dance halls and backdrops for the Howard Theatre, and "when customers came for posters to advertise a dance, I would ask them what they were doing about their music. When they wanted to hire a band, I would ask them who's painting their signs."[13] In Washington he formed his own group, Duke's Serenaders. "I was beginning to catch on around Washington," Ellington wrote, "and I finally built up so much of a reputation that I had to study music seriously to protect it."[14] With that confidence, he had to give New York City a shot. Having played in the city, and after having seen so many New York musicians play at the Howard, he had to prove that if he "could make it there he could make it anywhere." He said as much: "It was New York that filled our imagination. . . . We were awed by the never-ending roll of great talents there. . . . Harlem, to our minds, did indeed have the world's most glamorous atmosphere. We had to go there." And in 1923 he finally did.[15] In New York he wrote more than fifteen hundred compositions, and he also wrote a lot of music while on the road, in cars, and in hotels.

For the next fifty years Ellington made hundreds of appearances in his home-town, including at many stages shows, award ceremonies, and civic engagements, always making sure to pay homage to his city and its people. In 1931 he visited the gravesite of James Reese Europe at Arlington National Cemetery.[16] Over the years other musicians, like Randy Weston and Jason Moran have followed his lead.[17]

While the *Norfolk Journal and Guide* wrote that "Duke is the first colored entertainer ever to be received by the chief executive of the nation," this was not true.[18] What is true is that Duke Ellington did go to the White House and Herbert Hoover refused to see him. The *Afro-American*'s reporter Ralph Matthews Jr., who later covered Fidel Castro's trip to Harlem, wrote that "Hoover has covered more than half of his term and his record of never posing with a colored delegation is still intact. . . . He does not know that only the jazz sent over the air nightly by such chaps as Ellington and his ilk have helped America endure the Hoover administration and weather the depression."[19] Finally, on September 29, 1950, Ellington made his first visit past the White House gates, when he presented the score of his new creation, *Harlem,* to President Harry S. Truman.[20] The famed singer Kate Smith also presented a score, and Irving Berlin sent a song he had composed, " It Gets Lonely in the White House."[21] While he did not play at the White House when Dwight Eisenhower was president, he did perform at the White House Correspondents Dinner with the president present.[22]

Ellington also made his contribution to the desegregation of his native city. He knew well the works of the prolific African American historian Rayford Whittingham Logan, an old family friend, who in 1941 published *The Diplomatic Relations of the United States with Haiti.* According to Ellington biographer John Edward Hasse, Ellington "owned 800 books on black history, and had underlined passages about Denmark Vesey and Nat Turner."[23] Ellington was also familiar with the art of Jacob Lawrence, the poetry of Langston Hughes, and the prose of W. E. B. Du Bois related to the Haitian Revolution and Toussaint L'Ouverture.[24] Although some writers have noted Ellington's social conservatism, especially in his later years, Terry Teachout offers another view: "Ellington, like many other blacks, appreciated the Communist Party's stance against racism, and his sentiments were widely shared in Harlem." While noting that the maestro, like many of his generation, was a Republican, Teachout points out that Ellington "himself would actively support the candidacy of Benjamin J. Davis Jr., when he ran for New York's city council on the Communist ticket in 1943," siding with a Black man he admired for openly fighting racism.[25]

Ellington also made a statement with his symphony *Black, Brown and Beige.* Duke said that he composed the suite as "a tone parallel to the history of the Negro in America."[26] He told columnist Belle Ayer that "five of the 10 years which have gone into writing the piece were put into research, and the other five years were required to write the book and the music."[27] The suite was influenced by the story of the Black men who had fought at the Battle of Savannah and in appreciation of the Haitian Revolution. "I have gone back to the history of my race and tried to express it in rhythm," Ellington wrote. "We used to have a little something in Africa, a 'something' we have lost. One day we shall get it again."[28]

In 1943 *Black, Brown and Beige* was ready for its opening in New York. Ellington knew that when the film *Emperor Jones,* starring Paul Robeson, had premiered in September 1933, it opened simultaneously to segregated audiences. Whites viewed it at the Rivoli Theater in the downtown theater district and Blacks viewed it at the Roosevelt Theater uptown in Harlem. Duke wanted better.[29] On January 23, 1943, Ellington's *Black, Brown and Beige* premiered at New York's Carnegie Hall. Count Basie, Jimmy Lunceford, and Benny Goodman attended the performance, as well as First Lady Eleanor Roosevelt and Leopold Stokowski. According to the *Washington Afro-American,* "Frank Sinatra left his engagement at the Paramount to visit backstage."[30] Among the African American celebrities in attendance were Marian Anderson, Langston Hughes, and Alain Locke. Tickets to the concert sold out two weeks before the premiere, and "an overflow crowd of about 2,000 persons milled about the sidewalks and lobby of [the 3,000-person capacity] Carnegie Hall . . . in the hopes of securing tickets."[31] The concert, which was held in support of Russian war relief, grossed $7,000 and netted $5,000. The concerts were repeated in Boston on January 28, 1943, and in Cleveland on February 20, 1943, all for integrated audiences."[32] Ellington, who said that he was not a street protester, used his *Jump for Joy* (1941), *Symphony in Black* (1934), and *Creole Rhapsody* (1931)—in addition to *Black, Brown and Beige*—to express himself through his music. He wrote that "jazz is based on our native heritage. It is an American idiom with African roots—a trunk of soul with limbs, reaching in every direction, to the frigid North, the exotic East, the miserable, swampy South, and the wild swinging West."[33] Hasse states that Ellington

composed works that in effect asserted "black is beautiful" long before that phrase became popular in the 1960s. These works included celebrations of black history and culture—*Black Beauty* (1928), *Echoes of Harlem* (1936), *Harlem Airshaft* (1940), *Black, Brown and Beige: A Tone Parallel to the History of the Negro in America* (1943), the *Liberian Suite* (1947), *Symphony in Black* (1935), *Harlem* (1951), *My People* (1963), *La plus belle Africaine* (1966), and *Togo Brava Suite* (1971)—and compositions honoring African American cultural heroes, such as Martin Luther King, Jr., in *King Fit the Battle of Alabam'* (1963), as well as *A Portrait of Louis Armstrong* and *A Portrait of Mahalia Jackson* (both movements of his *New Orleans Suite,* 1970).[34]

In many ways Duke Ellington's contributions "to the cause" of Black rights have been neglected. But at the same time that Satchmo was speaking out on events in Little Rock, Ellington was making his "race statements." In a 1957 essay titled "The Race for Space," Ellington wrote that "America's inability to go ahead of Russian in the race for space can be traced directly to this racial problem."[35] Even though he was a committed anticommunist, he also saw beyond politics. Just as he had when he once raised money for Russian war relief, he now compared the race in space and the Soviet Union's launching of *Sputnik* as "a work of art in the sense that I view a great painting, read a great poem or listen to a great work of music." He added that as far as he could see, the country "doesn't permit race prejudice . . . to interfere with scientific progress."[36]

At another time he declared, "The music of my race is something more than an American idiom. It is the result of our transplantation to American soil and was our reaction in the plantation days to the tyranny we endured. What we could not say openly we expressed in music. . . . It expresses our personality."[37] In one interview, not long after the assassination of Medgar Evers in Mississippi, he was asked, "Why hasn't the Negro artist done more for the cause?" He answered without bitterness but with a deep sense of hurt, saying, "We had been working on the Negro situation in the south since the 30s, that we had done shows, musical works, benefits, etc. and the American Negro artists had been among the first to make contributions."[38] In Bombay, India, on a US State Department–sponsored trip in 1963, he noticed that local musicians were denied the right to attend his concerts and that the price of black market tickets proved prohibitive. He thought back to his early DC days, and he told the American officials that "all musicians are brothers in arms, and it distresses me terribly that they could not get into our concerts, so we go about the business of readjusting the conditions. I insist that from now on, no matter how limited the space, all musicians are to be admitted."[39]

Ellington did not receive an invitation to the White House from President John F. Kennedy.[40] Kennedy did not invite King to the White House either. Rumor spread that Kennedy, giving in to the sentiments about communism of the day, had said having King to the White House would be like inviting Karl Marx. During Lyndon B. Johnson's presidency Ellington visited at the White House seven times, sometimes performing, including at the White House Festival of the Arts in 1965.[41] The Ellington Orchestra performed in January 1969 at Richard M. Nixon's inaugural ball held at the Smithsonian Institution.[42] A few months later, on April 29, 1969, the Duke's seventieth birthday, Nixon presented Ellington with the Presidential Medal of Freedom, the nation's highest civilian honor, in a room filled with dignitaries and celebrities. With grace and elegance, Ellington said in his classic Ellingtonese, "There is no place I would rather be tonight except in my

President Richard M. Nixon presents Edward Kennedy "Duke" Ellington with the
Presidential Medal of Freedom on April 29, 1969, Duke's seventieth birthday, during a
gala tribute at the White House. White House Record Library, Courtesy National Archives
and Records Administration.

mother's arms."[43] After Nixon said a few words in praise of the maestro, Ellington
kissed him twice on each cheek. Momentarily stunned, Nixon asked, "Four
kisses? Why four?," to which Duke answered again to the president's amazement
"One for each cheek."[44]

Several events in the early 1960s changed Ellington's affection for his hometown. In 1960 the graves of his beloved parents and thirty-seven thousand others, primarily African Americans, were dug up in Columbia Harmony Cemetery
and transferred to National Harmony Memorial Park near Landover, Maryland.[45]
According to Hasse, "officials told Ellington that he had to dig up his parents'
graves, or else lose them."[46] Ellington's sister Ruth said that after this, Ellington
"had a completely different feeling about Washington. It was as if Washington
had disinherited him."[47] Other well-known interred African Americans whose
graves were also moved include Sgt. Maj. Christian A. Fleetwood, the Civil War
Medal of Honor recipient and long-time head of Dunbar's Cadet Corps; Henry
Lincoln Johnson, the DC recorder of deeds and husband of Georgia Douglass
Johnson; and Elizabeth Keckley, abolitionist and seamstress to the Lincolns.

Ellington transferred his parents' caskets to Woodlawn Cemetery in the Bronx, but the bitterness lingered. Whether he thought the matter would have been handled differently if the deceased had been white, he did not publicly say. It did not matter; they were his parents, and they were Black.

On December 5, 1966, Ellington again came back to Washington to perform his "Concert of Sacred Music" at Constitution Hall. This time the trouble did not come from the Daughters of the American Revolution, who had denied Marian Anderson's concert almost forty years before. It came from the Baptist Ministers Conference of Washington, which protested on the grounds that his music was too "wordly" and "not spiritual enough." His publicist, Joe Morgen, said, "This is the first time a thing like this ever happened to him. He's 67 and he's upset. This is his hometown."[48]

On March 27, 1968, a few days before Martin Luther King Jr. was assassinated, Ellington performed at the White House at a State Dinner for Liberian president William S. Taubman. It was one of the many Ellington concerts dedicated to Africa held over his lifetime. At a November 9, 1968, concert, at the National Guard Armory, he was presented a plaque by Mayor Walter E. Washington. Ellington had praised the mayor for his handling of the 1968 DC riots.

Exactly thirty years later, on April 29, 1999, on what would have been Ellington's one hundredth birthday, his "Concert of Sacred Music" was presented at Washington's National Cathedral. As jazz producer and presenter Bill Bower recounted, "that concert came about when the dean of the National Cathedral, Rev. Nathan Baxter, approached Maurice Jackson, a parent of children at the National Cathedral School for Girls and the St. Albans School for Boys, about the idea to commission a concert of sacred music. Jackson suggested that instead he and the dean reach out to the Smithsonian Jazz Masterworks Orchestra [SJMO] about performing a concert of Duke Ellington's sacred music," which had been presented only a few times before.[49] Unlike the 1966 half-full concert at Constitution Hall, which was known for its history of bigotry, the event at the National Cathedral, where Martin Luther King Jr. gave his last public sermon, was full, and a spirit of racial unity prevailed. The SJMO was conducted by David Baker and joined by "two singers who had actually sung the concerts with Ellington—Queen Esther Morrow and De Vonne Gardner—as well as Kevin Mahogany." As Hasse once wrote in a book dedicated to David Baker, "the nation's jazz orchestra, performing in the National Cathedral, a couple of miles from Ellington's birthplace, in the nation's capital, on the centennial of one of the nation's greatest creative artists, performing his sacred music before a huge stained-glass rose window and arches and flying buttresses reaching towards heaven," would have made Ellington proud.[50] Hasse recounted the story of a young girl who, after hearing one of his sacred concerts, told him: "You know, Duke, you made me put the cross back on."[51]

## Ahmet Ertegun and Friends

Ahmet and Nesuhi Ertegun, sons of Munir Ertegun, the Turkish ambassador to the United States, and his wife, Hayrunisa Rustem, had a profound impact upon the Washington jazz scene. Arriving in Washington in 1935, the young men and their sister, Selma, quickly developed a love of and appreciation for African American music of all kinds: blues, spirituals, gospels, jazz, and, later, rhythm and blues. They learned about the city and about African Americans from the embassy's custodian, Cleo Payne, an ex-prizefighter who taught Ahmet to box, took him to boxing matches, and "introduced him to beer [and] joints, and . . . gave him an appetite for soul food."[52] Often they traveled the streets of Black Washington while being driven by the embassy's African American chauffeur, spending long hours at record stores and visiting the homes of Blacks to listen to and purchase jazz recordings.

Despite segregation, the Erteguns socialized with the African American community. "In the forties, Washington was like a Southern town," Ahmet later wrote.[53] "There was total segregation. Black people had their own movie theatres in their own section of town and were not allowed in the white movie theatres." Except, that is, at the burlesque shows, where whites sat downstairs and Blacks were in the balcony. "Black and white musicians did play together, but it was not easy. It was more possible in New York, particularly Harlem, but in Washington at that time it was virtually impossible." The men began to meet "the black professors at Howard University, especially the Dean of the School of English Literature, Sterling Brown," and others of

> the black intelligentsia and members of the Washington black society. Our common interest in jazz brought all of us together. . . . We had a lot of friends in Washington, and we could never go to a restaurant together, never go to a movie, or to the theater with them. . . . It was impossible to go out. I couldn't even take Duke Ellington, who is one of the geniuses of our country, to a restaurant. Or Count Basie. That's how it was and we could not accept it.[54]

Beginning in 1940 the brothers invited musicians they had seen perform on a Saturday night at the Howard Theatre and elsewhere to the embassy for Sunday lunch. Jazz-loving friends gathered, and whichever musicians were in town would join in playing, including Duke Ellington, Louis Armstrong, Johnny Hodges, Benny Carter, Rex Stuart, Joe Marsala, Lester Young, and Meade Lux Lewis.[55]

In 1940 the Ertegun brothers began inviting visiting bands to visit the embassy on Sundays for lunch and casual jam sessions. The pictured ensemble includes members of the Ellington and Marsala bands (*left to right*): Johnny Hodges (partially hidden in back), Rex Stewart, unidentified saxophonist, Harry Carney, Adele Girard, Barney Bigard, unidentified person (partially hidden), and Joe Marsala. William P. Gottlieb Collection, Library of Congress Music Division, LC-GLB13-0267 DLC.

Some Washington residents with strong southern sensibilities were disturbed to see Blacks entering the embassy through the front door. Ertegun often told the story of one southern senator who lived nearby complaining to his father, Mehmet, about African Americans entering the embassy through the front door. Ahmet recounted, "My father would respond with a terse one-sentence reply such as: 'In my home, friends enter by the front door—however, we can arrange for you to enter from the back.'"[56]

Ahmet Ertegun called himself "leftish intellectually" while living "in an embassy with sixteen servants with a limousine," yet he detested segregation.[57] Frustrated, the Ertegun brothers decided to hold jazz concerts that were open to integrated audiences in 1942. While whites had long gone to U Street and the Howard Theatre to hear Great Black Music, no previous events had promoted Blacks and whites listening to music together. According to Ahmet,

As Nesuhi and I had become friends with Duke Ellington, Lena Horne and Jelly Roll Morton, we decided to put on the first integrated concert in Washington. We had black and white musicians onstage, people like Sidney Bechet, Joe Turner, Pete Johnson, Pee Wee Russell, and others—and also we had an integrated audience. We had a lot of trouble finding a place in Washington where we could stage this event. The first concert we held was at the Jewish Community Center, which was the only place that would allow a mixed audience and a mixed band. After that the National Press Club broke down and let us use their auditorium. Leadbelly used to come to some of our open jam sessions at the embassy and he sang at the first concert we gave at the National Press Club. When he peeked out from the wings backstage and saw the size of the crowd, he said "Man, you gotta give me double the price, otherwise I'm not going on." So of course we did—we gave him everything we could, and you know, we certainly weren't pretending to be experienced promoters, we were just doing it for the love of the music.[58]

Some years later Ellington returned the admiration to the Erteguns and wrote to the Norfolk, Virginia, *Journal and Guide* about seeing the brothers:

I might write about an afternoon last February while we were playing at the Howard Theatre in Washington, D.C. Our very good friend Bill Gottlieb, a columnist on one of the Washington papers, came backstage to see us and brought with him an invitation from Nezuhu Ertigan [*sic*], the son of the Turkish Ambassador to the United States (who, by the way, really has his boots zipped to the hip), to attend a "jam" session at the Embassy where we were all invited to "cut a Turkish rug." So, we "jammed" until the "wee" hours of the morning—all in the cause of cementing Turkish-American good will with American "jam." But I can't write about that without the approval of the Department of State.[59]

The Erteguns smashed boundaries imposed by culture and race when they organized this first interracial concert in Washington, on 16th Street about a mile north of the White House. As Nesuhi remembered in a 1979 interview with the *Washington Post*, "Blacks and whites couldn't sit together in most places. So we put on concerts . . . jazz was our weapon for social action."[60] According to Robert E. Greenfield, author of *The Last Sultan: The Life and Times of Ahmet Ertegun*, Ahmet remembered later that many who came to the Jewish Community Center "did not know it would be integrated" and that the Press Club relented and allowed their next concert, because Ertegun promised "to make a big scene out of it if they didn't let us rent it."[61] A racially mixed jazz orchestra played the music for a mixed audience. Interracial audiences began to be more commonly seen in the DC jazz clubs.[62] The Erteguns also saw this as an effort to bring African

Americans, Jewish people, and Muslims together. Perhaps they had read the evil words of Adolph Hitler, that "the large mass of Jews is a race culturally unproductive. That is why they are more drawn to the Negro than to the culturally higher world of the truly creative races."[63] The Erteguns wanted to denounce anti-Semitism and racial hatred of all kinds. They did so using the music of the truly creative African American people, Jewish Klezmer music, echoes of Moroccan Gnawa music, and even Turkish folk songs..

Soon the Erteguns were known throughout the city for their activities in the jazz scene. In a *Washington Post* article dated May 16, 1943, and titled "Two Turks, Hot for U.S. Swing," journalist and photographer William Gottlieb wrote that "from the beginning, the young Erteguns treated the music of Morton, Armstrong, Oliver, Ellington and the rest with sincere enthusiasm and scholarly discrimination, an attitude that, strangely enough, is more typical of Europeans than Americans."[64]

When Leadbelly performed in the Erteguns' second concert, he was familiar with the realities of segregation in Washington, having visited the city years before, in the 1930s. Born Huddie Ledbetter, Leadbelly was initially brought to the city by folklorist Alan Lomax to record music at the Library of Congress. According to Lomax biographer John Szwed, "The Ledbetters were to have stayed with the Lomaxes in their apartment, but when the landlord got word that they had Negroes as guests he threatened to call the police and, under Washington's segregated housing laws, have them all put out of the building."[65] The next day, Lomax and Leadbelly searched the town looking for a Black hotel or rooming house and when, with their wives, they sought a place to eat together, they were denied entrance to restaurants. Leadbelly wrote "Bourgeois Blues" to reflect his views of race and class in the capital city, first recorded in 1938:

> Me and my wife went all over town,
> And everywhere we went people turned us down
> Lord in a bourgeois town.

The song included this last stanza:

> I tell all the colored folks to listen to me
> Don't try to find no home in Washington, DC
> Cause it's a bourgeois town.

Over the years this song has been used to unflatteringly describe the city's "Black bourgeoisie." Lomax himself was known to call Washington a "Bush-wa Town."[66]

Ahmet Ertegun also got to know Jelly Roll Morton, who was born in 1890 as Ferdinand Joseph Lamothe, a Creole of both French and African ancestry.

Renaming himself Jelly Roll Morton, he was one of the founders of what we now call jazz, a mixture of opera, French quadrilles, and Latin American and European marching band traditions. Popular in the 1920s when jazz was centered in New Orleans, Morton moved between California, Chicago, and New York. As ragtime declined and when he was down on his luck, he moved to DC, where, Ertegun said, "he had hit rock bottom . . . didn't have a place to stay, didn't have anything."[67] Still, in 1935 Morton's music was influential, "as Benny Goodman's rendition of Morton's 'King Porter's Stomp,' arranged by Fletcher Henderson, ushered in the Swing Era."[68] In 1938, as with Leadbelly, Lomax conducted interviews with Morton for the Library of Congress, and the next year he made eight new recordings as a result of the interviews. Although Leadbelly recorded "Bourgeois Blues" in 1938, some of his words reflect those of Jelly Roll, who wrote to his wife in January 1937, "Darling Wife, I don't want you to worry. Things are tough everywhere and we are not the only ones that's catching hell."[69] Lomax sums up Morton's condition: "Another month of striving up and down U St.—another month of acting up to the part of top composer in jazz on coffee and cakes in the most class-ridden small town in the U.S.—the colored bourgeois ghetto of Washington, D.C." Ertegun recalled, "For me Jelly Roll is still, to this day, one of the greatest musicians of all time."[70]

Another musician who indirectly influenced the integration of the city was Elizabeth Cotton, the author of the monumental folk song "Freight Train." According to Mike Seeger, a folk singer and cousin to the legendary Pete Seeger, "beginning in the early 1940s she lived with her daughter and five grandchildren in Washington, D.C."[71] While working at Lansburgh's Department Store, she "returned a lost Peggy Seeger to her mother. They quickly became friends and soon Elizabeth Cotton was working for the Seegers. After a few years she recalled that she, too, used to play, took the family guitar down and started playing again, recalling one by one many of the songs and tunes of her childhood and youth." On the streets, near Lansburgh's Store, along 7th and E Streets in downtown DC, all races heard her and the message about the dignity of African Americans. With the help of the Seeger family she joined the folk festival circuit, playing at the Newport Folk Festival and the Smithsonian Festival of American Folklife on the National Mall.

Ahmet and Nesuhi Ertegun moved to New York and, in September 1947, founded Atlantic Records, where they worked with the greats of American and world music of all colors, races, and religions. They produced Ray Charles, Aretha Franklin, Ornette Coleman, John Coltrane, and later the Rolling Stones and others. The noted pianist, composer, jazz educator, and Dunbar graduate Billy Taylor later wrote in appreciation that, "in their own way, the Erteguns defied segregation to frequent our neighborhood and patronize our music. They also produced jazz concerts that featured racially mixed groups, shocking the Washington, D.C. establishment and delighting their friends."[72] In a 2007 PBS documentary about Atlantic Records, Ahmet comments, "All popular music stems from black music, be it jazz or rock and roll." Reflecting on his career, he adds, "I'd be happy if people said that I did a little bit to raise the dignity and recognition of the greatness of African American music."[73]

The Erteguns left Washington a somewhat different city than the one they had found when their family arrived. Through their insistence on breaking racial barriers, they cracked open a door to greater integration in entertainment venues and, ultimately, much more. In 1946 David Rosenberg, the owner of Club Bali, where legendary artists such as Lester Young, Billie Holiday, Louis Armstrong, and Sarah Vaughn had appeared, made news with plans to build an event space having a nondiscriminatory policy for both musicians and audiences. On January 12, 1947, Rosenberg opened the Music Hall—one of the first professional venues in Washington that allowed mixed-race bands and audiences—with great fanfare. The new hall at 9th and V Streets NW featured a one-week engagement by Louis Armstrong. By late April the Music Hall had hosted Billy Eckstine, Ella Fitzgerald, Cootie Williams, Lionel Hampton, Tony Pastor, Cab Calloway, Rex Stewart, Jimmy Lunceford, Illinois Jacquet, Erskine Hawkins, Andy Kirk, Dizzy Gillespie, Art Tatum, and Sam Donahue. Charlie "Yardbird" Parker also performed there, while he and Dizzy Gillespie were leading the new bebop revolution in jazz.[74]

The next year, jazz events continued to weaken the hold of segregation through concerts promoted by Willis Conover, a popular disc jockey heard on radio station WWDC. Conover held the first of many integrated jazz concerts on Saturday, April 24, 1948, at the All Souls Unitarian Church on 16th Street NW, a fitting place to hold a socially pioneering performance. Long a bastion of social liberalism, the church's bell rang on Emancipation Day, January 1, 1863, and again rang during the March on Washington on August 28, 1963. Among its founders in 1821 was John Quincy Adams, called by some "the Abolitionist" for his role arguing the Amistad case before the US Supreme Court.[75] The church has continued its activism for freedom and racial equality to this day.

Following the success of this first "jam session" at All Souls Church, the next, formally the "Willis Conover Presents Jam Session No. 2," was held on May 9, 1948, at the National Press Club, which by then had adopted a policy of nondiscrimination, in part because of the efforts of the Ertegun brothers, Gottlieb, and Conover. The third and last of that first series of concerts was held two weeks later, on Sunday afternoon, May 23, at the Music Hall, advertised in the *Washington*

*Daily News* as Dixieland vs. Bebop and featuring Charlie Parker.[76] Ron Frits writes that the Music Hall was a good choice: "Venues in the Washington area that would accommodate patrons regardless of race and charge reasonable rent, while offering amenities far and above the standard in 1948, [were] few and far between."[77]

Conover later became famous internationally as a jazz broadcaster for the Voice of America. Although he made thousands of American jazz fans around the world, he was little known outside the jazz community in this country. Conover described himself as a "lower case voice identified with the music that symbolized freedom," perhaps equating Black freedom with the Voice of America's broadcasts from "the free world" to behind the Iron Curtain.[78] "A program should play music, not talk about it," he continued, thinking he should not discuss US race issues on air. However, as noted author Gene Lees has written, "During his military service, [Conover] acted to desegregate Washington. His part in this effort was to present musicians in nightclubs, insisting that blacks be admitted. He also produced a series of Saturday midnight concerts at the Howard Theater. His opposition to racism was lifelong, and deeply felt."[79]

Pianist and jazz authority Bill Potts, who toured with the likes of Ella Fitzgerald and Stan Getz and who often led the house band at Olivia's Patio Lounge, wrote that, "in the fifties, Washington was a mecca for jazz in the country. There was an abundance of young, experienced musicians from all around the country living in the D.C. area."[80] These included Shirley Horn, June Norton, Bill Potts, Buck Hill, John Malachi, and many others. Willis Conover was producing shows under the name "Willis Conover Presents the Orchestra, Joe Timer, Musical Director," with guest musicians such as Dizzy Gillespie, Stan Getz, Lee Konitz, Zoot Sims, and Charlie "Yardbird" Parker when they were in Washington. On February 22, 1953, Bird appeared and may have played the plastic saxophone he was known to use whenever he had pawned his horn.

## Satchmo Speaks His Mind

In September 1957 nine African American students were blocked from entering the all-white Central High School in Little Rock, Arkansas. Defying federal law, Governor Orval Faubus stationed Arkansas National Guard troops around the school to prevent their entry.[81] Louis Armstrong, who had been approached by the State Department to visit the Soviet Union as part of the Jazz Ambassadors program, was angered.[82] After seeing pictures of white mobs throwing objects at young Black girls, Armstrong told a reporter, "My people—the Negroes—are not looking for anything—we just want a square shake. But when I see on television and read about a crowd in Arkansas spitting and cursing at a little colored girl—I think I have a right to get sore—and say something about it."[83]

Referring to his trips abroad representing the United States, on September 19 he told another reporter, "The way they are treating my people in the South, the Government can go to hell. The people over there ask me what's wrong with my country. What am I supposed to say?" Accusing the president of being "two faced" and having "no guts," he added, "It's getting so bad a colored man hasn't got any country."[84] Because of his outspokenness, some concerts and television appearances were canceled, but Armstrong found a new appreciation for his work among Black Americans and throughout the world. On September 24, perhaps affected by the man known as Satchmo, President Eisenhower sent twelve hundred paratroopers from the 101st Airborne Division to Little Rock, to escort the Little Rock Nine into Central High. Satchmo then sent a message to Ike: "If you decide to walk into the schools with the little colored kids, take me along, daddy. God Bless You."[85]

Dizzy Gillespie said of Satchmo, "No you, no me," meaning that without Satchmo there would have been no Dizzy Gillespie.[86] In summing up the meaning of Satchmo to society and to music, Bing Crosby said, "I am proud to acknowledge my debt to Reverend Satchel Mouth. He is the beginning and the end of music in America. And long may he reign." He told a friend later in life that Armstrong "was the greatest singer that ever was and ever will be."[87]

Crosby, one of the most successful persons in the history of American show business, said great things about Armstrong before Little Rock and he praised him and his music after. He did not have to mention the controversy. All he had to say was, "It's so simple, when he sings he makes you cry, when he sings a sad song you cry and when he sings a happy song you laugh. What the hell else is there in popular music?"[88] At an exhibit at the Louis Armstrong Museum in Queens, New York, the words of the great crooner Tony Bennett greet visitors: "The bottom line of any country in the world is 'What did we contribute to the world? We contributed Louis Armstrong.'"

Armstrong said in October 1957 that he would play in the Soviet Union before he would play in Little Rock, "because Faubus might hear a couple of notes—and he don't deserve that."[89] He was roundly criticized by some. Paul Robeson, perhaps the most courageous scholar-athlete-activist-entertainer the world has ever known, came to Armstrong's defense, even as he was himself being vilified for his political stances. Robeson said simply that Armstrong's "heartfelt outburst" was given "in stronger terms than I ever have."[90]

Armstrong's words and actions had a tremendous impact in Washington in the same year that African Americans became the majority population. In his

Paul Robeson in Washington, DC. 1942. Before Robeson launched his career as an actor, singer, and activist, he was an All-American football player at Rutgers University. Robeson was class valedictorian as well. He played three years in the American Professional Football League (Association), the forerunner of the NFL. Photograph by Gordon Parks, courtesy Farm Security Administration, Office of War Information, Library of Congress Prints and Photographs Division, LC-USF346-BN-013363-C.

own way, "Ole Satch" had reached the president: not just with his trumpet or his singing but with his spoken word. His actions directly contributed to democracy in the nation's capital.

Armstrong "continued to express his sympathy for the movement, and for the young generation of radicals," when in 1964 "he posed for a photo for *Ebony* magazine sitting in a chair in his home reading *Blues People*, by Amiri Baraka (LeRoi Jones)."[91] Indeed the photo ran front and center in *Ebony* in November 1964 in the midst of the civil rights battle. Perhaps to give the photo a less radical ring, the story was titled "Louis Armstrong: The Reluctant Millionaire."[92] No matter: Baraka, who had learned from Washington's Sterling Brown, was deeply moved by Armstrong's simple, dignified, forceful gesture. Years later he told National Public Radio, "You know Louis's expression was musical and artistic and transcended that," meaning old stereotypes. He added: "When it was possible for Louis to speak, he spoke."[93]

## Notes

1. Hasse, "Washington's Duke Ellington," 50.
2. Ellington, *Music Is My Mistress,* 10.

3. Hollie I. West, "The Duke at 70: Honor from the President," *Washington Post*, April 27, 1969, K10.

4. Ulanov, *Duke Ellington*, 13.

5. Armstrong was born to missionary parents in Maui, Hawaii, and after graduating from Williams College in 1862, he took his missionary zeal with him when joining the Union war effort soon after. In 1863 he was made commander of the USCT 9th Regiment, distinguishing himself at the Battle of Petersburg. While stationed at Camp Stanton in Maryland, he founded a school for Black soldiers, most of whom were formerly enslaved. At the war's end he joined the Freedmen's Bureau and, with the support of the American Missionary Association, helped establish the Hampton Normal and Agricultural Institute, now Hampton University.

6. After graduating from high school in 1956, Wood attended junior college in California for a year, becoming an All-American quarterback at the University of Southern California. He then was shifted to a free safety for the Green Bay Packers, where he led a defense on teams that won five NFL championships. Eckstine was inducted into the Pro Football Hall of Fame in 1989.

7. Saint Paul's was opened in 1888 as a school for teacher training and for agriculture and industrial training, much like Washington's Tuskegee Institute. It closed in 2013. Eckstine went on to perform in the Earl Hines Orchestra, where he sang and played the trumpet. In 1944 he formed a bebop orchestra featuring Art Blakey, Tadd Dameron, Miles Davis, Dexter Gordon, Fats Navarro, and Charlie Parker. He shared vocal duties with Sarah Vaughn.

8. Cohen, *Duke Ellington's America*, 9.

9. Ellington, *Music Is My Mistress*, 12

10. Ellington, 17.

11. Ellington, 23.

12. Ellington and Dance, *Duke Ellington in Person*, 9.

13. Ellington, *Music Is My Mistress* 32.

14. Ellington, 33. He formed Duke Ellington and His Washingtonians, sometimes called Duke Ellington's Washingtonians and at other times Duke Ellington and the Washingtonians.

15. Ellington, *Music Is My Mistress*, 35–36. Ellington's compositions, according to Hasse, "combined his musicians' instrumental voices in innovative ways. Most arrangers for big bands voiced instruments in sections—pitting, for example, the trumpet section against the saxophone section. Ellington voiced his instruments across sections, combining, for instance, the clarinet, trombone, and trumpet in an innovative fashion." Hasse, "Washington's Duke Ellington," 52.

16. Hasse, "Washington's Duke Ellington," 58. See a full list of Ellington's Washington life and appearances in tables 3.1 and 3.2.

17. Personal conversations with Randy Weston and with Jason Moran, 2016–18. Both pianists also performed the music of Europe at the John F. Kennedy Center in Washington, DC.

18. "The Duke after White House Visit," *Norfolk Journal and Gazette*, October 31, 1931, 29. See also "Duke Meets Herb at White House," *Philadelphia Tribune*, October 15, 1931, 7; and "When the Duke Met Hoover," *Afro-American*, October 24, 1931, 23.

19. Ralph Matthews, "Looking at the Stars," *Afro-American*, October 10, 1931, 9; "Where's Hoover's Picture? As Usual the President 'Sidestepped' Being Photographed with Visitors of Color," *Cleveland Gazette*, October 10, 1931, 9.

20. Hasse, *Beyond Category*, 296–97.

21. The song was later used in Berlin's 1962 Broadway show *Mr. President* (1962). Kirk, *Musical Highlights*, 127.

22. Ellington, *Music Is My Mistress,* 424–33.

23. Hasse, *Beyond Category*, 254.

24. Logan, *The Diplomatic Relations* ; Hasse, *Beyond Category*, 254; Jackson, "No Man Could Hinder Him."

25. Teachout, *Duke*, 226.

26. Ellington, *The Duke Ellington Carnegie Hall Concerts: January 1943* (Prestige, 1977). See also Jackson, "No Man Could Hinder Him," 141–64.

27. Cohen, "Duke Ellington and *Black, Brown and Beige*," 1006–7.

28. Collier, *Duke Ellington*, 216.

29. Vail, *Duke's Diary*.

30. Cohen, "Duke Ellington and *Black, Brown and Beige,* 1010–11.

31. Cohen, 1010–11.

32. Jackson, "No Man Could Hinder Him," 154–56.

33. Ellington, *Music Is My Mistress,* 436.

34. Hasse, "Washington's Duke Ellington," 59–60.

35. Ellington, "The Race for Space," 295.

36. Ellington, 294.

37. Ellington, "The Duke Steps Out," 49.

38. Dance, *The World of Duke Ellington*, 21.

39. Ellington, *Music Is My Mistress*, 318. Penny Von Eschen writes: "In Delhi, the band members were invited to the university, where they were given demonstrations of indigenous Indian instruments and introduced to several forms of dance." Von Eschen, *Satchmo Blows Up the World*, 294n77.

40. Cohen, *Duke Ellington's America*, 422–23.

41. Faine, *Duke Ellington at the White House*; Ellington, *Music Is My Mistress*, 428, 476.

42. ". . . And Dancing Through the Night: An At-Ease, Low-Keyed Nixon Goes Out on the Town," *Washington Post*, January 21, 1969, D1, D3.

43. Ellington and Dance, *Duke Ellington in Person*, 287.

44. Ellington, *Music Is My Mistress*, 427.

45. "Workers Start to Clear 100-Year-Old Cemetery," *Washington Post,* May 24, 1960; "Old District Graveyard Moving Set," *Washington Post*, September 1, 1959.

46. Hasse, "Washington's Duke Ellington," in *DC Jazz*, 60.

47. Cohen, *Duke Ellington's America*, 423

48. Phil Casey, "The Duke Will Play Despite Rebuff," *Washington Post*, December 3, 1966.

49. Jenkins, "Bill Brower," 81. In an ironic twist, the man who did so much to segregate Washington, Woodrow Wilson, is buried in the cathedral's main sanctuary.

50. Hasse, "Smithsonian Jazz Masterworks," 250.

51. Hasse, *Beyond Category*, 378. For a full listing of Ellington concerts, including the sacred concert, see Vail, *Duke's Diary*.

52. Wade and Picardie, *Music Man*, 29.

53. Ertegun et al., "*What'd I Say*," 12.

54. Wade and Picardie, *Music Man*, 30–31.

55. Recently a series of jazz events were held at the Turkish embassy to commemorate the 1940s events, sponsored by the embassy and Jazz at Lincoln Center.

56. Ertegun et al., "*What'd I Say*," 7. In 1944 Ambassador Mehmet Ertegun died and his widow and some of the family returned to Turkey. Ahmet and Nesuhi elected to stay in the United States to finish their studies.

57. Quoted in Jackson, "Great Black Music," 16.

58. Ertegun et al., "*What'd I Say*," 12.

59. Duke Ellington, "The Duke Takes Pen in Hand," *Norfolk New Journal and Guide*, August 1, 1942, 16. William Gottlieb's column *Swing Session* in the *Washington Post* regularly included photographs of jazz musicians in Washington and New York City. Gottlieb's photograph collection is now housed at the Library of Congress. For more on the Ertegun brothers' pioneering work in jazz, see also Hasse, "How the Turkish Ambassador's Sons," 107.

60. J. Freedom du Lac, "A Chord of Jazz History to Echo at Turkish Embassy," *Washington Post*, February 3, 2011.

61. Greenfield, *The Last Sultan*, 32.

62. Maurice Jackson, "Remembering the Turkish Brothers Who Helped Change Race Relations in America," *The Hill*, November 1, 2013; "Hon. Alcee L. Hastings, D. Fla.," recognition of Maurice Jackson on publication of *Remembering the Turkish Brothers Who Helped Change Race Relations in America*," *The Hill*, November 1, 2013, Congressional Record, Tuesday November 12, 2013, E1629, 4–5.

63. Adam, *Art of the Third Reich*, 62.

64. William Gottlieb, "Two Turks, Hot for U.S. Swing," *Washington Post*, May 16, 1943, L2.

65. Szwed, *Alan Lomax*, 105.

66. Szwed, 105.

67. Ertegun et al., "*What'd I Say*," 8.

68. Rolf, *The Definitive Illustrated Encyclopedia*, 61.

69. Lomax, *Mister Jelly Roll*, 276.

70. Ertegun et al., "*What'd I Say*," 8. See also Barlow, *Looking Up at Down*, 72–75.

71. Mike Seeger, liner notes to *Elizabeth Cotton: Freight Train and other North Carolina Folksongs and Tunes* (Folkways, 1989).

72. Taylor with Reed, *The Jazz Life of Dr. Billy Taylor*, 29.

73. Ahmet Ertegun, quoted in *Atlantic Records: The House that Ahmet Built* (PBS, 2007).

74. Ron Frits, liner notes to *Charlie Parker: Washington, D.C., 1948* (Uptown).

75. Rediker, *The Amistad Rebellion*.

76. *Washington Daily News* ad, May 23, 1948.

77. Frits, liner notes to *Charlie Parker*.

78. Conover, "Willis Conover"; Davenport, *Jazz Diplomacy*, 133.

79. Lees, *Friends Along the Way*, 253.

80. Bill Potts, liner notes to *Washington Concerts: Charlie Parker with Quartet and the Orchestra* (Blue Note, 2001, from the recording at the Howard Theatre, Washington, DC, October 18, 1952).

81. Von Eschen, *Satchmo Blows Up the World*, 63. See also Munson, *Freedom Sounds*, 1–2.

82. Teachout, *Pops*, 314, 336.

83. "Satch Blasts Echoed," 1–2.

84. "Satchmo Tells Off U.S.," *Pittsburgh Courier*, September 28, 1957.

85. David Margolick, "The Day Louis Armstrong Made Noise," *New York Times*, September 23, 2007.

86. Gillespie, with Fraser, *To Be Or Not to Bop*, 486–91.

87. Crosby interview with Gary Giddens, https://riverwalkjazz.stanford.edu/program/bing-and-louis-pocketful-dreams-gary-giddins. Crosby, who is considered the first superstar "multimedia" entertainer as an actor and singer, wrote to Armstrong's widow Lucille: "I know of no man for whom I had more admiration and respect." Quoted in Teachout, *Pops*, 380.

88. Giddins, *Satchmo*, 183.

89. Giddins, 183. See also Giddings, *Bing Crosby*. Crosby and Armstrong worked together many times, including in the 1956 film *High Society*, which was made before Little Rock. The two men also recorded many records together, one in 1960, *Bing and Satchmo*.

90. Erik Mosh, "Maurice Jackson: The former Laborer . . . , Community Organizer and Activist Who Became a Historian," History News Network, May 13, 2018, https://historynewsnetwork.org/article/168895.

91. Von Eschen, *Satchmo Blows Up the World*, 73.

92. Anonymous, "Louis Armstrong."

93. "Revisiting Louis Armstrong in the Context of Civil Rights," NPR, November 22, 2006.

# 4

# JAZZ EXPANDS ITS HORIZONS

## From the Local to the Global

### Howard University

The Howard University Music School was admitted into the National Association of Schools of Music (NASM) in 1943. Over the years, Howard's Rankin Chapel had hosted performances by opera stars like Todd Duncan, eventually producing opera singer Jessye Norman, class of 1967. Jazz music was not accepted by the Black, Washington, or Howard elite. The DC-born and -raised George Walker (1922–2008), who attended Dunbar High School, participated in Howard's Junior Department of Music recitals, and was the first African American to win the Pulitzer Prize for Music, summed this up: "Only classical music was studied in this preparatory school. Jazz was for dancing and the uncultured rung of Black society in Washington, DC."[1] But jazz could not be denied to Howard students or to "high class" music lovers. Some formed a social club, calling themselves the "What Good Are We" in 1915. The club's members were "seeking respite from a demanding workload imposed by a new cadre of brilliant black educators" like Kelly Miller and Alain Locke. The year after its founding, What Good Are We "organized its first chaperoned house party. Entertainment was provided by a young pianist who lived near the campus. He was the soon to be world famous pianist Edward 'Duke' Ellington, son of James and Daisy Ellington, who were also talented musicians."[2]

Billy Eckstine, born in Pittsburgh, Pennsylvania, attended Armstrong High and then Howard until he dropped out to launch his singing career after winning an amateur contest at the Howard Theatre in 1933.[3] He formed his revolutionary bebop band in 1944 with Dizzy Gillespie, Miles Davis, Fats Navarro, Charlie Parker, Dexter Gordon, and Art Blakey, with Washington's own John Malachi on the piano and Sarah Vaughn as vocalist. In 1982 the Howard Jazz Repertory Orchestra performed the music of the Billy Eckstine Band of the 1940s, featuring Malachi on piano.[4]

Years later poet Sterling A. Brown played a major role in bringing jazz to the campus. In a new introduction to his now classic *Blues People,* first published in 1963, poet and playwright Amiri Baraka (formerly Leroi Jones) writes that "it was Sterling Brown, the great Afro-American poet and English teacher at Howard University, who first hipped A. B. Spellman and me to the fact that the music was our history, in our English 212 class."[5] He adds: "Sterling 'signified' to A.B. and me that we wasn't as hip as we thunk." Brown took them to his home at 1222 Kearney Street NE. There they listened to his Folkways and Commodore, Bluebirds, and even a Gennett recording. Jones recounts that Brown told his students, "This is the history. This is your history, my history, the history of the Negro people." Brown also "began to give a few informal talks on our history as Black Music, in the lounge of the old, then new, Cook Hall and we sat, literally, at his feet, taking those priceless teachings in. The Music, The Music, this is our history."[6]

At the Monterey Jazz festival in 1959, Brown gave a talk titled "The Social Background of Jazz." He "pointed out that contemptuous stereotypes of jazz and its musicians have turned many middle-class Negroes against it," adding that "the closest thing to jazz that ha[d] been played over the Howard University public address system [was] Paul Whiteman's version of 'Rhapsody in Blue.'"[7] Brown often spoke of his life at Howard. In his description of his years there, poet E. Ethelbert Miller, who first attended Howard in the fall of 1968 as a freshman, wrote that Brown used his poetic ability to tell stories "as a distillation of the black experience." Like the blues and jazz that Brown taught about, he "unlocks the door of transformation and embraces a future of infinite possibilities" of the African American people, their history, and their culture.[8] Brown was named Poet Laureate of the District of Columbia on April 11, 1984, the first to hold the position and the highest honor ever given to a poet or any other literary figure in the city.

Saxophonist Benny Golson went to Howard in 1947. When he arrived at the Hilltop, the school offered no jazz courses and formal training in classical music only. Golson's answer was to "gather with a few like-minded classmates and play together for no credit in the school jazz band."[9] He also performed with and wrote music for the Howard Swing Masters. Eventually, in 1950–51 he left to go on the road with Bullmoose Jackson and His Buffalo Bearcats because he felt that jazz music was "frowned upon" at Howard.[10] Golson later said that in the school's formal classes, he "was disappointed . . . because there were so many music rules," and he found it necessary to "break the rules" and "question every-thing in college" since "so many of the lessons [he] was taught contradicted the ideas [he] had in [his] head."[11] Years later, in 1996, the Benny Golson Jazz Master Award was created. Golson was conferred an honorary doctorate from Howard

At Howard University, ca. 1982: (*left to right*) Michael Winston, vice president for academic affairs, Professor Rayford Logan, DC Poet Laureate Professor Sterling Brown, James Early, and Professor Stephen E. Henderson. Courtesy James Early, Former Assistant Secretary of Education and Public Service and Former Director of Cultural Heritage Policy Folklife and Cultural Heritage Center, Smithsonian Institution.

in 2014, a moment which he calls "fantasy at its best," making him feel that his "life was [then] complete."[12]

John Malachi, although born in North Carolina, attended Armstrong High just like Duke Ellington, Billy Eckstine, and his good friend and DC legend Buck Hill. With Billy Taylor, another friend and fellow pianist at Dunbar High, he "hung out at the Jungle Inn," at 12th and U Streets NW, "where Jelly Roll Morton was the manager" and where "in the early 1940s he would accompany Pearl Bailey as her career was getting started."[13]

While he did play with the Eckstine band and was Sarah Vaughan's pianist in the early 1950s, Malachi preferred to live in Washington like Hill. Rusty Hassan, jazz show host and a longtime Malachi friend, put it best when noting that Malachi's "decision to make DC his home base and not tour extensively may have limited his name recognition, but it certainly didn't diminish the love and respect his more famous peers had for him."[14] Over time, Malachi accompanied the most acclaimed vocalists of his time, including Billie Holliday, Dinah Washington, Bailey, and Vaughn. Indeed, Malachi faced the dilemma of staying or leaving home, which many musicians have faced, such as greats Vaughn Freeman in Chicago, Ellis Marsalis in New Orleans, and Washington's own Buck Hill, Shirley Horn, and, later, Rueben Brown. The life of a musician was hard enough, and with family responsibilities a good nine-to-five, such as what Hill had at the US Post Office, offered a steady income. Local familiarity—even in Washington, a place full of bigotry—offered needed solace. In their cases, it was better to face

Pearl Bailey with two Georgetown University professors on the day of her commencement in 1985. Courtesy Georgetown University Library.

the prejudice that they knew in Washington and could work around than the one that they might come to know in other cities such as New York. Those who stayed home often made a living teaching and playing locally to jazz-wise and jazz-adoring audiences and to audiences in New York on weekends.[13] At Howard, Malachi taught piano to saxophonist Frank Wess, before the student left school to join the saxophone section in the pit band at Howard Theatre.

Wess was born in Kansas City, Missouri, but came to DC as a young child, like James Reese Europe. Going into the military, also like Europe albeit during a different war (World War Two), he joined the 54th Army band as a solo clarinetist. Mustered out in 1945, he joined the Billy Eckstine Orchestra and, like Eckstine before him, joined Bull Moose Jackson's band. But "determined to take his flute lessons seriously," Wess enrolled at the Modern School of Music in Washington under the GI Bill in 1949 and was tutored by Wallace Mann, the National Symphony Orchestra's flute soloist, eventually earning his degree."[16] The Modern School of Music, located at 3109 Georgia Avenue NW, was featured in the *Baltimore Afro-American,* in a picture of the school's head, Arthur E. Smith, an African American veteran, giving guitar instructions to a student, Jason Tillman, under the title "Vet Studies Music Under GI Bill."[17] Some years later Charlie Hampton, like Frank Wess, studied at the Modern School of Music. He

was also a onetime student at Howard University, where he studied classical clarinet starting in 1957; an Army veteran, Hampton was the last bandleader at the
Howard Theatre (1964–70).

The Modern School is an example of what pianist Jason Moran calls the
importance of the history of how a "space gets started" and "begins to tell the
story of how jazz in DC is also related to community."[18] Moran says, "We focus on
who it was and what they played, but we have somehow forgotten about where
it's played," adding, "when will America think about its relation to space—about
where culture happens?"[19] When there was no place for Blacks to get advanced
training in music, the Modern School provided it. It was a cross between Booker T.
Washington's notion of self-help, of creating your own institutions, and W. E. B.
Du Bois's concept of the right of African Americans to seek the highest form of
advanced learning.[20] The Modern School filled the gap that Howard University, a
few blocks away, failed to fill or to even realize existed, as the Howard music program did not yet recognize jazz as the unique contribution of African Americans
to the nation and the world.[21]

Photos and video of pianist Jason Moran are featured in the acclaimed multimedia performance "Harlem Hellfighters: James Reece Europe and the Absence of Ruin" by Moran and
cinematographer Bradford Young. This audiovisual homage to James Reese Europe has
wowed audiences at Barbican UK, Jazzfest Berlin, and the Kennedy Center in the Unites
States. Photograph by Jati Lindsay. Courtesy Jati Lindsay.

Pianist Geri Allen, one of the first students to graduate from Howard University with the bachelor of arts degree in jazz studies, at the 2014 NPR Piano Jazz Christmas Concert. Allen is pictured with Truly Hassan, granddaughter of Rusty Hassan, jazz educator and WPFW jazz programmer. Courtesy Rusty Hassan.

Malachi later taught pianist Geri Allen, who in 1979 received a bachelor's degree in jazz studies from Howard.[22] Allen was a graduate of Cass High School in Detroit, the school that produced many other jazz greats, such as bassist Ron Carter. On her 1992 album *Maroons*, Allen included a song "For John Malachi." She fondly remembered her Howard University years as "a very special experience," surrounded by "a lot of people we could look at in terms of excellence and what would be required of us in the professional world."[23] Allen joined the ancestors on June 27, 2017, and jazz musicians far and wide mourned her passing.[24] The book *DC Jazz: Stories of Jazz Music in Washington, DC* was dedicated to the memory of Geri Allen, Buck Hill, and Reuben Brown.[25]

Malachi later worked for a quarter of a century with Keter Betts, known as the bassist for Ella Fitzgerald, and with Dinah Washington, Stan Getz, and Charlie Byrd.[26] As Rusty Hassan has noted, "When he was not traveling with Ella he performed extensively in DC."[27] He made the DC area his home "and was undoubtedly one of the best teachers about jazz," in addition to being a "great storyteller." Beginning in 1963 John Malachi taught at Howard University and later for the Washington Performing Arts Society, the Wolf Trap Institute for Early Learning, and the Prince George's County Public Schools. He also conducted afternoon workshops and jam sessions at the Pig Foot, the club and restaurant owned by guitarist Bull Harris located on Rhode Island Avenue NE. He later taught at the Duke Ellington School of the Arts, while at one time also playing with the Smithsonian Jazz Masterworks Big Band.[28]

In 1960, Washington-born Andrew White arrived at Howard to study classical oboe. He had also won a scholarship to study the instrument at Tanglewood in 1963. Like Golson, White "found it difficult to reconcile the 'dualistic nature' of studying at Howard" and "felt he was 'a disappointment' to the HU administration because he was being groomed to be a classical music great, yet he had interest in both worlds."[29] Nonetheless, White did transcend many worlds. He became the bandleader and saxophonist with the J.F.K. Quintet, which was made up of Howard musicians and other locals who played most often at the Bohemian Caverns. White went on to play electric bass and woodwinds with R&B musicians like Stevie Wonder and Otis Redding, as well as with the Fifth Dimension. From 1968 to 1970 he was the principal oboist with the American Ballet Theater. A prodigious jazz talent, White played with McCoy Tyner, Kenny Clarke, Beaver Harris, and so many others.[30] White is perhaps best known for his transcriptions of the works, improvisations, and innovative music of saxophonist John Coltrane and Charlie Parker.[31]

Another Howard alumnus is trombonist Calvin Jones, who earned a master's degree in music education from the university in 1970. He broke the "color line" as the first African American to play in the Washington Redskins Band (1965–83) and in the Ice Capades in Washington, and he was one of the first African Americans to play in the pit orchestra of the National Theater.[32] He eventually went on to help found the jazz program at the University of the District of Columbia (UDC) and played a leading role in establishing the jazz archives at the University of the District of Columbia.

Howard University's student newspaper, the *Hilltop*, ran articles publicizing special student admission rates at jazz clubs like Abart's Internationale at 1928 9th Street NW.[33] In 1961 the Abart's performance schedule included Slide Hampton, Stan Getz, Dizzy Gillespie, Thelonious Monk, Max Roach, Miles Davis, Horace Silver, Art Blakey, and John Coltrane, among others.[34] Places like Abart's, in the words of pianist Jason Moran, inspired connections "not just to the musician, the hero, or the music, but also to the space that inspired the pieces they played and where the musicians felt comfortable to share them with us."[35]

Taking on Sterling Brown's mantle, Donald Byrd became the founding director of jazz studies at Howard in 1968, the year Martin Luther King was killed.[36] Byrd brought a prolific knowledge of jazz and music in general, having played with the greats such as Thelonious Monk, Charlie Parker, and John Coltrane. At

Omrao Brown, owner of Bohemian Caverns, with Robert Glasper at the club. Photograph by Jati Lindsay. Courtesy Jati Lindsay.

Howard he founded and toured with his band, the Blackbyrds, which included Howard students.[37] Byrd even earned a law degree and taught law, so that "he could teach himself and others how to protect their rights under the law."[38]

As a leader of Howard's music program, Saïs Kamalidiin, has written:

> He [Byrd] arrived on campus in 1968 with a larger-than-life persona and planted seeds for what would later become one of the greatest collegiate jazz programs in the world. Professor Fred Irby, III, Director of the Howard University Jazz Ensemble since 1975, has often said that, "Donald Byrd and Benny Golson are the most important figures in the history of the Howard University Jazz Studies program." During the turbulent '60s, Howard University faced student protests over the Department of Music curriculum that consisted of only the study of European art music. Performing or studying jazz in the Howard University Department of Music was strictly forbidden. Students were expelled for practicing jazz in the on-campus practice rooms and were strongly discouraged from performing it off-campus. Benny Golson actually withdrew from the university because of this policy. . . . The university administration finally relented by agreeing to create a Jazz Studies Program and recruited Donald Byrd to be its first Director.[39]

Howard University Jazz Ensemble in Japan, 2009. Courtesy Fred Irby III.

In 1970 Howard offered its first bachelor of music degree in jazz studies and in 1983 a master of music degree in jazz studies. In 1972 Cramton Auditorium held a memorial concert for trumpeter Lee Morgan, given by fellow trumpeters Donald Byrd and Freddie Hubbard, the day after Morgan had been murdered in New York City.[40] The two men played Hubbard's "Red Clay" and one of Morgan's best-known tunes, "Sidewinder." Then, on March 10, drummer Max Roach joined Byrd, who also conducted the Howard Gospel Choir, in performing at Cramton.[41] A few months later the auditorium held a series of concerts sponsored by the Left Bank Jazz Society of Washington, DC, featuring vocalist Leon Thomas, Argentine saxophonist Gato Barbieri, and poet Gil Scott Heron, with a focus on "third world politics, black power advocacy, and jazz."[42] Cramton also hosted convocations where honorary degrees were bestowed on jazz legends such as Lionel Hampton and Ella Fitzgerald.[43] In 1977 the university awarded its first jazz studies degree to Noble Jolley Sr., a Roosevelt High School graduate. Pianist Geri Allen received the same degree in 1979.

### University of the District of Columbia

In 1968 three institutions—Federal City College (FCC), District of Columbia Teachers College (DCTC), and Washington Technical Institute (WTI)—merged and opened as the University of the District of Columbia. Indeed, "from its founding, University of the District of Columbia [UDC] has been a hot spot for jazz performance, education and history."[44]

An important link between the programs at Howard and UDC provides the connection between the two universities' faculties that taught jazz studies in the 1970s. When trombonist Robert "Bobby" Felder joined the UDC faculty and became director of instrumental music, he was already well known as the leader of Bobby Felder and His Blue Notes. Felder recruited saxophonist and educator Arthur Dawkins from T. C. Williams High School in nearby Alexandria, Virginia, in 1970. When Fred Irby joined the Howard University faculty in 1974 and founded the Howard University Jazz Ensemble (HUJE) in 1975, Dawkins left Federal City College (UDC) to head the jazz studies program at Howard. In 1976 Felder recruited Calvin Jones from Cardozo High School to replace Dawkins. Jones and Dawkins played together in the Capital Jazz Quintet and as members of pit orchestras for shows that came through DC; they were friends among the close-knit jazz community in DC area, particularly the African American jazz community.

The name "jazz programs" at Howard and UDC refers not only to degree programs but also to jazz studies curricula and sets of courses. Judith Korey, professor of music and curator of the Felix E. Grant Archives at UDC, has noted that the story "begins at the Federal City College, a predecessor institution that was a leader in urban higher education."[45] Hildred Roach, pianist and scholar on the history of African American music, joined the faculty at Federal City

The UDC Jazz Ensemble with director Allyn Johnson at the Calvin Jones Big Band Jazz Festival, April 30, 2007. Photograph by Andrew Elwell. Courtesy Felix E. Grant Jazz Archives, University of the District of Columbia.

Maurice Jackson, the founder and leader of SUPERNOVA, Nasar Abadey, Joe Ford, James King, and Allyn Johnson shared their experiences as jazz musicians during this era and beyond. (*Left to right*): James King (bass), Allyn Johnson (piano), Maurice Jackson (moderator), Nasar Abadey (drums), and Joe Ford (saxophone), September 17, 2013. Photo by Ana Spoljaric. Courtesy UDC Archives

College at its inception in 1968. The school offered courses in music, including both jazz history and music performance.[46] By 1970 the Department of Music had established a bachelor of music education degree and an associate of arts in music degree.[47] UDC jazz groups also played at Lorton Reformatory as part of the Cultural Arts Forum in the university's Lorton Prison College Program during 1979 and 1980.[48]

### Lorton Jazz Festival and Concerts

Events in the Washington area also influenced Louis Armstrong. On July 2, 1957, Armstrong and his All Stars with trombonist Jack Teagarden appeared at the Second Annual Lorton Jazz Festival. The festival was established in 1956 at the Lorton Prison complex, where offenders from Washington were sent. Conceived by the prison's Catholic chaplain, Father Carl J. Breitfeller, the first concert featured Sarah Vaughn. Performing before a large audience of Black and white inmates, Satchmo told the large audience that he learned to play the trumpet at the Waifs Home in New Orleans when he was sentenced for eighteen months for shooting a pistol when he was twelve years old. Armstrong stated, "They made me the bugler—I didn't know one end of the horn from the other—and later I picked up the cornet." He added, "If it had not been for Professor Jones, the man who headed the Waifs home, who got me interested in music—well, thank God for the good men he put on this earth."[49] Armstrong appeared at the Lorton Festival again in 1960, that time with the great singer Velma Middleton.

In 1965, at the Tenth Annual Lorton Jazz Concert, Frank Sinatra appeared with the Count Basie Orchestra and Ella Fitzgerald with the Tommy Flanagan Trio. The crowd of fifteen hundred inmates witnessed history, as this was the first time that Sinatra and Fitzgerald had ever performed on the same program. A documentary on Sinatra, narrated by the legendary broadcaster Walter Cronkite, tells of the chaplain inviting him, and notes the obvious fun that "Ole Blue Eyes is having" and "that he not only came but brought the whole Count Basie Band with him." Cronkite added, "At this affluent point in his career he responds more quickly to the request for a benefit performance than to the opportunity to make money."[50] Also appearing were Eddie Harris, Ramsey Lewis, Bobby Timmons, and Quincy Jones.[51] This was Fitzgerald's fourth appearance, Basie's second, and Sinatra's first; inmates from the District of Columbia jail and the Women's Reformatory at Occoquan were bused in.[52] Washington's hometown hero Duke

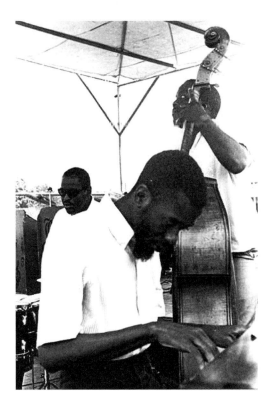

Pianist Bobby Timmons with Keter Betts, bassist for Ella Fitzgerald and longtime DC area resident, and drummer Harry T. "Stump" Saunders at the Lorton Jazz Festival in Lorton, Virginia. September 1964. Courtesy Felix E. Grant Jazz Archives, University of the District of Columbia.

Pianist Oscar Peterson, drummer Ed Thigpen, and bassist Ray Brown at the Lorton Jazz Festival in Lorton, Virginia. September 1964. Courtesy Felix E. Grant Jazz Archives, University of the District of Columbia.

Ellington held a special concert for a thousand at Lorton on July 16, 1967, in the midst of a five-day run with Ella Fitzgerald taking place at the Carter Baron Amphitheatre—both were owned by the federal government.[53] Some years later, in 1979 and 1980, UDC jazz combos played at Lorton Reformatory as part of the school's Lorton Prison College Program.[54]

## The New Thing

It was at this moment when the New Thing Art and Architectural Center began to play a major role in bringing Black, white, and brown people of different ages and classes together to listen to jazz, to socialize, and to help educate young people of color. The New Thing was founded in 1967 by Collin "Topper" Carew, a one-time member of the Student Nonviolent Coordinating Committee.[55] The twenty-eight-year-old former Howard University architecture student had dropped out, saying he "wanted to be a people's architect. So, I opened a storefront in the Adams Morgan community."[56] Soon the kids would "come by and stare in the window at me, wondering 'Who is this guy?' . . . So one day I just opened the door, let the kids come in, and started explaining what I did. They began coming by every day after school." He asserted, "We were taking kids past drugs and stimulating the whole cultural community of Washington."[57] Carew estimated that between 1967 and 1970 the center held many performances and brought different groups of people together, which "usually involve thirty, but in workshops there are many more," employing the "collective energies of 100 to 125 people." Up to "250 kids are involved on a continuing basis, seventy-five young adults" and "fifty older adults." The New Thing gave performances with as many as "2,500 people in attendance," and had six hundred monetary contributors.[58] Its most noteworthy events were weekly jazz concerts held at St. Margaret's Episcopal Church on Connecticut Avenue. Shirley Horn and Andrew White were among the performers there.

Eric Gravatt, a student at Howard University, played a special role. Carew observed that "the little boys have a cat named Eric, who's their idol, teaches them percussion, but its more than just teaching percussion, it's a whole relationship. . . . When he comes in, he just has a whole line of kids walking behind him. It's partly because they can go see him at the jazz workshop."[59] Carew added, "Eric's twenty-one. He's played with Pharaoh Sanders, he's recorded about three albums, Miles David wants him to play." Gravatt was best known for his long association as the drummer and percussionist with pianist McCoy Tyner, who himself came to prominence playing with John Coltrane. Carew later said, "I wanted jazz recognized as the only true American art form. This was really important. But you know, what I was trying to say was that black artists deserved their due. I wanted cultural institutions in Washington to acknowledge and accept the reality of Washington's black population."[60] A magnificent outgrowth of the concerts was the launching, in July 1969, of a legendary jazz program on radio station WAMU, a program later hosted by Rusty Hassan and aptly named *The New Thing Root Music Show.*[61]

Carew noted that The New Thing hosted young people at its storefront spaces, giving training in "photography, film making, African American design, Afro-American sculpture, karate, black history, and a workshop on practical life experiences."[62] The center, located in the area of the city populated by African Americans and Latinos, offered classes in "Afro-Cuban percussion, Latin percussion, blues guitar, blues harmonica, and blues theory." The New Thing operated out of five buildings and gained national recognition. One location sat near the headquarters of the local branches of the Students for a Democratic Society and the Black Panther Party.

Melvin Deal was also a member of The New Thing. As founding director of the African Heritage Dancers and Drummers, he became known worldwide for his pioneering instruction of African dance and drumming, most notably to young people in Wards Seven and Eight. As reported in the *Washington Post*, "The troupe was started in 1967 with 15 children. Demands now are heavy on the 38 positions in the troupe. There are nearly 100 youngsters in the dance workshops."[63] Among those who came to work with the kids was legendary Nigerian percussionist Babatunde Olatunji. In late 1968 and early 1969 alone the troupe played concerts at several colleges, including Yale University, Bennington College, Columbia University, and Williams College in Massachusetts. The youth drummers also visited the South American nation of Colombia.

Deal's vision, along with Carew's efforts, the guidance and leadership of Peggy Cooper Cafritz and the dancer Michael Malone, among others helped to lay the foundation for the Duke Ellington School for the Performing Arts. Deal, in summarizing the need for groups like The New Thing, believed that "so many advances are being undone. I see a tremendous need for another New Thing in about 10 years. Because it was a conscience for the power establishment. It received great impetus after the riots of '68. The way things are going, there might be more trouble. And then it will be needed again."[64]

The New Thing also sponsored the Washington Blues Festival at Howard University in November 1970. It was the first such effort in the city and the first-ever major blues festival organized by Blacks. "We wanted to bring the blues back home and make people more conscious of their cultural heritage," said Carew.[65] Performing at the festival were B. B. King, Howlin' Wolf, The Junior Wells–Buddy Guy Blues Band, and Richard Haven, the famed folksinger who performed for free. On three successive nights Blacks and whites attended en masse, with fifteen hundred in the audience on Thursday, twelve hundred on Friday, and a thousand on Saturday. At one point protests arose among Howard University students and other Blacks from the city who were unable to attend because tickets were sold out; they noted large numbers of whites in the audience. "Why do those whites from Georgetown get all the privileges? This is black music," said some of the protesters.[66] Carew, who had received funding from organizations like the Friends of the John F. Kennedy Center, explained that the tickets had been sold by mail, so sales were color-blind. Carew said the festival was intended to be an assault on cultural racism: "Washington is 70 percent black, but the city's cultural style is neo-European," he told the *Washington Post*.[67] In the end, though plagued by disorganization and faulty audio equipment, the festival was deemed a success. Never before had so many whites gone to a musical event at Howard University, and never had the school seen such an integrated audience at such a venue.

Ron Clark, executive director of RAP INCORPORATED, presenting award to DC GO GO pioneer Chuck Brown. Brown and the Soul Searchers recorded "It Don't Mean a Thing If It Don't Have the Go Go Swing," a take on Duke Ellington's "It Don't Mean a Thing If It Ain't Got That Swing," in 1986. Ron Clark collection, courtesy Angela Owens Clark.

## Notes

1. Walker, *Reminiscences*, 13.

2. Courtland Milloy, "What Good Are We? Turns Out Not So Bad, Especially for a Black Social Club Turning 100," *Washington Post*, October 20, 2015. The club still exists today and serves the same purpose.

3. Obituary of Croner Eckstine, "A Modern Jazz Pioneer," *Afro-American Gazette*, April 5, 1993. He sang with the Earl Hinds Orchestra, and later sang now-classic songs like "Prisoner of Love," "Cottage for Sale," "Blue Moon," and the song he became best known for, "Jelly Jelly." Eckstine formed his revolutionary bebop band in 1944 with Dizzy Gillespie, Miles Davis, and Fats Navarro on trumpet; Charlie Parker and Dexter Gordon on saxophone; and Art Blakey on drums. Sarah Vaughn was the vocalist. Washington's own John Malachi also played with the band, as did Sonny Stitt, who later moved to Washington.

4. W. R. Stokes, "Jazzing Up the Curriculum: At Howard U., Thelonious Monk's Music," *Washington Post*, March 13, 1985,

5. Baraka, *Blues People*, ix.

6. Baraka, viii–ix. A. B. Spellman was a Baraka classmate and author of *Four Jazz Lives*. Spellman a renowned music critic and poet and part of the Black arts movement of the 1960s and 1970s, worked for many years at the National Endowment for the Arts (NEA) in Washington. The NEA has since established the A. B. Spellman Awards for Jazz Advocacy, which inducts new NEA Jazz Masters (its Hall of Fame) every year it names others who have played a major role in promoting jazz and in aiding ailing and struggling musicians. See Gates and Smith, "A. B. Spellman," in *Norton Anthology*, 749–50.

7. L. P. Jackson, "Race that Bred Jazz Lends It a Top Scholar," *Washington Post and Times Herald,* July 9, 1959.

8. Miller, "Sterling Brown and the Browning of My Life," 107.

9. Sims, "Benny Golson," 23.

10. Sims, 23.

11. JazzWax, "Interview: Benny Golson (part 1)," http://www.jazzwax.com/2008/09/interview-benny.html. Golson, the NEA Jazz master, died on September 24, 2024. Richard Williams, "Benny Golson Obituary," The Guardian, September 25, 2024.

12. Benny Golson's honorary doctorate speech, quoted in Sinclair, "No Church Without a Choir," 136. Recipients have included multi-instrumentalist Yusef A. Lateef (2001), pianist Geri Allen (2005), saxophonist and oboist Andrew White (2008), and drummer T. S. Monk, the son of Thelonius Monk (2010). Doris McGinty, who for many decades had done so much to bridge the gap in Howard's music program and to support its Jazz Ensemble and jazz studies program, was awarded the Benny Golson award in 2002. Doris Evans McGinty Music Professor," *Washington Post*, April 8, 2005. She also wrote liner notes for the Howard University Jazz Ensemble's recordings every year from 1976 until her death.

13. Hassan, "Jazz Radio in Washington, DC," 99.

14. Hassan, 99.

15. Richard Harrington, "John Malachi, The Professor of Jazz," *Washington Post,* February 13, 1987.

16. Vacher, "Remembering Jazz Legend Frank Wess," *Guardian*, November 4, 2013.

17. *Baltimore Afro-American,* "Vet Studies Music Under GI Bill," February 16, 1946, 6. After playing with the Eckstine Orchestra and many others, Wess became a mainstay with the Count Basie Orchestra beginning in 1953.

18. Moran, Foreword.

19. Michael J. West, "Crescendo in Blue: If These Walls Could Talk," *Washington City Paper,* June 19, 2018.

20. Washington had many such institutions for African Americans. Of special note is the Jones-Haywood Dance School, established in 1941. Haywood School has sent students to careers with the Alvin Ailey American Dance Theater, the Washington Ballet, the Paul Taylor Dance Company, the Royal Netherlands Ballet Company, and more.

21. For a review of how musicians like Benny Golson, Frank Wess, Shirley Horn, and others felt about Howard University's ambivalence to early jazz studies, see Sinclair, "No Church Without a Choir."

22. Richard Harrington, "The Rising Scale of Geri Allen: Jazz Piano and the Composer's Art Jazzy Geri Allen," *Washington Post*, October 1, 1988. Among Allen's contemporaries at Howard were Greg Osby (saxophone), Gary Thomas (saxophone, flute), and Wallace Roney (trumpet).

23. Harrington, "The Rising Scale."

24. S. Mervis, "Fellow Musicians Pay Tribute to Geri Allen," *Pittsburgh Post-Gazette*, July 5, 2017.

25. The deep respect accorded to Allen is in part due to her great dexterity across genres, playing folk music with artists such as Charlie Haden, free jazz with Ornette Coleman, and electro-acoustic jazz with Steve Coleman.

26. I grew up partly in Newport News, Virginia, where my stepfather, Pete Ballard, was then known as the state's premier saxophonist. He had been a member of the US Army Air Force band and served in World War Two. He had played with Dinah Washington and other jazz greats when they passed through Newport News, often leaving their usual reed players behind while Pete would sit in with them. Sometimes his band, The Mellow Tones, would also be on the program. Pete had played with Lloyd Price and Ruth Brown and even with the famed R&B group The Five Keys, led by Rudy West. But, like many, he chose to stay home. He sat in with Ella Fitzgerald and Pearl Bailey, both from Newport News. He and Keter Betts were old friends who bragged about their golfing game. Whenever I saw either one of them, in DC or in Newport News, they would ask me if I had seen the other and if I had brought the money owed to them, which they claimed they were owed because they had beaten the other in a round of golf. Whenever Charlie Haden came to DC he would come over to borrow one of Betts's basses and would ask if Pete sent him his money. Both Pete and Keter were masterful storytellers. Betts, in fact, first met Ella Fitzgerald by playing golf with her ex-husband and business manager, the great bassist Ray Brown.

27. Hassan, "Jazz Radio in Washington, DC," 101.

28. Hassan, "Jazz Radio in Washington."

29. Sinclair, "No Church Without a Choir," 133.

30. Karina Porcelli, "Weekend Best," *Washington Post,* January 22, 1988.

31. White is also an influential jazz collector and scholar, and received the 2006 Gold Medal from France's Ordre des Arts et des Lettres.

32. Matt Schudel, "D.C. Jazz Band Leader Charlie Hampton, 75, Dies," *Washington Post*, August 26, 2005.

33. The same year as the *Hilltop* article, the newly opened Cramton Auditorium on the Howard campus began to book a wide range of cultural performers. Concerts extended well into the1970s. See "Washington; Les McCann; Nick Kirgo; Howard University; Phi Mu Alpha; Approximately," *Chicago Metro News*, December 9, 1978. Abart's Internationale had a name representative of the times. Recently it has been the location of the Expo Lounge. Jazz writer Mike West notes that "John Coltrane and Cannonball Adderley played there, and that " Andrew White, playing with the JFK Quintet at Bohemian Caverns, would run down to Abart's between sets to check out the headliners." Michael J. West, "Crescendo in Blue: If These Walls Could Talk," *Washington City Paper*, June 19, 2018.

West interviewed pianist Jason Moran, who spoke about the space and historic jazz spots, the subject of a talk given at Georgetown University in 2018, where he was Distinguished Artist in Residence.

34. Collis Davis Jr., "Jazz Greats Galore Coming, Club Offers Student Rates," *Hilltop,* October 27, 1961.

35. West, "Crescendo in Blue."

36. Hon. John Conyers Jr., "A Tribute to Jazz Master Dr. Donald Byrd," US Congressional Record, Vol. 149, February 26, 2003, https://www.govinfo.gov.

37. "Jazz Great Donald Byrd at George's," *Chicago Metro News,* December 31, 1983. The Blackbyrds also recorded "Rock Creek Park," about the city's largest open space, which runs throughout the city as part of the Appalachian Trial.

38. "Byrd Makes Music to Recreate Heritage," *Milwaukee Star,* September 18, 1971.

39. Saïs Kamalidiin, liner notes to Howard University Jazz Ensemble (2013), https://www.howard.edu/library/music@howard/huje/2013-notes.htm.

40. Hollie I. West, "A Sad Occasion," *Washington Post and Times Herald,* February 22, 1972. I attended that concert as a young college student.

41. "Sidewinder" (1964) was one of Morgan's best-known albums and title song, at the time Bluenote Records's number one recording. On March 24 of that year Gary Bartz joined Rene McClean for a tribute concert held at the University of Maryland in College Park.

42. Hollie I. West, "Left Bank Jazz," *Washington Post,* May 15, 1972.

43. "Lionel Hampton to Be Honored at Howard," *Afro-American,* February 24, 1979; "Howard University to Honor Ella Fitzgerald," *Washington Informer* September 25, 1980, 15; Brian M. Walton, "What's Going On in Arts & Entertainment," *Washington Informer,* January 22, 1997; "All That Jazz," *Washington Informer,* May 2, 1984.

44. Lightman and Zeisel, *Since 1851,* 176.

45. Korey, "From Federal City College to UDC," 145.

46. Department of Music, "Chronological Chart of Faculty Progress and Music Curriculum Development, September 1968–January 1972," Federal City College Collection, University of the District of Columbia Archives. Course offerings at the time included "The History of Afro-American Music"; by 1969 Stage Band and The Voices (Gospel Music Ensemble) were added.

47. For an excellent history of jazz at the University of the District of Columbia, see Korey, "From Federal City College to UDC." In 1968 a course in jazz history was designed to provide insight into the role of jazz in the social, historical, economic, and literary development of a people's culture. "The Sound of Soul" discussed the history and development of gospel, rhythm and blues, and soul music, and examined the musical influences and social impact surrounding the growth of each form. In 1970 the FCC Department of Music established a bachelor of music education degree and an associate of arts in music degree. In addition to the traditional music curriculum required by national accrediting agencies, jazz and gospel music courses were offered for credit as part of the program of study. The bachelor of music degree in jazz studies degree was first offered in 1984.

Bobby Felder and Calvin Jones recruited students from schools all over the city (including Southeast). Calvin Jones brought many students from Cardozo High School. One noted example of UDC's recruiting students locally is Davey Yarborough, who graduated from Coolidge Senior High School. He was the founding director of the jazz program at Duke University, as well as a recording artist in his own right.

48. Gloria O. Stokes, quoted in Korey, "From Federal City College to UDC," 150.

49. *Washington Post and Times Herald,* "Jail Sentence Started Him on Music, Satchmo Tells 1600 Lorton Inmates," July 3, 1957. For a look at Armstrong's own life in prison see Brothers, *Louis Armstrong's New Orleans,* 74–109.

50. Walter Cronkite in *"CBS News* Special: Sinatra," November 17, 1965, Don Hewitt, executive producer, excerpted in the HBO documentary *Sinatra: All or Nothing at All* (Alex Gibney, dir., 2015). For an interesting take on the social and political views of Sinatra, see Jones, *Q,* 180–85, 194–96, 282–83.

51. "Ella, Sinatra, Basie, Quincy Jones Send Inmates," *JET* 28, no. 16 (July 29, 1965): 54.

52. Leroy F. Aarons, "Stars Visit Prison—and It's a Near Riot," *Washington Post,* July 15, 1965; "Only Invited May Watch Show," *Washington Post,* July 10, 1965, B2.

53. Hasse, "Washington's Duke Ellington," 57, 73.

54. Korey, "From Federal City College to UDC," 150.

55. Anderson, "The Young Black Man" 132.

56. Alan Bunce, "Breaking Down the Color Barrier: Producer Topper Carew Uses TV to Help Shape Values," *Christian Science Monitor,* February 2, 1988.

57. Michael Kernan, "That Summer Thing," *Washington Post,* August 19, 1984.

58. Wallace Roberts, "Black Arts for Black Youth: An Interview with Topper Carew," *Saturday Review,* July 18, 1970, 47–48.

59. Blackman et al., "Interview with Topper Carew," 112.

60. Juan Williams, "Roads from the Riots: How the Events of '68 Changed Three Lives," *Washington Post,* April 3, 1988.

61. Hassan, "Jazz Radio in Washington," 77.

62. Blackman et al., "Interview with Topper Carew," 46.

63. "Children Drum Up Interest in African Dance," *Washington Post,* January 30, 1969. See also Michael Kernan, "A Dancer's Homage: Heirs A Series on The American Family, A Dancer's Homage," *Washington Post,* January 19, 1977.

64. Kernan, "That Summer 'Thing.'"

65. Hollie I. West, "Blues Festival," *Washington Post,* November 9, 1970.

66. West, "Blues Festival at Howard."

67. Hollie I. West, "Blues Festival: Top Stars in 3-Day Event," October 9, 1970.

# 5

# TWO WHO STAYED HOME

### Shirley Horn and Buck Hill

Perhaps the greatest of those who decided to stay home in Washington to raise children was Shirley Horn, who stayed home to raise her daughter. As Bridget Arwine has noted, the Washington-born Horn "was groomed for success early on. Her family wanted her to grow up to be a concert pianist, so she began taking lessons before she could read or write."[1] While at Dunbar High School, she studied classical piano as a teenager at the Howard University Junior School of Music. Although she won "offers to attend Julliard and Xavier University, Horn stayed in Washington," married Charles "Shep" Deering, and had a daughter they named Rainey. Years later Horn said, "I'm going to stay home and take care of my baby, you know, I had to do that. I mean, it was no other way for me. . . . I couldn't live with myself because I'd seen so many cases where, oh boy, it's sorry."[2]

Horn stayed home and formed her own bands, playing at all the "in" spots, like Olivia's Patio Lounge at 713 13th Street NW and the Crystal Caverns (Bohemian Caverns) at 11th and U Streets NW. Like so many Washington musicians, Horn had kind words for Buck Hill. In speaking about the difficulty African American women jazz instrumentalists and vocalists faced especially in the 1950s, 1960s, and 1970s, Horn once told a *Washington Post* interviewer: "'Buck was the only person who was nice to me the couple of times they let me sit in. I didn't know anything about jazz, just what I had heard, and imitations of Erroll Garner didn't fit in with what the guys were doing then. Their attitude was 'Let's bear down on her.' Which was the best thing for me, trying to come out of the classical tradition. I was nervous but I was stubborn."[3]

She went on the road for a while, as a pianist and vocalist. She had recorded her first album, *Embers and Ashes,* in 1960, and when Miles Davis heard it, he sent for her to come to New York as the opening act for his shows. Much in the spirit of Buck Hill, Davis both admired Horn's musical genius as a vocalist and pianist and promoted her. Arwine writes, "The woman who some perceived as an unwelcome addition to the jam session now was in demand."[4]

Horn subsequently took a ten-year break from working on the road, mainly to be with her family, but kept performing in the DC area and parts nearby. She also began to spend a good deal of time in Europe starting in the late 1960s. There she may have found the racial climate gentler and the life of a Black woman musician a bit less burdensome. In 1981 she recorded *Violets for Furs,* and the success of the album and the spreading word among jazz hipsters of her performances at the North Sea Jazz Festival in Holland propelled her back on the road. She again worked with Davis, who considered her one of his favorite vocalists and pianists because of her spacing, phrasing, and lyricism. In 1991 she recruited Davis to play on the title track of perhaps her best-known work, *You Won't Forget Me,* now considered a jazz classic.[5] Her longtime friend Buck Hill appeared on other tracks of the album, and Washington-born drummer Billy Hart, who is considered one of the greatest of all time, also appeared. Hart credits Horn and Hill as being the two established musicians who took a chance on him. A few years later she produced the album *I Remember Miles,* dedicated to Davis, who she credited with revitalizing her career. She also won a Grammy for Best Vocal Performance for the record. Known for her loyalty, especially to DC musicians, she kept the same rhythm section for over twenty-five years and included them on her recordings.

As Rusty Hassan, her neighbor and longtime friend in the Brookland neighborhood in Washington (not far from Catholic University) notes, "her unique vocal styling and piano accomplishments eventually landed her a recording contract with Verve Records, and world tours followed, but she and her husband Shep, continued to live in their house on Lawrence Street."[6] Hassan relates that her increased income allowed "her to build additions to her house and she was especially proud when she could finally accommodate a grand piano in her home." By then, she told friends, the city government began to deny her any more building permits. Even as she began to travel, as her daughter grew into adulthood, she retained her local fan base and was equally loyal to them. Her home was also a drop-by place for out-of-town musicians wanting a good home-cooked meal and hometown soul. One was bassist Charlie Haden, who made a point of visiting, especially as Horn developed some health problems. She sang and played piano on several of his albums, and her rendition of "The Folks Who Live on the Hill" carried special meaning to the people of her hometown.[7] The 109th US Congress (2005–7) recognized her for "her many achievements to the world of jazz and American culture."[8] The resolution was read by Congressman John Conyers Jr. of Michigan, a founder of the Congressional Black Caucus and original sponsor of HR-57, which declared jazz an American treasure.[9] Conyers's words read that "importantly, Ms. Horn never forgot her background. She was dedicated to the Washington, DC community and, as a result, earned the Mayor's

The author with friends Charlie Haden (bassist, composer, *Downbeat* Hall of Fame member, and NEA Jazz Master), Ron Clark, and Carletta Cherry (with her daughter and granddaughter) at the Black Entertainment Television studio. (*From left to right*): Maurice Jackson, Ron Clark, Charlie Haden, Carletta Cherry, and her daughter and granddaughter. Ron Clark collection, courtesy Angela Owens Clark.

Arts Award for Excellence in an Artistic Discipline."[10] In 2005 she was inducted as a "jazz master" by the National Endowment for the Arts.[11]

Buck Hill, like Horn, was a link between the days of rigid segregation in the city and a more modern form in present-day Washington. The Armstrong graduate spent over forty years as a mail carrier. A "good post office job" was a "good government job," but unlike working inside the mail room, where hours of sorting mail often led to undiagnosed carpel tunnel syndrome, Hill "walked the route," keeping fit by day and playing his horn by night. Although the Woodrow Wilson administration reestablished segregationist practices at the US Post Office, for some the old saying still rang true: "There's always work at the Post Office." Amzie Moore, the heroic civil rights leader, "got a job as a postal custodian in Cleveland, Mississippi, and kept at it until his retirement in 1968 despite attempts to fire him for his civil rights activism."[12] Others, like "Dick Gregory worked at the Chicago post office during the day while polishing his comedy act at night"; Richard Wright worked at the post office in Chicago in the 1920s and 1930s, and his novel *Lawd Today* posthumously published in 1963 was based on his experiences as a postal worker, as well as his observations of what he called "the broken dreams of his black coworkers." Charles Mingus, one of the world's greatest bassists and jazz composers, worked at the Los Angeles Post Office between 1949 and 1950. The Marvelettes even had a hit song, "Please Mr. Postman," released in 1961 on the Motown label.

Although Hill stayed home, his admirers were legion. In the tough late 1950s he once sat in with Miles Davis during one of John Coltrane's absences, and Davis offered him a regular job. But he declined, for he could not give up his day job and regular income. One stout admirer was Jimmy Heath, of Heath Brothers fame, who said of his fellow tenor sax man: "A lot of cats came into DC who were heralded, who played the horn," and "nobody warned them about Buck Hill. . . . Man, you get into a jam session with Buck Hill, you gonna come out skinned up."[13] On August 27, 2019, a seventy-foot-high mural of Hill, the "wailin' mail-man," was unveiled near the corner of 14th and U Streets NW in the center of gentrified Washington. Mayor Muriel Bowser proclaimed it "Buck Hill Day."[14] Still others had long since paid tribute to Hill.[15] As Hassan notes, "In 1978 drummer Billy Hart wanted to pay back those who helped him get started with his career and arranged for Buck to record for the Danish Steeplechase label and perform in Europe at the North Sea Jazz Festival in 1981"; the event led to a live recording of the album *Easy to Love.*[16] This was the same event that had played an important role in Shirley Horn's latter career.[17]

Lawrence Levine has observed that "culture is not a fixed condition but a process, the product of interaction between the past and the present. Its toughness and resiliency are determined not by a culture's ability to withstand change, which indeed may be a sign of stagnation not life, but by its ability to reach creatively and responsively to the realities of the new situation."[18] The many forms of Great Black Music changed, developed, and played a major role in the struggle for equality in the nation's capital. It started with Will Marion Cook, who wrote that "we must strike out for ourselves; we must develop our own ideas and conceive an orchestration adopted to our own abilities and instincts."[19]

The Great Black Music created in Washington and by Washingtonians highlights how this music advanced both music and society. It helped to bring the races together in the fight for equality. By the 1960s DC was moving slowly, if not to becoming a city of "equals," then at least to becoming a place where "equal rights" were the law. By this time it had become the first major city in the country

The Shirley Horn Trio—Horn (vocals and piano), Chares Ables (bass) and Steve Williams (drum)— at the Benefit for the Free Festival at Duke Ellington School for the Arts, November 3, 1989. Courtesy Michael Wilderman, jazzvisionsphotos.com.

with a majority Black population. The Twenty-Third Amendment was ratified in 1961, allowing Washington residents, Black and white, to vote in a presidential election. The following February 13, at Pierce Hall in All Souls Church, guitarist Charlie Byrd, tenor sax giant Stan Getz, and bassist Keter Betts recorded their groundbreaking session *Jazz Samba*, bringing the multiethnic Brazilian sounds to the nation.

In 1964 Washingtonians were able to vote for president for the first time since 1800, and the Civil Rights Act was passed. That same year the Ramsey Lewis Trio recorded *The Ramsey Lewis Trio at the Bohemian Caverns*; in 1965 the group repeated its success at the venue by releasing the Grammy-winning *The In Crowd with the Ramsey Lewis Trio*. Al Clarke of WOOK Radio writes in the album's liner notes, "Nowhere in the country has the trio been more enthusiastically received than in the nation's capital, where they enjoy the praise of fans of all nations. It is a small wonder that hundreds of global neighbors waited in line to enter the beautiful, sculptured, world-renowned Bohemian Caverns, the home of the 'In' crowd."[20]

Shortly after the Voting Rights Act of 1965 was passed, James Reeb, the former white assistant pastor of All Souls Unitarian Church—where both Blacks and

2019 mural by Joe Pagac at the Corner of U and 14th Streets NW, Washington, DC. Flickr, no. 22711505@N05/52202187412. Courtesy Ron Cogswell.

whites, such as Keter Betts and Charlie Byrd, performed—was murdered by a gang of white men in Selma, Alabama, because of his efforts to win equality for African Americans. Great Black Music—and the men and women, Black and white, who performed, promoted, and went to hear it—played a part in integrating the city and the nation. As Washington, DC, educator Thomas J. Porter has pointed out, "National consciousness has always been inherent in Black music, but the music has always embodied both the class and national characteristics in its criticism of the society."[21] Nowhere has this been more evident than in Washington, DC, the nation's capital, where Great Black Music played a role in securing the rights that Reverend Reeb had died for.

Washington-born musicians continued to express their desire for equality. Billy Taylor, who graduated from Dunbar High in 1939, reflected on his years in Washington, DC, in saying, "I had much reinforcement in terms of who I was, what I was about and the tremendous contributions that black people have made to science, music, art, government. Black accomplishment was very visible in Washington what with judges, lawyers and other over achievers."[22] Doctor Taylor, as he was universally known, wrote of the racial situation in America when he recorded "I Wish That I Knew How It Would Feel to Be Free" two weeks before the assassination of President John Kennedy.[23] In his book Taylor says "The lyrics were about freedom, which for African Americans was the clarion cry of that era."[24] He believed that the song "captured the essence of the Civil Rights Movement" and that Martin Luther King was especially fond of Nina Simone's popular recording of it in 1967. Taylor notes that King "was a lover of Jazz" but because he could never remember the title always asked him to play "that Baptist sounding song."

In May of 1971 the May Day Peace Protest against the war in Vietnam, one of the largest demonstrations in American history until that time, was held in the capital city. That same year Washington-born Marvin Gaye released one of the highest-selling albums in history, *What's Going On*, with the opening track of the same name. The album also ranks among the top musical recordings of social protest. Gaye was deeply moved by the letters his brother had sent from Vietnam and the conditions of Black people in America. One of the songs on the album, "Inner City Blues (Makes Me Wanna Holler)," reflects the chaos of the times and with it the violence, poverty, and plight of ghetto youth, who took the song as their own. The beginnings words, "Rockets, moon shots / Spend it on the have nots," took "the government to task for probing outer space while leaving the poor to fend for themselves."[25] The song is about inequality and the denial of democratic rights. Gaye said, "What mattered was the message. For the first time I felt like I had something to say."[26]

Gaye was shot in the chest by his father, Marvin Gaye Sr, on April 1, 1984, at the father's home. He died soon after at the California Hospital Medical Center.[27] On April 5 over ten thousand mourners viewed his casket at the Hollywood Hills Forest Lawn Memorial Park Hall of Liberty. Another ten to twenty thousand mourners were said to have been turned away.[28] After cremation, Gaye's ashes were scattered in the Pacific Ocean.

Duke Ellington's last concert in the city of his birth was at Georgetown University on February 10, 1974.[29] Although ill with terminal lung cancer, Ellington soldiered on, "with Jackie Byard assisting at the piano."[30] The orchestra played over twenty of his compositions as well as "New York, New York," a song for his adopted hometown.[31] Ellington died in New York on May 24, 1974, a few weeks after his seventy-fifth birthday. He is buried next to his father and mother at Woodlawn Cemetery in the Bronx. His hometown has often honored him. Western High School, the first public high school in the city to fully desegregate, was renamed the Duke Ellington High School for the Arts; a bridge in the Adams Morgan neighborhood overlooking Rock Creek Park bears his name; a statue in his honor was erected outside the renovated Howard Theatre; a giant mural of him decorates the side of True Reformer Building; the side of a US Post Office

Marvin Gaye (born Gay) was born at the Freedman's Hospital of Howard University on April 2, 1939. His album *What's Going On*, released on May 21, 1971, at the height of the Vietnam War, marked an important new stage in Gaye's career. The title song is considered one of the greatest protest songs in US history, from one of the greatest R&B protest albums of all time. "Inner City Blues," from the same album, is a lament of the Black urban condition. Wikimedia Commons.

bears his image; and a tiny triangle of land at M and 21st Streets NW, near his birthplace, is named Duke Ellington Plaza. The Smithsonian Institution Museum holds the Ellington Collection, his repository of musical scores and other arti-facts, drawing researchers and scholars from the world over. The archive also holds his Presidential Medal of Honor.[32] It rests in the Smithsonian, now headed by an African American, Lonnie G. Bunch III. Though Ellington's remains rest in the Bronx, much of the fruits of his work and his soul rest in Washington, DC.

Gil Scott-Heron, who had lived in DC and once taught at Federal City College, also wrote songs about life in Washington, his most famous being "The H20Gate Blues." He said that many of his "songs began taking shape in DC" as he observed the Black condition, and "instead of just glossing over the problem" he wanted to use "an individual or an individual circumstance as an example of a larger thing": the plight of impoverished Black Washingtonians.[33] Washingtonians still do not have a voting representative in the US Congress, so the struggle for democracy and equal rights continues. Scott-Heron said it best in a song on his 1982 album, *Moving Target*. Titled "Washington, D.C.," a key verse reflects the city in 2023: "It's a mass of irony for all the world to see / It's the nation's capital / It's Washington, DC."[34]

In November 1973 Bernice Reagon, a civil rights activist and former mem-ber of the SNCC Freedom Singers, who had been the vocal director of the DC Black Repertory Company, founded and became vocal director of Sweet Honey in the Rock, the all-Black women a cappella ensemble, while in graduate school

The Listening Group stands in front of the Duke Ellington mural at 1200 U Street NW. (*Front row, left to right*): Howard McCree, Sam Turner, Joe Selmon, Fred Foss, Keith Hunter, Tom Porter, (unidentified), Bill Brower, and Michael Wallace. (*Middle row, left to right*): John Whitmore, Tariq Tucker, Bill Shields, Aminifu Harvey, James Early, Gaston Neal, Norval Perkins, Phil Roane, Lew Marshall, Ron Clark, Medaris Banks, and David Truly. (*Back row, left to right*): Askia Muhammad, Willard Jenkins, Maurice Jackson, Wilmer Leon, Muneer Nassar, Elijah "Smitty" Smith, Ralph Matthews, Michael Thomas, and Barry Carpenter. Author's collection, courtesy Marvin Tupper Jones.

at Howard University. The name was a biblical reference to the Bible verse Psalm 81:16, which "describes a land so rich that honey pours from the rock." The verse reads: "But you would be fed with the finest of wheat; with honey from the rock I would satisfy you."[35] Their voices became a voice of the Black community, but also far beyond it. National Public Radio reported, "Sweet Honey's mission of using music to obtain a better world is nothing if anyone is excluded."[36]

One of the company's most memorable songs, "Ella's Song," is dedicated to civil rights legend Ella Baker:

> I am a woman who speaks in a voice and I must be heard
> At times I can be quite difficult, I's bow to no man's word
> We who believe in freedom shall not rest
> We who believe in freedom shall not rest until it comes.

Gil Scott Heron worked as a full-time lecturer at Federal City College, now the University of the District of Columbia, throughout his recording career. Wikimedia Commons. Courtesy Roger Woolman.

A month after Sweet Honey's founding, President Richard Nixon signed the District of Columbia Self-Government and Reorganization Act, and on December 24, 1973, Congress approved the District of Columbia Self-Government and Governmental Reorganization, establishing an elected mayor and a thirteen-member district council.[37] Blacks in Washington did not yet have full equality and they would "not rest until it comes," but they were at least "halfway to freedom."[38]

## Notes

1. Arnwine, "The Beautiful Struggle," 119.

2. Shirley Horn interview for the Smithsonian Institution Jazz Orchestra Oral History Program, June 13, 1996, quoted in Arnwine, "The Beautiful Struggle," 121.

3. Richard Harrington, "The Wonder of the Way She Sings," *Washington Post*, October 18, 1992.

4. Arwine, "The Beautiful Struggle," 121.

5. Wynton Marsalis and Branford Marsalis also appear, along with native DC artists Buck Hill and Billy Hart, on *You Won't Forget Me* (Verve, 1990).

6. Hassan, "Jazz Radio in Washington, DC," 98. I had the opportunity of visiting Horn's home with bassist Charlie Haden, who she had previously recorded with.

7. Charlie Haden, *The Art of the Song*, featuring Shirley Horn and Bill Henderson (Verve, 1999).

8. Horn also performed at the White House several times and received an honorary doctorate from the Berklee College of Music. She recorded several other albums as well, most notably *Here's to Life* (Verve, 1992).

9. H. Con. Res. 57(IH), Expressing the sense of Congress respecting the designation of jazz as a rare and valuable national treasure." See also Celenza, "Legislating Jazz."

10. John Conyers Jr., "Paying Tribute to Shirley Horn in Recognition of Her Many Achievements and Contributions to the World of Jazz and American Culture," US Congressional Record, vol. 151, November 16, 2005, https://www.govinfo.gov.

11. DC Delegate Eleanor Holmes Norton and Congressman John Conyers of Michigan entered into the Congressional Record these words: "Recognizing 2005 NEA Jazz Master Shirley Horn, who passed away on October 20, 2005" (US Congressional Record, Vol. 152, February 15, 2006, https://www.govinfo.gov).

12. Rubio, *There's Always Work at the Post Office*, 3. Black radicals like Hubert Harrison, the West Indian socialist leader in New York in the early 1900s, and James Ford, the Fisk University graduate, World War Two veteran, and Communist Party USA leader, worked at the Post Office when they could not find other good "white collar" jobs.

13. Michael J. West, "Legendary D.C. Jazz Musician Buck Hill Dies," *Washington City Paper*, March 22, 2017.

14. Amanda Michelle Gomez, "D.C.'s Tallest Mural," *District Line Daily, Washington City Paper,* August 28, 2019.

15. In the mid-1950s Hill, a World War Two veteran, was known as perhaps the best saxophonist in DC, a scene that at the time included such fellow travelers as Charlie Rouse, Frank Wess, and Benny Golson.

16. Buck Hill, *Easy to Love* (Steeplechase, 1981). The recording included Hill, Billy Hart on drums, Wilbur Little on bass, and DC's Rueben Brown on piano. Brown wrote most of the compositions.

17. Hassan, "Jazz Radio in Washington," 100. Hill also recorded *This Is Buck Hill*, featuring bassist Buster Williams, pianist Kenny Barron, and DC's Billy Hart on drums.

18. Levine, *Black Culture and Black Consciousness*, 5.

19. Peress, *Dvořák to Duke Ellington,* 199.

20. Al Clarke of WOOK Radio, liner notes to *The In Crowd with the Ramsey Lewis Trio* (Chess, 1965).

21. Porter, "The Social Roots," 268.

22. Clarke, "Conversations with William (Billy) Taylor," 182.

23. Taylor received a PhD from the University of Massachusetts in 1975. He also taught at Howard University, at the University of Massachusetts, at the Manhattan School of Music, and at East Carolina University.

24. Taylor with Reed, *The Jazz Life of Dr. Billy Taylor*, 148.

25. Dyson, *Mercy, Mercy Me*, 66.

26. Marvin Gaye, *The Very Best of Motown*, with liner notes by David Ritz (UTV, 2001).

27. "Marvin Gaye Is Shot and Killed; Pop Singer's Father Faces Charges," *New York Times*, April 2, 1984.

28. "Tribute to Marvin Gaye," *Washington Post,* April 6, 1983; Rojas, "The Private Funeral."

29. "Gaston Hall Performances Present New Faces," *The Hoya,* January 18, 1974. Mary Lou Williams presented her own Jazz Mass at Georgetown the year before. See "G'town Has Jazz Mass," *The Hoya,* November 9, 1973. Dave Brubeck played parts of his Jazz Mass at the inauguration of Georgetown president John DeGioia; see "Inauguration: DeGioia Shows Resolve, Humility During Ceremonies," *The Hoya,* October 16, 2001.

30. Green, *The Cambridge Companion to Duke Ellington,* 168.

31. Timner, *Ellingtonia,* 520.

32. Fitzgerald, "Researching Jazz History," 174–75.

33. Scott-Heron, *The Last Holiday,* 177.

34. Gil Scott-Heron, "Washington, DC," *Moving Target* (Arista, 1982).

35. At Spelman College Reagon also founded the Harambee Singers, which came about during the Black Consciousness Movement in South Africa, spearheaded by South African anti-apartheid activist Steve Biko. In addition to the music of Sweet Honey in the Rock, Reagon was a prolific author: *If You Don't Go, Don't Hinder Me: The American Sacred Song Tradition* (University of Nebraska Press, 2001) and *We'll Understand It Better By and By: Pioneering African Americana Gospel Composers* (Smithsonian Institution Scholarly Press, 1912). For the Bible passage see Bible Gateway, "Passage: Psalm 81:16, New International Version."

36. Kim Ruehl, "Turning the Tables" and "We Who Believe in Freedom Shall Not Rest: Sweet Honey in the Rock's Four Decades of Music and Freedom," NPR, January 16, 2018.

37. US Congress Act, P.L. 93-198. In February 2010 Reagon and former members of the SNCC singers and her daughter, Toshi, performed at a Black History Month concert organized by the White House in celebration of music in the civil rights movement. In 2014, as a response to police brutality following the shooting and death of Michael Brown by a white police officer in Ferguson, Missouri, Reagon substituted the line "Ain't gonna let nobody turn us around," from the old civil rights song, with "Ain't gonna let no Ferguson turn me 'round." She died at the age of eighty-one on July 16, 2024. See "Bernice Johnson Reagon, a Musical Voice for Civil Rights, Is Dead at 81," *New York Times,* https://www.nytimes.com/2024/07/19/arts/music/bernice-johnson-reagon-dead.html; and "Bernice Reagon Musical Memory Icon" at abdulslist@lists.illinois.edu.

38. Maurice Jackson, *Halfway to Freedom: The Struggles and Strivings of Black Folk in Washington, DC.* (Duke University Press, forthcoming)..

# Interlude

# THE PETERS SISTERS

For decades, a common refrain—and myth—was that Black people excelled in sports using big balls, like football and basketball, and white people excelled at sports using little balls, like tennis and golf. Yet for as long as the myth was perpetuated, both Black and white athletes disproved them. Two Black athletes from DC who challenged this myth were Margaret Peters (1915–2004) and her sister, Matilda Roumania Peters (1916–2003). Known as "Pete" and "Repeat," the pair first began playing tennis on the clay courts at the Rose Park playground in Georgetown, right across the street from their home at 2710 O Street NW. In describing the court, Matilda once remarked that "sand, dirt, rocks, everything. We would have to get out there in the morning and pick up the rocks and sweep the line and put some dry lime on them. That's what we played with. We didn't have any fancy courts. We learned there."[1]

Because the sport of tennis, like all of Washington, was segregated, the sisters competed in the American Tennis Association (ATA), founded in 1916 by African American lawyers, doctors, professors, and businesspeople to offer aspiring Black athletes an opportunity to compete nationally. In 1917 Lucy Diggs Slowe, a founder of the Alpha Kappa Alpha (AKA) sorority and Howard University's first college dean, won the ATA's inaugural tournament, becoming the first African American national tennis champion.[2] The Peters sisters competed in the 1936 ATA National Championship at Wilberforce University in Ohio, where Matilda lost in the final to three-time champion Lulu Ballard. Cleve Abbott, the tennis coach at Tuskegee Institute, soon recruited both sisters to attend Tuskegee. Margaret, not wanting to leave for Alabama alone, decided to wait one year for her sister to graduate from high school. In 1937 they both went to Tuskegee and played basketball as well as tennis. Matilda became the Southern Intercollegiate Athletic Conference (SAIC) tennis champion. After graduation in 1941 the sisters continued to compete and won fourteen doubles championships between 1938 and 1953. Matilda won her first

ATA National Singles title in 1944, and in 1946 defeated the soon to become legendary Althea Gibson, who won ten ATA National Singles titles before the integration of tennis in 1950. (That 1946 loss was one of Gibson's few losses on the ATA circuit.[3]) The next year Gibson, who would go on to become a national champion before the era of Serena and Venus Williams, beat Matilda and went on to win nine straight ATA tittles, on her way to becoming one of the sport's greatest champions. In 1956 Gibson was the first African American to win a Grand Slam event, the French Open. In 1957 she won both the US Open (then called the US Nationals) and Wimbledon. Overall Gibson won eleven Grand Slam titles (five singles, five doubles, and one mixed doubles).[4]

The sisters practiced often with a variety of notables, including actor Gene Kelly, when he was stationed in the city during World War Two. Both earned master's degrees in physical education from New York University. Later Matilda taught at Howard University and in the DC public school system from 1964 until 1981, mainly at Dunbar High. She also directed tennis camps for inner city youth for the DC Department of Recreation. Margaret, after some years in New York City, returned to Washington to work as a special education teacher. Both sisters were inducted into the Tuskegee Hall of Fame in 1977. But it was only in 2003 that the United States Tennis Association (USTA) recognized the triumphs of the Peters sisters, presenting them with an achievement award and induction into the Hall of Fame of the USTA Mid-Atlantic Section.[5]

## Notes

1. Lesko, Babb, and Gibbs, *Black Georgetown Remembered*, x, xv, 71–74.
2. Miller and Pruitt-Logan, *The Life of Lucy Diggs Slowe*.
3. Brown, *Serving Herself*, 58.
4. Jacobs, *Althea*, 74, 159, 279–84, 366–67.
5. In his three-volume *A Hard Road to Glory,* tennis champion Arthur Aske makes a one-line mention of the sisters. He writes: The "twosome won the ATA Women's Doubles Crown a whopping fourteen times unmatched by any doubles team, male or female" (2: 62). In *Arthur Ashe: A Life*, Ashe's biographer, Raymond Arsenault, refers to Romania with one line about her 1946 victory over Gibson (29).

# JAMES REESE EUROPE

James Reese Europe was the first African American officer to experience combat in wartime, on April 20, 1918. During his recuperation from an injury sustained in Germany, he penned "On Patrol in No Man's Land" from his hospital bed. It begins:

> When war broke out I enlisted as a private in Colonel Hayward's regiment, and I had just passed my officer's exam when the Colonel asked me to form a band and I told him that it would be impossible, as the Negro musicians of New York were paid too well to have them give up their jobs to go to war. However, Hayward raised $10,000 and told me to get the musicians wherever I could get them. . . . These are the men who now compose the band, and they are all fighters as well as musicians, for all have seen service in the trenches."[1]

## Note

1. Europe, "A Negro Explains Jazz," 239. Europe wrote that "the reed players I got from Porto Rico [*sic*], the rest from all over the country. I had only one New York Negro in my band—my solo cornetist."

# PART II

# Sports

## The Great Equalizer, the Great Unifier

"The city's soul on a roll."
—Christian Williams, "A City's Soul on a Roll,"
*Washington Post,* January 31, 1983.

# 6

# BASEBALL

## The Ball Rolled Toward Bigotry

As with music, sports played a major role in the lives, culture, well-being, and development of the Black community in Washington, DC. Baseball found a home near where Black folks lived. Starting in the late 1860s, baseball was played at the "White Lot." Officially controlled by the Army Corps of Engineers, the White Lot, also called "the President's Grounds," was located on the southwest grounds of the White House, between the executive mansion and the uncompleted Washington Monument. This highly popular location among baseball clubs was not far from where Blacks lived in Foggy Bottom and not far from the government jobs some of them held. Near what is now called the Ellipse, Black and white teams took turns playing—just not against each other. Some liked the arrangement while others did not. "One will sometimes find white and colored teams sitting around disconsolately because the other color has the only diamond which is in good order," a white player who preferred separate grounds wrote to the *Washington Post*.[1] This player did not propose stopping African Americans from playing ball, but he did call for separate and equal playing fields, adding, "If that little point could be settled, each color would keep his ground in good condition, cutting the grass and throwing out the stones."

One of the early proponents of Black baseball in Washington, DC, was Charles Douglass, Frederick Douglass's youngest son. Charles became the first Black man to enlist in the Union Army, when he joined the 54th Massachusetts Regiment in March of 1863 at age eighteen, along with his older brother, Lewis, who was twenty-two. They explored the idea of emigration and colonization but decided that the fight against the Confederacy was their fight to win. Charles's father reeled with pride. "Charley, my youngest," he wrote to Gerrit Smith, the New York abolitionist, "was the first to put his name down as one of the company."[2] On March 21, 1863, the elder Douglass penned his immortal broadside "Men of Color to Arms!" with: "Words are now useful only as they stimulate to blows."[3] But as Douglass biographer David Blight noted, his "effusive public words urging young black men to join the fight may have masked the private family anguish of a father recruiting his sons to go to war for their reasons as well as his own."[4]

But Charles did come back from war and moved to Washington to work for the Freedmen's Bureau. After he lost his job there in 1869, he worked for the US Treasury. Young Douglass also joined the Social Equality Republican Club.[5] As Blight aptly writes, "Charles' life in Washington was not all consumed with seeking government jobs and observing politics. During the five years after the war, he was directly involved in organizing two Black baseball teams, the Alert and the Mutual Base Ball Clubs."[6] He had learned the game playing second base for the Rochester Excelsior Club. The importance of sports to African Americans was as relevant then as it is today. Blight notes:

> For Charles, and for so many of the other young government workers, black and white, baseball was a personal and community outlet. . . . Black baseball clubs, not unlike fraternal orders and churches in black communities, took on a social-political function. In these years the goal was never to gain full integration into white teams and leagues, but to achieve full access to the best playing grounds and to book matches with the best clubs such as the famed Washington Nationals.[7]

Baseball was still a fairly new sport, and solid color lines were not yet set. Rather than the complete breakage of a long-established tradition, an early level of fluidity of racial mingling in baseball developed. Just as the color line was indeed being created, the Alert Baseball Club in Washington challenged it in 1869, with a well-attended match against the white Olympic Club.[8] The New York press reported:

> The game yesterday on the National Grounds being rather a novel sight here, that of a white and colored club playing together, attracted a large concourse of spectators, comprising the friends of both organizations. . . . Good feelings prevailed throughout, the game being equally enjoyed by the contestants and spectators. In Washington that meant to play official games on the White Lot.[9]

The Olympics defeated the Alert, 56–4.

President Andrew Johnson was known to stop by the White Lot to catch a few innings.[10] Reporters noted President U.S. Grant's presence at games in the 1870s.[11] The field was shared with "junior ball clubs" as well as the Washington and American Cricket Clubs, which brought their sport from the United Kingdom by way of New England. The White Lot seemed the embodiment of a "public space," featuring so many different games at a time that one reporter observed, "What a crowd of ball players there are on the field every day. In fact, the way the balls fly in every direction is enough to remind a veteran of the army of the [war] time."[12]

Being so close to government buildings, the White Lot was often the first destination at the end of the business day for ballplayers who worked at the many federal agency offices nearby. The ball field and the White House were both located near the Black neighborhoods in the First Ward, near Foggy Bottom, which had one of the highest concentrations of Black residents of any ward in the city.[13] This led to some struggles over the use of the White Lot and other public spaces in general where Blacks and whites might come into contact, especially in the waning years of Reconstruction. Blacks held out hope when an apparent ally, Sayles Bowen, was elected mayor in 1868. In 1870 the city council passed its first antidiscrimination bill, which forbade restaurants and theaters from denying service to Blacks (though the measure only solidified a previous decision already on the books).[14] In June 1872, Councilman Lewis Douglass introduced another bill to strengthen the city's nondiscrimination statutes. Though the bill passed, the District Supreme Court struck it down.[15]

The battle for control of the White Lot brought baseball firmly into the struggle for equality, due process, and equal rights as promised in the Reconstruction amendments. It also demonstrates how difficult it had become for Black ballplayers after the 1870s. First, in 1869 a general order prohibited all baseball on the White Lot, supposedly over security concerns for the president.[16] But the order was largely ignored, and games continued with regularity, as the grounds remained open to all. In September 1871 much of Washington's Black population gathered at the White Lot to celebrate Lincoln's one-hundred-day freedom proclamation. The festivities included a parade, complete with a salute by the Black militia organization, the Stanton Guard.[17]

Once a rough plot of land open to almost anybody who wanted to throw and catch a ball, the White Lot soon became a regulated public space restricted for upper-class whites. For a while the fields were steadily improved. Frederick Douglass noted as much in his *New National Era*, writing, "The citizens and visitors of Washington are indebted for the splendid resorts to avoid the heat and dust, furnished by our parks. . . . Lafayette Square and the White Lot have been greatly improved, and are now beautiful and fashionable resorts."[18] If he knew of forthcoming restrictions, he did not write of them.

In 1873 the White Lot became restrictive and the Creighton Baseball Club became its unofficial baseball tenant.[19] The September 6, 1874, edition of the *Sunday Herald* noted, "The White Lot has been closed to all ball players except the Creighton. The gangs of lazy negroes and other vagrants infesting the grounds made this action necessary."[20] Henceforth all "baseball clubs were required to apply for permission just to play ball on the White Lot."[21] A sign may not have been posted but the message was clear: baseball at the White Lot was for whites only.

By 1891 the Olympic Grounds at 7th Street and Florida Avenue NW, not far from Howard University (and the present location of Howard University Hospital), was becoming a place of play. The Washington Nationals were established in 1859 by men who worked as clerks in the federal government. The name derived from newspapers that had begun to call baseball "the national game" and "the national pastime."[22] The team played some of its first games, according to the White House Historical Association, in an area called Swampoodle Park or Capital Park, at a location near where Union Station now sits.[23] Throughout the 1890s the Nationals, at that time a member of the National League formed in 1876, played near Howard University at Boundary Field. When the wooden stadium there was destroyed by fire in 1911, a new ballpark was built near 7th and T Streets NW. In 1919 Clark Griffith became the majority owner of the then Washington Senators, which had been founded in 1911. In 1920 the park was renamed Griffith Stadium after the team's owner.[24] All kinds of events were held at the stadium, including "championship fights featuring African American boxers such as Joe Louis, and outdoor jazz concerts with performers such as Louis Armstrong."[25]

Such events brought the stadium closer to the community, and, as a business venture, was partly welcoming to Blacks. Griffith Stadium was somewhat unique because it did not have "officially" segregated seating areas. In theory it was integrated; but, like many places, it had an unspoken racial boundary and invisible rope that Blacks dared not cross; it was an invisible roped-off area that made up most of the stadium.[26] In short, "African Americans were expected to sit in the right field pavilion."[27] African American religious leaders like Elder Lightfoot Michaux of the Washington Church of God held baptismal services there, one time with seven thousand congregants present. One of the biggest sports series in Black Washington, the Lincoln University versus Howard University Thanksgiving football game, was held there in the 1930s and 1940s.

With the almighty dollar in mind, Griffith was more open to allowing Black people go to events at his stadium than many other team owners, but only if they knew and kept to their place—in the bleachers. Like anywhere else in Washington, de facto (customary) segregation trumped de jure (legal) integration every time and in every place. One Washingtonian who had the baseball bug also visited the stadium: Duke Ellington. He said, "Washington was in the American league and every day I had to see the game." To be able to see the Senators' games, he got a job selling peanuts and popcorn at the stadium. He first got stage fright working

"Homestead Grays of 1931"
Colored 43-31 Champions

The Homestead Grays, ca. 1931. The photo includes Hall of Famers pitcher Ray Brown, catcher Josh Gibson, left fielder Cool Papa Bell, first baseman Walter "Buck" Leonard, and third baseman Judd Wilson, as well as center fielder Jerry Benjamin and second baseman Howard Esterling. Wikimedia Commons, courtesy Heritage Auctions.

at those games—not playing music. "I was completely terrified at the Washington ballpark, it was like going on stage. Everybody in the park was looking at me! All I wanted to see was the baseball game."[28]

Griffith found other ways to profit from Black baseball without integrating the seats. In 1937 he made an arrangement with the Homestead Grays, one of the best teams in the Negro Leagues.[29] The Grays' official home was Forbes Field in Pittsburgh, but the team split its home games between Pittsburgh and Washington.[30] Formed in Homestead, Pennsylvania, the Grays were owned, for a time, by the former Black baseball and basketball star Cumberland Posey. For some years Posey had associated his team with the old American Negro League but, like the economy, the league failed during the Depression. After trying to start his own league, he brought his team into the Negro National Leagues in 1935.

When the Senators were on road trips beginning in 1940, Griffith rented out the stadium for "home games" to the Grays, which attracted more fans in DC than at Forbes Field in Pittsburgh. In 1943 Griffith made at least $100,000 in profits from renting the stadium to the team in DC. His decision was based on racism, on the one hand, and pure capitalism on the other—at times the Grays even outsold the Senators in attendance. Still, white baseball owners refused to allow Black players on their teams.

Most of the time the Grays were just as good as the Washington Senators were bad, and they made profits as the white team suffered. Griffith was steadfast against integrating Major League Baseball (MLB), but he saw nonwhite players as highly skilled and cheap.[31] In 1938, nine years before Jackie Robinson broke baseball's color barrier, Griffith reportedly said, "There are few big league magnates who are not aware of the fact that the time is not far off when colored players will take their places beside those of other races in the major leagues."[32]

The Senators, and the park they played in, were an integral part of the Black community, especially in the U Street neighborhood. "Standing as it did at the intersection of U and 7th streets—next to the Howard Campus—the park became a meeting ground for middle class, intellectual, and working-class African Americans in 1920."[33] Still, Griffith was slightly more amiable to Black fans and outside events than other owners were. Even if only motivated by profits, he wanted them to come to his games and he hosted their events.

Griffith knew the advantage of propaganda and of appearing to be concerned. He once met with Negro Leaguer and future Hall of Famer Josh Gibson. Gibson had also played in the Cuban, Dominican, and Mexican Leagues, and was one of the greatest ever long-ball hitters, with a career batting average purportedly over .350. Griffith also met with the left-handed Black first baseman Walter "Buck" Leonard, who had a .320 batting average and played on the Grays for seventeen years. Leonard recalled the meeting years later, remembering that "[Griffith] talked to us about Negro baseball and about the trouble there would be if he took us into the big leagues. . . . But he never did make us an offer."[34] Both Gibson and Leonard played on 1943 and 1944 Negro League Championship teams with the Grays. Many of the Negro Leagues players were drafted into the military, just like the whites from the MLB, but Satchel Paige and Gibson "were both declared 4-F. Paige had flat feet and Gibson creaky knees."[35]

Along with Gibson and Leonard, the team had three other future Hall of Famers: Jud Wilson, Ray Brown, and Cool Papa Bell.[36] They often drew crowds of over twenty thousand—and once drew over thirty thousand, at a game when they faced the Kansas City Monarchs and the legendary pitcher LeRoy "Satchel" Paige.[37] Blacks gave sterling performances at the stadium, especially when the Grays featured catcher Josh Gibson and first baseman Buck Leonard. With both men regularly knocking balls "over Griffith's Stadium's 30-foot-high right field wall," and with the team's "popularity growing among black fans, the clamor to integrate the Senators increased."[38]

At the same time, George Preston Marshall, owner of the Redskins football team, rented Griffith Stadium for $100,000 a season. He "banned local high school football teams and the all-black professional Washington Lions from playing their games" there, as he held veto rights over "any perceived competition from playing there."[39] Unlike Griffith, his racism came before his profits, though he profited aplenty.

Brad Snyder, author of a definitive book on the Negro Leagues teams, has argued that for the love of money, Griffith, along with the notorious racist and anticommunist Larry MacPhail, the general manager of the Cincinnati Reds, "led the opposition to integration."[40] In fact, a secret document aptly named "The Race Question" was first circulated by a secret Major League committee in August 1946, then formally submitted to a congressional committee in 1951. "Club owners in the major leagues are reluctant to give up revenues amounting to hundreds of thousands of dollars every year," it read. "They naturally want the Negro Leagues to continue."[41] In other words, racism and segregation paid well in the big leagues and in Griffith's Washington.

Legendary sportswriter Sam Lacy apparently believed that integration in the nation's capital was more important than it would be in any other city—and as meaningful as Blacks playing baseball in the White Lot almost a century earlier. He saw the symbolism of a "large black population and a stadium in the midst of the city's largest black neighborhood."[42] On April 1, 1950, Lacy wrote, "If the reports emanating from this quarter are so glowing as to give the impression everything in baseball's integration experiment is now honey and whipped cream, let me assure you that is far from the truth."[43]

Instead of being the first team to field a Black player, the Senators were one of the last. Although Jackie Robinson had integrated Major League Baseball in 1947, Griffith still refused to sign Blacks. In his last season, prior to his death in September 1954 and "four months after the *Brown* and *Bolling* decisions, Griffith finally integrated his team but in his own perverse way," Snyder observes.[44] He used Carlos Paula, a twenty-six-year-old Black Cuban player.[45] The *Pittsburgh Courier* editorialized, "Mr. Griffith would give Washington fans dark players from other lands but never an American Negro."[46] Indeed, the Senators "had been the most active pursuer of Latino talent during its segregated era."[47] The team's first African American player did not appear until three years later, making the Senators among the last to integrate. The team gave real meaning to the popular refrain of wartime years, "First in war, first in peace, and last in the American League."

*Washington Post* sportswriter Shirley Povich wrote that Griffith planned to pass the team to his nephew and adopted son, Calvin Griffith, who learned baseball "at the knee of his uncle" and who made sure that there was "no deviation, necessarily, from Clark Griffith's policy even in the distant future."[48] Povich added that in 1960, "Calvin Griffith, for financial reasons and to flee a city that was majority African American, moved the team to Minnesota."[49] In the very white twin cities of Minneapolis and St. Paul, the name was changed to the Minnesota Twins. The replacement team in Washington, also known as the Senators and often called the "Expansion Senators," played just as poorly as their predecessors.[50] The new team got a new stadium, playing their games in the newly constructed DC Memorial Stadium, while Griffith Stadium was purchased by Howard University and destroyed in 1965 to make room for the construction of Howard University Hospital.[51] This ripped a longstanding landmark from the U Street neighborhood and effectively removed baseball from the area. The closing and destruction of Griffith Stadium marked the end of an era that had featured some of the best Black baseball players playing in front of large Black crowds. The new Senators—even the 1969 team, which won eighty-six games and was managed by the legendary Ted Williams—could not gain Black support. Two losing seasons later, in 1971, owner Robert E. Short was granted permission to move to the team to Arlington, Texas, where they became the Texas Rangers.[52] Baseball did not return to Washington until 2005, when the Montreal Expos moved to Washington and became the Nationals.[53]

In May 2024 the statistics from the Negro Leagues were incorporated into the Major League Baseball records.[54] The Homestead Grays' Josh Gibson became the new MLB all-time career batting leader, with a .372 average, placing him ahead of Ty Cobb. He also now holds the single-season highest batting average, at .466. This recognition came seventy-seven years after his death in 1947. Gibson died three months after Jackie Robinson integrated the MLB. With the 2024 change, Satchel Paige moved to third place on the all-time earned run average list, with an ERA of .101 in his 1944 season.[55]

## Notes

1. *Washington Post*, July 22, 1901.

2. Blight, *Frederick Douglass*, 385.

3. "Men of Color to Arms!," Rochester, New York, March 21, 1863, quoted in Douglass, *The Life and Writings of Frederick Douglass*, 3:317.

4. Blight, *Frederick Douglass*, 385.

5. Johnson, "The City on a Hill," 217–18.

6. Blight, *Frederick Douglass*, 507.

7. Blight, 508.

8. For a wonderful look at how Blacks and whites played baseball in the nineteenth century, see Swanson, *When Baseball Went White*.

9. *New York Clipper,* October 2, 1869. "National Grounds" was another name for the White Lot.

10. Benson, *Ballparks of North America,* 406.

11. *Sunday Herald and Weekly Intelligencer,* June 20, 1873.

12. *New York Clipper,* May 5, 1866.

13. Schweninger, *Black Property Owners in the South,* 200–204.

14. Green, *The Secret City,* 96.

15. Johnson, "The City on a Hill," 220.

16. *New York Clipper,* May 15, 1869; *Sunday Mercury,* April 25, 1869.

17. *New National Era,* September 28, 1871.

18. *New National Era,* May 23, 1872.

19. *Sunday Herald and Weekly National Intelligencer,* June 30, 1872.

20. *Sunday Herald and Weekly National Intelligencer,* September 6, 1874.

21. Swanson, "Less Than Monumental," 24.

22. Washington DC Genealogy, "Genealogy and History: John G. Sharp," accessed 2009, http://genealogytrails.com/washdc/sports/1860to1869baseball.html.

23. White House Historical Association, "Washington Nationals Play Baseball at Swampoodle Grounds," https://www.whitehousehistory.org/photos/fotoware?id=DAF8557F60A14767%20A2A34B8DC5097DD4.

24. Hubler and Drazen, *The Nats and the Grays,* 8.

25. Ruble, *Washington's U Street,* 152–53.

26. Synder, *Beyond the Shadow of the Senators.*

27. Swanson, "Less Than Monumental," 26.

28. Carter Harman interview of Duke Ellington, 1964, Carter Harman Interview Collection, Archives Center, National Museum of American History, Smithsonian Institution, quoted in Hasse, "Washington's Duke Ellington," 41.

29. Swanson, "Less Than Monumental," 27.

30. Ruble, *Washington's U Street,* 152.

31. Ruble, 152.

32. Ribowsky, *A Complete History of the Negro Leagues,* 251.

33. Ruble, *Washington's U Street,* 152.

34. Peterson, *Only the Ball Was White,* 169.

35. Swanson, "Less Than Monumental," 29–30.

36. Ruble, *Washington's U Street,* 162.

37. Carter, "Black Baseball in Washington," 26.

38. Brad Snyder, "When Segregation Doomed Baseball in Washington," *Washington Post,* February 16, 2003.

39. Synder, *Beyond the Shadow of the Senators,* 207.

40. Snyder, 233.

41. Tygiel, "The Race Question," 129–31. See also Snyder, *Beyond the Shadow of the Senators,* 233.

42. Hubler, *The Nats and the Grays,* 29.

43. Lacy, "Campy, Jackie as Dodgers," 211.

44. Snyder, *Beyond the Shadow of the Senators*, 285.

45. Walker, "Uniting a Divided City," 166.

46. Snyder, *Beyond the Shadow of the Senators*, 286. See also Frommer, *The Washington Nationals*, 69.

47. Burgos, *Cuban Star*, 213.

48. Povich, *The Washington Senators*, 244.

49. Walker, "Uniting a Divided City," 166.

50. Walker, 166.

51. Swanson, "Less Than Monumental," 30.

52. Walker, "Uniting a Divided City," 180.

53. Hartley, "Washington Baseball Fans," 291–92.

54. Bob Nightengale, "Negro Leagues' Statistics Will Be Incorporated into the Major League Baseball's Historical Records on Wednesday," *USA Today,* May 28, 2024.

55. Stephen J. Nesbitt, "The MLB–Negro Leagues Stat Change: What Happened and Why?," *New York Times/Athletic,* May 29, 2024. The all-time ERA leader is Tim Keefe, who had a 0.86 average in 1880.

# 7

# BOXING

## The Great Black Hope

African Americans in Washington and across the country were glued to their radios on July 4, 1910, "when the indomitable and pompous Jack Johnson knocked out Jim Jeffries . . . the Great White Hope."[1] Whites disliked Johnson simply because he was a big Black man and more so because he boastfully displayed white women as his companions and wives. A *Los Angeles Times* editorial after the fight might as well have appeared in the *Alabama Klansman*. Entitled "A Word to the Black Man," it read: "Do not swell your chest too much. Do not boast too loudly. . . . You are just the same member of society you were last week . . . deserve no new consideration, and will get none."[2] A few days before the fight Booker T. Washington's chief deputy, Emmett Scott, had written to J. Frank Wheaton, an African American attorney and former Republican leader in New York. He wrote, "We all believe that he can defeat Jeffries but I think it would be much better for him not to boast about what he is going to do in that particular, but simply stand on his record and on the statements that he 'would fight any living man for the Heavy Weight Championship of the World.'"[3]

White organizations such as the United Society of Christian Endeavor launched a campaign to halt theaters from showing the film of the fight. Several sent Western Union telegrams to the governor of every state, proclaiming "race riots and murder in many places following announcement of Johnson's victory."[4] Washington's Black community protested a proposed ban on showing the fight films in theaters. David L. Lewis, W. E. B. Du Bois's biographer, wrote that "in the beginning, far more African Americans had known the name Jack Johnson, ex-world heavyweight boxing champion, than they had that of W.E. B. Du Bois, civil rights militant."[5] Lewis believes that Johnson's "genius in the ring had nearly launched a race war and finally driven congressional racists to outlaw the interstate sale of prizefighting films."

The *Washington Bee* editorialized, "There are separate moving picture theatres among whites and blacks in this country. . . . Let the pictures be shown, and if

111

Jack Johnson was born in 1878 to former enslaved people in Galveston, Texas. He won the World Colored Heavyweight title in 1903 and in 1908 became the first African American heavyweight boxing champion. In the "Battle of the Century" in 1910 he defeated the white former champion Jim Jeffries, who came out of retirement at the behest of whites, including novelist Jack London, who dubbed Jeffries the "Great White Hope." Courtesy George Grantham Bain Collection, Library of Congress Prints and Photographs Division.

the whites get mad with themselves and fight themselves, they are to blame. The blacks on the other hand will shout among themselves only."[6] The *Bee* underestimated Black determination and resolve, as African Americans defended themselves and celebrated. The Associated Press reported that in Washington "several small race riots broke out at several points on Pennsylvania Avenue" when the result of the Jeffries-Johnson fight was announced. There were a number of arrests, the Associated Press (AP) reported, but no one was seriously hurt. United Press International (UPI) reported that in Washington, "in a race riot one white man Thomas Mundle, an enlisted man of the United States Marine Corps," was killed, while "another white man was found unconscious after a free for all fight. He later died."[7] The AP issued dispatches from Atlanta about events "where Negros were chased by crowds" and where "three Negroes were badly hurt by white men inside an hour." From Little Rock came a dispatch that "two Negroes are reported killed by white men." In Charleston, Missouri, "a third lynching within twenty-four hours was threatened here." In Augusta, Georgia, white violence led to "the killing of three negroes. . . . So far no whites have been killed." The Mann Act, commonly known as the White Slave Traffic Act, was passed in 1910. Its stated purpose was to prevent (white) girls and women from being forced or tricked into prostitution and transported across state lines. The act was named after Illinois Republican congressman James Robert Mann, who said: "The white slave traffic . . . is much more horrible than any black-slave traffic ever was in the history of the world." Jack Johnson, while married to a white woman named Lucille Cameron, was charged and sentenced in 1912 to a term of one year and one day for violating the Mann Act, after he crossed state lines with a different white woman, Belle Schreiber, in 1910. To avoid imprisonment he fled to Canada, then to Paris. He returned in 1920 to serve his sentence in the federal penitentiary at Leavenworth, Kansas. The Mann Act was called by newspapers like the *New York Times* "the White Trade Act."[8]

One hundred years later Senator Harry Reid (D-Nevada) and Senator John McCain (R-Arizona), supported by the Congressional Black Caucus, introduced legislation calling for a posthumous pardon for Johnson. Reid, a former amateur boxer, described Johnson's legal troubles as an "unjust conviction under the Mann Act in 1913" and called him the "greatest athlete of his time and a barrier-breaking boxer" whose name was tarnished by an "unjust and racially motivated conviction." McCain, who boxed at the Naval Academy, called Johnson "a boxing legend and pioneer whose reputation was wrongly tarnished by an unjust and racially-motivated conviction more than a century ago." Both he and Reid called for America to "right a historical wrong and repair the legacy of this great man."[9] When the senators first introduced legislation to pardon Johnson in 2014, they were joined by Peter King (R-NY) and Gregory Meeks (D-NY). Johnson received a presidential pardon when Donald Trump signed the order on May 24, 2018.[10]

Former Barack Obama administration attorney general Eric Holder said that there was "no question" that Johnson had been unfairly convicted," but "his history of abusing women stood in the way" of President Obama signing the legislation.[11] At the time of Johnson's pardon, boxing historian Mike Silver wrote, perhaps partly correctly and partly wrongly, that "Johnson was one of the few people in sports who transcended sports. He transcended the athletic world to become really part of the culture and the racial history of the country."[12]

## Notes

1. Collins, *All Hell Broke Loose*, 31. See also Godshalk, *Veiled Visions*, 137. In 1967 James Earl Jones starred with Jane Alexander in *The Great White Hope* at the Arena Stage in Washington, DC. The play is based on the true story of Johnson (fictionalized in the play as Jack Jefferson) and his fight against white champion boxer Jim Jeffries. The play went to Broadway in 1968 and in 1969 won both the Tony Award for Best Play and the Pulitzer Prize for Drama.

2. "A Word to the Black Man," *Los Angeles Times*, July 6, 1910, quoted in Ward, *Unforgivable Blackness*, 216.

3. Emmett Scott to J. Frank Wheaton, March 23, 1909, Booker T. Washington Papers, Library of Congress.

4. Ward, *Unforgivable Blackness*, 230.

5. Lewis, *W. E. B. Du Bois*, 3, 99.

6. "What Folly!," *Washington Bee*, July 9, 1910.

7. All quotes in this section are from Ward, *Unforgivable Blackness*.

8. John Eligon and Brandon K. Thorp, "Champion's Race Was the Story for the Times," *New York Times*, May 25, 2018, B8.

9. Senator Harry Reid and Senator John McCain joint press release, February 26, 2014. See also Yvonne Wingett Sanchez, "Trump Pardon of Boxing Legend Jack Johnson Closes 'Shameful Chapter' in History," *Arizona Republic*, March 24, 2018; and Guy Clifton, "U.S. Senators Reid, McCain Again Urge Jacks Johnson Pardon," *Reno Gazette Journal*, February 12, 2014.

10. White House Office of the Press Secretary, press release, May 24, 2018.

11. Malika Andrews, "The Fight to Clear Jack Johnson's Name," *New York Times*, May 9, 2018, B8.

12. Eligon and Thorp, "Champion's Race." James Earl Jones, the brilliant actor who took Johnson to the screen and to modern America in the film "The Great White Hope," died on September 9, 2024. His many obituaries and tributes brought renewed attention to Jack Johnson. Robert D. McFadden, "James Earl Jones, Whose Powerful Acting Resonated Onstage and Onscreen, Has Died at 93," *New York Times*, September 9, 2024.

# 8

# FOOTBALL

## Washington "Has No Negroes and No Victories"

Football as an organized national and professional league began in 1920 with the American Professional Football Association (APFA) and was then renamed the National Football Association in 1922. From the start most players were white, but a few were Black. Before the APFA existed Charles W. Follis "became football's first black professional when he signed to play for the Shelby Athletic Club on September 15, 1904."[1] The first African American in the APFA was Frederick Douglass "Fritz" Pollard, who had played at the collegiate level at Brown University.[2] He was joined on the Akron Indians team, renamed the Akron Pros, by legendary singer, actor, and activist Paul Robeson, known as "Robie of Rutgers," who had been a two-time All American yet was stripped of this distinction during the infamous McCarthy years, when "at least one publication listed only a 10-man All-America team for 1918 rather than print Robeson's name. The Football Hall of Fame took a similar tack."[3] Additionally, "newsreel footage of [Robeson] was destroyed, recordings erased," and Jackie Robinson, who had integrated modern baseball on April 15, 1947, was called to testify at the House Un-American Activities Committee hearing against Robeson." Years later, near the end of his life, Robinson wrote, "I would reject such an invitation if offered now. I have grown wiser and closer to the painful truths about America's destructiveness. And I do have increased respect for Paul Robeson."[4] In 1988 Robeson was inducted into the Rutgers University Sports Hall of Fame and posthumously into the College Football Hall of Fame in 1995.

In the APFA, thirteen black players played in the NFL before the creation of a defined color barrier in 1933. While there was no written policy against their inclusion on a team, African Americans were effectively banned from 1933 until 1945. The same was said of the white-only/colored-only practices in the city. Sports historian Charles K. Ross has noted that while "the NFL's color barrier only lasted twelve seasons. . . . The creation of the color barrier in the NFL appears to have happened informally, in that there is no written documentation between owners. Instead there seems to have been a gentlemen's agreement among owners not to sign black players to team contracts."[5] The reasoning was that the owners had "decided informally to emulate the policy of racial exclusion that prevailed in major league baseball."[6] The owners wanted their teams to reflect the segregated United States.

Professional football was one of the last bastions of rigid segregation in the nation's capital city. George Preston Marshall bought the Boston Redskins and brought the team to DC in 1937, making the city the home of the first professional football team located in a city below the Mason-Dixon line. In addition to bringing the team to DC, Marshall also brought his own racist viewpoints. As an early leader of the NFL, his ideas held sway in part because, along with his ideas about Blacks, he helped push through rules that opened up the game, added teams, and instituted a championship format, all of which led to increased ticket sales. He is credited with inventing the extravaganza-type half-time show, complete with a one-hundred-piece orchestra, and, eventually including animal acts, clown shows, cheerleaders, and show business stars.[7]

Marshall "claimed that he did not sign black athletes because white southerners on the team would have balked . . . that using black players would drive away advertisers and his white southern audience. . . . Washington was a southern city that adhered rigidly to segregation during the 1930s and 1940s."[8] He appealed to whites in nearby Virginia, Maryland, West Virginia, North Carolina, and South Carolina.

The first team to attempt desegregation was the Los Angeles Rams, which moved to Los Angeles from Cleveland in 1946. Soon, however, the team ran into the wall of racism in the California city. The Rams "hoped to use the 103,000 capacity Municipal Stadium, which was publicly owned, as their home," but "several black writers, including Harley Harding of the *Los Angeles Tribune* and Herman Hill, the West Coast correspondent of the *Pittsburgh Courier*, objected to the use of the coliseum by any organization that practiced racial discrimination."[9] Public pressure led to the Rams signing Kenny Washington on March 21, 1946, making him the first African American player in the NFL since 1933. This was a few months after Jackie Robinson integrated baseball on October 23, 1945. The Rams also signed Woody Strode, who later became a Hollywood actor.

As with baseball, Black footballers faced segregated housing and eating facilities, the bigotry of white teammates, and relentless threats and harassment by fans, both at home and on the road.[10] The Redskins did not employ any Blacks as team employees during the twenty-four years they played at Griffith Stadium."[11]

Black citizens' frustration grew into action, and in February 1957 "the DC branch of the NAACP sponsored a picket line that was maintained throughout the two-day meeting of the National Football League . . . in Philadelphia."[12] This effort, although failing to convince Marshall to integrate the team, united diverse organizations, including the United Auto Workers and other labor unions, local branches of the NAACP, and religious leaders— all of which threatened pickets, boycotts, and a public campaign to put pressure on the Redskins and other NFL teams. Members of the NAACP and the Congress of Racial Equality picketed both Marshall's house and the DC stadium, as well as venues in other cities across the country when the team played exhibition games. Even future owners who were members of team boards of directors or stockholders, like Edward Bennett Williams and Jack Kent Cooke, urged Marshall to change his policies. He would not.

*Washington Post* Columnist Thom Laverno writes, "The Redskins were the only NFL team south of the Mason-Dixon Line, and the owner milked those southern connections for all they were worth, often drafting less talented players just because they came from southern schools. It was this mentality of pleasing his southern audience that would hold back the franchise for many years to come."[13] Laverno notes that even as whites started moving to the suburbs, their connection to the city remained because of federal government jobs. For Blacks, "there was a connection for the city to the South as time went on but not one Marshall wanted. More black Americans began leaving the South, and those in Virginia and North and South Carolina came to Washington, seeking to leave rural poverty behind and find a better life in cities such as Washington." He concludes, "They would not be welcome at Redskins games, at least not by Marshall." After all, this was his team, and his wife, Corrine, even wrote the lyrics to the team's fight song, "Hail to the Redskins." The first stanza goes:

> Hail to the Redskins
> Hail victory
> Braves on the warpath
> Fight for old DC

To add to his segregationist credentials and to show that he would not bow to public pressure, in 1959 Marshall changed the song's last line: "Fight for old DC" now went "Fight for Old Dixie." The team's band also played the segregationist fight song "Dixie" before every game. And why not—for many, DC was, indeed, "the land of Old Dixie."

Shirley Povich, a Maine-born Jewish American who had once worked as a caddie at a country club where Jewish people were excluded, wrote for the *Washington Post* about the team and its policies. In more than one column he noted that "the Redskins' end zone has frequently been integrated by Negro players, but never in their lineup."[14] He became well known for lines that grew synonymous with the team: "George Preston Marshall is trying to restore the Confederacy, ninety-four years after everyone else has quit. The décor Marshall has chosen for the Redskins is burgundy, gold and Caucasian."[15]

When John F. Kennedy was elected president, he appointed Stewart Udall as secretary of the interior. Udall, raised a Mormon, had served in World War II and in the US House of Representatives from Arizona's second district. Many in Kennedy's administration, including his brother, Robert, the attorney general, wanted to proceed with caution on issues involving race—but not Udall. The Interior Department had control over the Redskins' stadium because it sat on federal land. In October 1961 the new secretary signed a thirty-year lease for the team to play at the stadium, which was still under construction. With the stadium, costing $24 million and being located on lands under the authority of the Interior Department and the National Capital Parks Authority (NCPA), and being guided by the Eisenhower administration policy of denying any federal dollars to any who discriminated on federal property, Udall held the upper hand. During the process, the Arizona outdoorsman Udall realized that of the nearly five hundred National Park Service rangers, only one was African American. He immediately ordered that fifty new minority rangers be hired.

Sometime later Udall wrote that he held "personal convictions about civil rights and considered it outrageous that the Redskins were the last team in the NFL to have a lily-white policy." He said he "instinctively felt that JFK and RFK would applaud" his actions, as he had not consulted them.[16] At the time, the Kennedys were not so clear about their civil rights views and policies, and many African Americans had high hopes on the one hand and a deep distrust on the other.

At the time, Povich wrote, "Marshall does have a racial problem. Not only is Secretary Udall threatening literally to run his team out of their new park unless they integrate, but in their thirteenth straight defeat, his Redskins have been beset by very pushy Negroes on other teams on the other clubs, perhaps in their awareness of what has been Marshall's aversion to living color on his own team."[17] A month after this column appeared, Povich surmised that "at the first suggestion by Interior Secretary Steward Udall that he dismantle the Redskins' color line and hire a Negro player, George Marshall last spring made the counter suggestion that Mr. Udall go jump in a lake."[18]

Povich was relentless. It had been more than fifteen years since the Los Angeles Rams had integrated, and Povich saw only good had come out of it—for the players and for the fans. His reasoning was simple: "Integrated pro football long ago was accepted by the players and the fans. Marshall has been the only holdout. He has keyed the Redskins' promotion to his Southern radio-TV network to exploit Nordic supremacy, which in the case of the Redskins has been nil for 17 games in a row."[19]

Dave Brady, a colleague of Povich's at the *Post*, joined the campaign with an article titled "83 Negroes on Pro Teams, Including Seven at Dallas, but None on Redskins," on November 30, 1961. With sarcasm and truth, Brady penned: "The Redskins have no Negroes and no victories, which may be coincidental, except that the latest NFL statistics indicate otherwise."[20] Brady wrote about the wins and losses of the various teams and analyzed their records in respect to having Black players. Teams with Black players, especially those that played the Washington Redskins at home in DC stadium, won.[21]

Readers of the more conservative *Washington Evening Star* had their say too. In a letter to the editor dated October 27, 1961, reader Nick Showers wrote, "The Washington Redskins keep losing ballgames. The NAACP keeps informing management the reason they don't win is because there isn't a Negro on the club. Perhaps the NAACP, America's number one policy framer in all matters, could set us straight on why the Washington Senators baseball team made such a poor showing during the past season. There are several Negroes on the team."[22]

But facts were facts. As a whole, in the 1950s at least 143 African Americans played in the NFL but zero played for the Washington franchise. During the 1960 season, 61 Blacks played in the league but still, zero played in Washington.[23]

Like many young Black athletes, Sam Lacy, the legendary African American sportswriter for the *Baltimore Afro-American* newspaper, had his dreams of playing Major League baseball. And, like a few of them, when he could not make it as a player he got a job—in his case, as a journalist. Lacy contributed a crucial African American point of view regarding the debate in the city where Blacks were, at that time, a population majority yet underrepresented in almost all facets of power, whether politics, large-scale media outlets, and so on. He engaged the issue of race explicitly and head-on, an approach reflective of the larger civil rights movement's rhetoric and goals, both nationwide and locally.

Lacy's critique of Marshall and his views and policies only increased after the 1960 NFL draft, when the Redskins failed to acquire a single Black player once again. Lacy opined, "This column has never advocated suicide, but in George Preston Marshall's case, it would be readily forgivable."[24] Lacy was crucial in turning popular opinion against Marshall and the Redskins, urging mass action and agitations, including urging Blacks and whites to picket games at Griffith Stadium.

In 1950 Marshall told the *Pittsburgh Courier*, a Black newspaper, "I have nothing against Negroes but I want an all white team." He also said. "I believe in states' rights both in government and in football."[25] To this, Lacy shared the opinion of a New York sportswriter, that the team name ought to be changed to the "Washington Confederates" or the "Washington Lilywhites."[26]

When Lacy visited Marshall at team headquarters, the owner greeted him by saying, "It has been a long time—fifteen, twenty, twenty-five years." Lacy responded, "All of twenty, possibly twenty-five. I couldn't afford to be seen in your company." He added, "You have shown good faith in drafting three colored athletes." Marshall then said, "This is something you can write that hasn't been written before. For years I was one of the city's largest employees of colored people. I was the first laundry operator to use all colored men. How many do you see on the laundry truck today? I was the first to use colored ushers and vendors at Griffith Stadium athletic contests and at one time there were nearly five hundred colored persons employed in this very building when the (Palace) laundry plant was situated here." Lacy seemed astonished: "But you must admit there is quite a difference between menial work and a professional job. . . . For years colored people have been able to do laboring work and find employment as washers of clothes and dishes and floors. But like everyone else, the colored man has no desire to make that his ceiling. The complaint is that you have shown evidence that you think this which you gave him in the past, is his level." Marshall responded, "The complaint comes from my refusal to exploit the colored athlete." To this Lacy simply said, "But you have exploited Jim Crow. Exploitation, as I understand it, means to use an individual or an issue in such a way as to derive benefits from it, financial or otherwise. You've been capitalizing on discrimination. [27]

Racism robbed the city of Washington of good football and good football players—and the nation knew it. Gordon Cobbledick of the *Cleveland Plain Dealer* wrote that Marshall's race-based policy was "spotting their rivals the tremendous advantage of exclusive rights to a whole race containing excellent football players."[28] He added, in a well-intentioned but partly in error comment, that recruiting African Americans "is not an argument for racial equality. It's a matter of practical football policy." No matter: it was costing Marshall as well. Cobbledick's column was reprinted in the *Washington Post* on December 24, 1960.

Players, like Ollie Matson of the Chicago Cardinals, spoke up. Povich quotes him in his column as saying that Blacks "try a little harder when we play the Washington team."[29] NFL teams jumped in when, "in early November, the Philadelphia Eagles turned down the opportunity to play the Skins in the fall of 1962 at Norfolk's Kiwanis Bowl. The Eagles cited segregated seating as the club's reason for turning down the offer."[30] Vince McNally, general manager of the Philadelphia Eagles, stated that "the Eagles felt obliged to decline the invitation in 'deference to their colored players—fullback Clarence Peaks and halfbacks

Ted Dean, Tim Brown and Irv Cross.' The four athletes said they preferred not to play before a segregated audience such as Virginia laws required."[31] More surprisingly, this statement came after a meeting between NFL commissioner Pete Rozelle and Marshall, which resulted in a verbal agreement by the owner of the Redskins to draft a Black player.

Marshall tried to downplay the seriousness of the issue and resolve matters on his own terms. For example, when he was criticized for being late for a meeting of team executives and fined $500 dollars, he tried to divert the issue while portraying his attitude to women: "Well she was worth every penny."[32] Another time he quipped, "We'll start signing Negroes when the Harlem Globetrotters start signing whites."[33] Though none attributed the words to him around the league and the nation, he did not care about protest, protesters, or Blacks. For him, "the NAACP stood for 'Never at Any time Any Colored Players.'"[34] When asked about his policies, he always tried to downplay the issue. "All other teams we play have Negroes; does it matter which team has the Negroes?"[35]

Finally, the voices represented by Povich and Lacy and the federal government prevailed. With public pressure mounting within Washington as well as outside of it, George Preston Marshall signed an African American athlete. On December 4 the Redskins drafted its first Black player, Ernie Davis, the Syracuse All-American who followed Jim Brown to the school and in 1961 became the first African American to win the Heisman Trophy, awarded to college football's finest athlete. Davis was immediately traded to the Cleveland Browns.[36]

Even though Davis never ended up playing for the team, the off-season trades before the 1962 schedule resulted in the acquisition of several African American players who did indeed play for the Redskins the following year, including wide receiver and future Hall of Famer Bobby Mitchell. Mitchell was obtained from the Cleveland Browns and became the first Black player to play for the team.

Bobby Mitchell said, when traded to the city, "When I found out about the trade, I thought 'I'm going to Washington, of all places?' When I went to a kick-off luncheon there, everybody stood up, and I thought they [the Redskins band] were going to play the national anthem. Then I heard, 'I wish I was in the land of cotton [Dixie].' But in the black community I was a shining light, the player they had waited for all those years."[37] Mitchell continued, "I wasn't accepted by a lot of white guys on the team. The fans would yell, 'Run n——r run.' I was spat on in Duke Zeibert's [restaurant]." Mitchell had a fantastic first season with the Redskins, was named to the Pro Bowl Team, and helped make 1962 the best season the team had since 1956. Mitchell was a reluctant spokesman for racial progress, choosing to let his playing speak for itself. Not a few whites disagreed with the decision to integrate, as "outright racists, such as the American Nazi Party, paraded outside DC stadium with swastika-emblazoned signs reading 'America Awake' and 'Keep Redskins White!'"[38]

The Washington football team added Blacks to the team just as the city was going through "tremendous changes, from a provincial southern town to a city with a growing Black power and identity—the presence of Black football players was a long awaited victory for the black community in Washington—a victory in a battle that the community fought for many years with Marshall from lobbying him to eliminate 'Dixie' from the Redskins fight song to his eventual surrender to the times."[39] Marshall left active involvement in the team in 1963 due to illness.

To this day, on any given Sunday with a game between the Washington football team and the Dallas Cowboys, much of the Washington community—including the suburbs—remains divided by team. In Giant food stores, cashiers and other workers garner their Dallas blue and white or their Washington burgundy and gold, then banter all day. The same goes on at Georgetown University the day after a game, as the employees from Maintenance and the Provost's Office wear their colors and the winners boast. For many Washington-area African Americans, Dallas is the team of choice, representing for them what Washington—the southernmost team—never did. Many new arrivals to DC do not know about the rivalry, and many bring with them the loyalties of the teams they grew up in San Francisco, Chicago, Houston, New Orleans, Buffalo, or elsewhere.

On July 20, 2020, the Washington football team officially retired Mitchell's No. 49. It also renamed the lower seating area the Bobby Mitchell Level, replacing the name of George Preston Marshall. Mitchell was inducted into the NFL Hall of Fame in 1983. This came a day after the team dismantled and removed the team founder-owner's statue from outside RFK Stadium. Doug Williams, an African American, the team's quarterback during its victory in Super Bowl XXII in 1988, said, "It's a terrible thing to go to work every day for a man who didn't [want?] any black men on his football team. Can you imagine what that was like every day for Bobby? There isn't a human being alone who could have worn Bobby's shoes."[40]

In 2020, after years of contentious debate with Native Americans, along with African Americans, labor unions, and many others—and in the midst of demonstrations and protest around the police killing of George Floyd, an African American man in Minneapolis, Minnesota—team owners "retired" the name and logo of the Washington Redskins. The owners had resisted and spent millions of dollars lobbying NFL owners to be allowed to keep the name. But public pressure and eventually common sense over the bottom line, that is, dollars and cents, prevailed. *Newsweek* magazine reported that companies like Nike, FedEx, and PepsiCo "received a letter signed by 87 different investors and shareholders—

Parade on Pennsylvania Avenue, Washington, DC, in 1988, celebrating the Washington Redskins' victory in Super Bowl XXII. Photograph by Carol M. Highsmith, courtesy Library of Congress Prints and Photographs Division, LC-HS503-4593.

whose total net worth is $620 billion—urging them to pull their sponsorship unless the Redskins change their nickname."[41] In 2022, the team that had been officially called Washington Football for two years renamed itself, with public input, as the Washington Commanders.

## Notes

1. Ross, *Outside the Lines*, 10.
2. See Ashe and Rampersad, *A Hard Road to Glory*, 1:108.
3. Kirshenbaum, "Paul Robeson."
4. King, "What Paul Robeson Said."
5. Ross, *Outside the Lines*, 20, 48–50.
6. Smith, "Civil Rights on the Gridiron," 193.

7. George Preston Marshall, "Pro Football Is Better Football," *Saturday Evening Post,* November 19, 1938, 20–21. See also Corrine Griffith (Marshall), *My Life with the Redskins,* 39–46.

8. Smith, "Civil Rights on the Gridiron," 194.

9. Ross, *Outside the Lines,* 78.

10. Tygiel, "Jackie Robinson," 168.

11. Laverno, *Hail Victory,* 37, 38.

12. Ross, *Outside the Lines,* 136.

13. Smith, *Showdown,* 49, 141.

14. Shirley Povich, "This Morning with Shirley Povich," *Washington Post,* October 20, 1961.

15. Shirley Povich, "This Morning with Shirley Povich," *Washington Post,* December 1, 1959.

16. Smith, "Civil Rights on the Gridiron, 197.

17. Povich, October 20, 1961.

18. Shirley Povich, "This Morning with Shirley Povich," *Washington Post,* November 17, 1961.

19. Povich, November 17, 1961.

20. Dave Brady, "83 Negroes on Pro Teams, Including Seven at Dallas," *Washington Post,* November 30, 1961.

21. Ross, *Outside the Lines,* 138.

22. Nick Showers, "Letter to the Editor," *Washington Evening Star,* October 27, 1961.

23. Smith, "Civil Rights on the Gridiron," 194.

24. Ross, *Outside the Lines,* 148.

25. Quoted in O'Toole, *Fighting for Old DC,* 1.

26. Smith, *Showdown,* 121.

27. All quotes in this section are from Sam Lacy, *Baltimore Afro-American,* December 16, 1961.

28. Gordon Cobbledick, quoted in Smith, "Civil Rights on the Gridiron," 195.

29. Shirley Povich, "This Morning with Shirley Povich," *Washington Post,* April 27, 1961.

30. O'Toole, *Fighting for Old DC,* 148.

31. Ross, *Outside the Lines,* 154.

32. O'Toole, *Fighting for Old DC,* 144.

33. Sam Lacy, *Baltimore Afro-American,* October 8 and November 26, 1960. See also *Newsweek* 60 (October 15, 1962), 99; and Smith, "Civil Rights on the Gridiron," 204nn48–49.

34. Smith, "Civil Right on the Gridiron," 194.

35. Smith, 194.

36. In the summer of 1962 Davis was diagnosed with acute monocytic leukemia. He died on May 18, 1963. "Ernie Davis Succumbs in Battle with Leukemia," *Toledo Blade,* May 19, 1963.

37. Laverno, *Hail Victory*, 53.

38. Smith, "Civil Rights on the Gridiron," 201.

39. Laverno, *Hail Victory*, 52.

40. Liz Clarke, "Redskins Retire Bobby Mitchell's Number, Remove George Preston Marshall's Name from Seating Level," *Washington Post,* June 20, 2020. Bobby Mitchell died on April 5, 2020. In addition to being one of the team's greatest players, after his retirement he served for almost three decades as a scout and executive for the team. Doug Williams served as the team's senior VP of player development.

41. McDonald, "Washington Redskins Urged to Lose Name."

# 9

# BASKETBALL

## The Ball Bounced Toward Fairness

### E. B. Henderson: Molder of Men

Basketball was brought to Black Washington by Edwin Bancroft Henderson, a native son born in the Southwest section of the city in 1883. He attended Bell School, not far from Capitol Hill. With his parents' encouragement, Henderson often visited the Library of Congress and even watched debates in the US Senate and House of Representative from the galleries, learning what he called the "perplexing social, economic and political problems of the day."[1] He attended M Street (later Dunbar) High School, where he played all sports; and in 1904 he graduated from Miner's Normal School (later DC Teachers College) and then from Howard University. Some years later, in 1922, he received the doctor of chiropractic (DC) degree from Central Chiropractic College in Kansas City, Missouri.

Henderson began a career as a physical education teacher at Bowen Elementary School in the city. While working at Bowen he also attended Howard University Medical School at night, but when the night school closed, he took another direction.

Henderson spent the next two summers at Harvard University Dudley Sargent School of Physical Training, which was associated with the YMCA in Springfield, Massachusetts.[2] There he learned the game of basketball in depth. Nearby, James Naismith, a Canadian-born physical education innovator, created the game of modern basketball while working as an instructor at the YMCA school. During one particularly hard New England winter, Naismith was ordered to create an indoor game to contain rowdy young boys—without having them harm each other and to be played on a hardwood floor.[3] Using his knowledge of soccer, rugby, hockey, baseball, and other sports and games, Naismith had the lads, nine to each side, toss soccer balls at goals made of peach baskets.

Shortly after returning from Harvard, Henderson began teaching physical education in the DC schools, where he wrote, "I taught three days a week in the elementary schools" and "returned to M Street and Armstrong in the afternoons, three days a week."[4] There he taught basketball for the first time in the Washington, DC, public schools to African American boys. He rode to his jobs on his bicycle. Later he became the lead instructor in physical training and athletics for the Washington DC Colored School System. Henderson said that in Washington, "Basketball was not a popular sport for boys in 1906. The boys preferred the major sports of the day, such as football and baseball. All this was about to change. Boys, being boys, the game took on a rougher, more competitive tone upon its introduction. The mix of heat and testosterone meant more rough play and fouling, whereas the girls were more into pure fundamentals."[5] He was mentored by Anita Turner, the assistant director of physical education in the Colored School System, who was teaching the sport to girls.[6] In 1909 Turner took up the call of Nannie Helen Burroughs to form a girls team at the National Training School for Women and Girls. The next year he and his childhood sweetheart and life-long partner, Mary Ellen Meriwether (Henderson), were married.

Henderson had a lifelong affiliation with the Twelfth Street YMCA. Its story began in 1853, when the former enslaved African Anthony Bowen, who was born in 1805 in Prince George's County, Maryland, and purchased his freedom in 1830 for $425.00. He formed the Colored Men's Christian Association in 1853, and it became associated with but was never financially supported by the YMCA, which had been founded in 1851. Bowen's home near the 6th Street wharf became a stop on the underground railroad. The CMCA never really had its own permanent structure, but for thirty-eight years Bowen funded what became a sort of YMCA for "colored men and boys," the first such in the nation.

In 1903 Bowen's dream appeared as the 12th Street Branch, which moved to the True Reformers Building at 12th and U Streets NW, which had been designed by the Black architect John A. Lankford. In 1905 plans were made for a permanent home. Henderson joined in the effort and helped secure funds from people like philanthropist John D. Rockefeller, Julius Rosenwald, who had funded hundreds of "Rosenwald Schools" in the South, and Booker T. Washington. The cornerstone was laid for a new YMCA building in 1908, with President Theodore Roosevelt giving the main address at the ceremony. Three years later President William Howard Taft addressed a gathering at the Howard Theatre, which helped raise money, and in 1912 the new YMCA was completed. It was named the Twelfth Street YMCA.[7] In 1972 it was renamed the Anthony Bowen YMCA.[8]

*Washington Post* sports columnist Kevin B. Blackistone wrote that "basketball became as much the heartbeat of Black Washington as Howard University, as U Street, as half smokes and go-go."[9] He notes that in 1907, when the sport was introduced to the city by Henderson, "the game was still less than two decades old" and "was largely a segregated enterprise in those days, taking a cue from the broader set of symptoms that plagued America during the period of Jim Crow."[10]

In 1906 Henderson and five colleagues founded the Interscholastic Athletic Association (ISAA), whose purpose was to "promote the well-being of black students in Washington and Baltimore"[11] through organized competitions of football, baseball, and track. The next year Henderson and his future brother-in-law, Benjamin Brownley, went to the whites-only Central YMCA located downtown to watch a basketball game. Just as African American Protestant ministers Richard Allen and Absalom Jones were asked, by whites, to leave their seats at the St. George's Methodist Church in Philadelphia in 1787, the two men were asked to leave the YMCA. Just like the preachers founded their own churches, Mother Bethel and St. Thomas, in "the city of brotherly love," Henderson founded his own league in December 1907. The first game was played at the True Reformers Hall on U Street, when a Howard University team lost to a team of Washington high school players.[12] At the conclusion of these early games, basketball would often meet jazz when "Henderson turned the lights down low . . . [and] while the Lyric Orchestra thrummed through the numbered selections on the printed dance card, couples danced and waltzed away their cares."[13]

In 1908 Henderson officially added basketball as a regulated sport in the ISAA.[14] Henderson was also driven by an additional motivation: the reality that crowded, unsanitary conditions in Washington hindered both the physical and intellectual development of Black children. He was determined to "build a pipeline to send forth the city's best black student athletes to Harvard, Yale, and other top white colleges in the North," as well as to Howard University, the center of Washington's Black intellectual and sports movement.[15] In 1910 Henderson co-authored the *Official Handbook: Inter-Scholastic Athletic Association of Middle Atlantic States,* describing the nature of segregation in Black schools. By 1910 the ISAA had begun overseeing basketball competitions for nearly a thousand young African American athletes on forty teams. From Washington's 12th Street YMCA a national rivalry developed with team clubs in New York City, the other birthplace of Black basketball. The 12th Street Team, composed mostly of Howard students, some of whom were in medical school, became the Howard University Big Five, which played teams from all over the East Coast, from Virginia to Philadelphia to Pittsburgh and New York. When Woodrow Wilson was elected president in 1913, bringing increased segregation to the federal workforce and reducing Black appointees allowed in top federal positions from over thirty to just one, Henderson kept building the sport. With the city's population growth to 100,000 between 1905 and 1915, basketball and sports played a pivotal role in aiding the development of Black unity and the ability to cope.[16]

Henderson worked with the superintendent of Black schools, Roscoe Bruce, who was the son of former senator Blanche K. Bruce, to start the Public Schools Athletic League (PSAL). The goal of the league was to bring organized sports like soccer, baseball, cross-country, track, swimming, handball, and tennis to Black elementary and secondary school students. On Saturday nights, basketball brought crowds to the True Reformers Hall and Murray's Casino on U Street. Spectators came to experience a PSAL doubleheader, followed by the Howard Big Five—often playing New York City teams—before jitterbugging, dancing, and listening to jazz, sometimes with Duke Ellington and his Washingtonians providing the music. Ellington even wrote about those days: "I played my first date at the True Reformers Hall, on the worse piano in the world. . . . I played from 8 p.m. to 1 a.m. and for 75 cents. Man, I snatched that money and ran like a thief. My mother was so proud of me."[17] Ellington, who enjoyed playing sports, however, noticed that "when you were playing piano there was always a pretty girl standing down at the bass-clef end of the piano. I ain't been no athlete since."[18]

At the True Reformers Hall the gathered crowds would move to the popular songs of the time, with the "Waltz, Tango, Turkey Trot, Grizzly Bear, Ballin' the Jack, One-Step, Fox Trot, Two-Step, and Texas Tommy."[19] Weekly at the hall "five local bands . . . competed for the most audience applause to determine the most popular." Some who could afford it would step over to the Howard Theatre, which had opened at 620 T Street on August 22, 1910. Some of the basketball fans and working-class Blacks would sit in the audience but, as the *Washington Bee* reported, "the private boxes were filled with ladies of society. The Orchestra was monopolized with the social elite of Washington, gayly and gorgeously dressed in gowns fit for goddesses."[20]

By the 1920s, "an entire generation had been raised on basketball in the Washington public schools."[21] The sport grew in Washington along U and 7th Streets around the same time as a number of Black movie theaters appeared, including the Lincoln at 13th and U Street, the Republic at 14th and U, and the Dunbar at 7th and T. Together, by the mid-1920s these theaters sold nearly 1.5 million tickets a year.[22] After games, revelers would go to the "Lincoln Colonnade in the basement of the Lincoln Theatre, the Murray Palace Casino at Tenth and U street, the Scottish Rite Temple near Eleventh and R streets, and the Press Club a couple of blocks away."[23] In the 1930s amateur basketball flourished and some played in a Black semipro circuits

Blackistone wrote that "Henderson spawned the all-Black Washington Bears, who won the 1943 World Professional Basketball tournament. They begot Elgin Baylor, who begot Tom Hoover and John Thompson, who begot Dave Bing," and so many others.[24] The Washington Bears had been formed in 1941 by

In 1954, when *Brown v. Board of Education* supposedly made his job obsolete, E. B. Henderson celebrated his retirement from DC Schools with a professional portrait by famed photographer Addison Scurlock. Courtesy City of Falls Church, Virginia.

sports businessman and journalist Harold "Hal" Jackson, a Washington native. Jackson was also the radio play-by-play announcer for the Homestead Grays and the Howard University Baseball Team. The Bears played their home games at Turner's Arena at 14th and W Streets NW and were financed by Abe Lichtman, a part owner of the Howard and Lincoln Theatres. Other East Coast teams in the Black league included the New York Renaissance (a.k.a. the Harlem Rens), the Paterson Crescents, the Philadelphia Toppers, and the Baltimore Mets."[25] Like other Black teams, the Bears squad was composed of everyday working men. Teams played games once or twice a week in various cities. Over time Jackson signed a few of the Harlem Rens' top players, including two future Naismith Hall of Famers, Tarzan Cooper and William "Pop" Gates. In 1943 Cooper and Gates led the Bears to a 41-0 record. In 1943 the Bears defeated the Oshkosh All-Stars in the World Professional Basketball Championship (WPBC), an invitational tournament sponsored by the *Chicago Herald American*. With this victory the Bears became the first undefeated African American team to win a championship in the WPBC.[26] At the time, Shirley Povich wrote in the *Washington Post* that "the city has not quite appreciated the skill of these Bears who haven't been on display in a hall as large as Uline's, and the game should be an awakening of some sort."[27] The team played a few more seasons before the NBA was integrated in 1950.

While Henderson modernized the game for Black youths, he also modernized the use of sports for social advancement. For example, he fought to end racial restrictions at Rose Park playground in Georgetown. With his growing family, he and Mary had moved to Falls Church, Virginia, in 1915, to a lot they purchased from his parents.[28] From there he commuted to his work in Washington. He led in the formation of the Falls Church NAACP in 1918 and years later he served as the state president.[29]

In 1935 he was appointed to the Planning Committee for Coordinating Plans for Recreation Facilities in the city while also serving with the several organizations under FDR's New Deal. That year he was also appointed to the newly formed DC Recreation Committee, the only African American member. He participated in the "Marian Anderson Concert Committee" in 1939, in protest at the National Theater with Todd Duncan and the Committee for Racial Democracy in the 1940s in the campaign to force the Washington football team to integrate in the 1950s and 1960s, and in the March on Washington in 1963.[30] He died in 1977. He and his wife Mary Henderson's ashes are interred in Woodlawn Cemetery in Washington.

## Charles Drew: Medicine and Sports

One of Henderson's prized students was Charles Drew. Like Sterling Brown, Drew was DC-born and attended Dunbar High School. He then studied at Amherst College. Henderson coached him at Dunbar, where, as Alison Stewart writes, he was known as "a super jock, not necessarily someone who would become a super scientist. He played football and basketball, swam, and ran track." Stewart continues, "As the eldest of five and the son of a carpet layer, Charlie needed an athletic scholarship to go to college."[31]

At Amherst, Drew excelled in academics and athletics. He received his medical degree from McGill University in Montreal, Quebec, where he hit his intellectual stride, winning the annual prize in neuroanatomy and being elected to Alpha Omega Alpha, the honorary medical scholastic fraternity. Drew won the Williams Prize, which was given to the top five students in each class, graduating second in his class in 1933.

After graduation Drew held a one-year residency, split between Royal Victoria Hospital in Victoria, BC, and Montreal General Hospital. While in Montreal he worked with bacteriology professor John Beattie, developing ways to treat shock with fluid replacement. Drew expressed a desire to do training in blood transfusion therapy at the Mayo Clinic, but racial prejudices severely limited where African American medical scholars could train or practice at that time. In the

United States, Drew's options were limited to Freedmen's Hospital in Washington, DC, and Meharry Medical College in Nashville, Tennessee.

When Drew's father died in 1935, his passing placed a severe financial burden on the family. That same year the dean of Howard University College of Medicine, Dr. Numa P. G. Adams, aspired to elevate the school's Surgery Department to a higher standard and offered Drew a position in the Department of Pathology and in the Surgery Training Program, which he accepted. The same year, Adams hired a white surgeon from Yale, Edward Lee Howes, as chief of surgery, to advance the program. Howes's goal was to mentor a young African American surgeon to take over as chair. The Rockefeller Foundation provided funds for Drew to get additional training and conduct research under Dr. Allen Whipple in 1938 at Presbyterian Hospital in New York. Whipple assigned Drew to work in the laboratory of Dr. John Scudder, who was doing research on blood transfusion and preservation. Whipple, according to some sources, was motivated in this assignment by a desire to deny Drew the customary training pathway that his white peers enjoyed, seeing patients and gaining experience in operating rooms and surgical wards. Under Scudder, Drew wrote his doctoral thesis about numerous aspects of blood storage. Scudder described Drew's thesis as a "masterpiece" in form and content. In 1940 Drew became the first African American to be awarded the doctor of science in medicine at Columbia University.

Drew wrote a personal letter to Henderson, who had coached him at Dunbar. The year before, in 1939, Henderson had authored *The Negro in Sports*.[32] The letter read, "I personally feel a great debt to you. You have set the pace continually, and we who have the privilege of coming under your influence cannot but feel just a bit 'chesty' when we say, 'Mr. Henderson, sure I knew him, he taught me in high school and you bet he's okay.'"[33] Drew also reminded Henderson of his own days as coach of the Morgan State Basketball Team, while he was teaching chemistry and biology to earn money for medical school. Drew told Henderson that "in American surgery there are no Negro representatives" but, rather, "country practitioners capable of sitting with the poor and the sick of their race but not given to too much intellectual activity and not particularly interested in advancing medicine," something "I should like to change." The man who would one day be regarded as one of the nation's preeminent surgeons and scientists concluded: "If at the end of another 25 years I can look back over my steps and feel that I have kept the faith in my sphere of activity in a manner comparable to that on which you have carried on in yours I shall be very happy. Again, I congratulate you." Sports gave Drew, a man from a working-class background who had grown up in segregated Washington, the opportunity to attend college and later to earn money for medical school. In short, sports enabled him to succeed.

Because of his expertise in blood preservation, Drew was chosen to lead the Blood for Britain Project during World War Two, helping to develop standard techniques and safety protocols for the large-scale collection, processing, and storage of blood. Lessons learned from the Blood for Britain Project led to the realization that procurement of blood products and their distribution could be effectively carried out through the organizational framework of the American Red Cross. Notably, the availability of blood is limited due to its degradation, allowing storage for forty days at most. Drew studied the changes that occur in stored blood and developed a large-scale method for separating plasma from blood. Plasma can be stored for twelve months and is effective in replacing loss from severe bleeding, as it contains the necessary clotting factors often missing from stored blood.[34] Drew also found that plasma can be stored for many years if dried and then reconstituted when needed, and he concluded that the infusion of plasma, instead of whole blood, would be the best way to save lives in an immediate time frame.[35]

At the time, the military said, "It is not advisable to indiscriminately mix Caucasian and Negro blood for use in blood transfusions for US military."[36] Drew soon resigned and returned to Washington, where some years later he said, "It is fundamentally wrong for any great nation to willingly discriminate against such a large group of its people," adding that "it is unfortunate that such a worthwhile and scientific bit of work should have been hamstrung by such stupidity." Drew concluded: "One can say quite truthfully that on the battlefields nobody is very interested in where the plasma comes from when they are hurt."[37]

On April 1, 1950, while driving back from a medical clinic in Tuskegee, Alabama, Drew and several other African American colleagues were in a serious car accident in North Carolina. The others received minor injuries but Drew, who was driving, was severely injured. He was taken to the hospital and died less than an hour later. Rumors and myths soon spread that he had died because he was Black and refused medical attention and that he either had bled to death or was refused a transfusion. While the rumors proved false, they were plausible: he was a Black man traveling in the South. He had put enormous effort into teaching and institutional development at the Howard College of Medicine, where he became chief of surgery at Freedmen's Hospital. This resulted in the elevation of the training of African American surgeons who had been deprived of exposure, opportunity, and resources that would enable them to become world-class leaders in the field. African American academic surgery was dealt a severe blow by the loss of Drew. Many African American surgeons since have labored prodigiously and sacrificed against numerous societal restrictions in order to reach the high intellectual standard that he envisioned.

In the midst of the battles to integrate DC public schools, Henderson wrote a letter that was published in the *Washington Post* on June 26, 1951. It read, in part, "The current suits . . . are causing turmoil in the minds of politicians, racial bigots, whites and Negroes. . . . In those social areas where sudden elimination of segregation has come about almost nowhere have any of the fears materialized."[38] Henderson believed that sports, especially basketball, presented Blacks with the opportunity to achieve. In 1968 he wrote *The Black Athlete: Emergence and Arrival,* which inspired Arthur Ashe to write his own history, *A Hard Road to Glory.*[39] Henderson was inducted into the Naismith Hall of Fame on September 8, 2013, over one hundred years after that first game at the YMCA.

## Notes

1. Dave Ungradle, "E. B. Henderson Brought Basketball to the District," *Washington Post*, September 6, 2003.

2. Henderson was the first African American certified to teach physical education in the United States.

3. Naismith earned his medical degree in 1898, then went on to become the basketball coach and athletic director at the University of Kansas. There Naismith coached Phog Allen, who went on to coach at Kansas for thirty-nine years. Among Allen's students were two legendary coaches, arch-segregationist Adolph Rupp and enlightened integrationist Dean Smith, who coached Michael Jordan at the University of North Carolina.

4. Coursey, "The Life of Edwin Bancroft Henderson," 154.

5. Henderson and Joiner, *Spaulding Handbook History*, 19.

6. Henderson, *The Grandfather of Black Basketball*, 36–37.

7. Henderson, 93–94.

8. The Bowen Y was named a National Historic Landmark in 1994. H.R. 2301, US Congress, 101st Congress (1989–1990).

9. Kevin B. Blackistone, "Losing NBA Would Sting Black D.C. to Its Core," *Washington Post*, December 16, 2023.

10. Blackistone, "Losing NBA Would Sting." Blackistone names other hoopsters with DC-area roots: Fatty Taylor, Austin Carr, Kermit Washington, Adrian Dantley, Penny Toler, Adrian Branch, Johnny Dawkins, Thurl Bailey, Tom Sluby, Walt Williams, Randolph Childress, Steve Francis, and Kevin Durant.

11. Henderson and Joiner, *Spaulding Handbook History*, 19.

12. Ungradle, "E. B. Henderson Brought Basketball to the District."

13. Kuska, *Hot Potato*, 3.

14. Kuska, x–xi.

15. Kuska, 13.

16. Kuska, 11, 12, 13, 25, 35–39.

17. Gwen Dodson, "Luncheon with . . . Duke Ellington," *Washington Evening Star*, April 23, 1971.

18. Ellington, *Music Is My Mistress*, 22.

19. Hasse, "Washington's Duke Ellington," 45.

20. Gardner and Thomas, "Cultural Impact."

21. Kuska, *Hot Potato*, 51, 95.

22. McQuirter, "Claiming the City."

23. "Basketball," *Washington Afro-American*, April 25, 1964.

24. Blackistone, "Losing NBA Would Sting."

25. Al White, "Small Group of Players Dominate Eastern Teams," *Baltimore Afro-American*, February 28, 1942.

26. Johnson, *The Black Fives*, 395–96.

27. Shirley Povich, "This Morning with Shirley Povich," *Washington Post*, January 28, 1944.

28. Henderson, *The Grandfather of Black Basketball*, 118–19. The Hendersons purchased a Model 225 home from the Sears and Roebuck catalog and placed it on the lot.

29. While serving as the president of the Virginia Council of the NAACP from 1955 to 1958, he helped found the Colored Citizens Protective League and fought against the white-led "Massive Resistance" campaign against integration that came after the *Brown v. Board of Education* decision in 1954. See chap. 16, "Protest in Virginia," in Henderson, *The Grandfather of Black Basketball*, 123–47.

30. See Henderson, *The Grandfather of Black Basketball*, chap. 17, "Protest in the Nation's Capital," 149–64.

31. Stewart, *First Class*, 156–57.

32. Henderson, *The Negro in Sports*. Henderson published many articles in the *Crisis*, the *Journal of Negro Education*, the *Journal of the American Association for Health, Physical Education and Recreation*, and other magazines and journals. He wrote over three thousand Letters to the Editor and published hundreds of articles in the *Washington Tribune*, the *Washington Afro-American*, and the *Baltimore Afro-American*.

33. Charles Drew to E. B. Henderson, May 31, 1940, Historical Society of Washington. The letter was sent from the Columbia University College of Physicians and Surgeons, where Drew was working on a postdoctoral fellowship. His Columbia thesis was titled "Banked Blood: A Study in Blood Preservation." Drew was also granted a patent by the US Patent and Trademark Office for a device that preserved blood. The patent lists Scudder as the inventor but Scudder assigned ownership of the patent to Drew, probably because, as is true even today, at many institutions only faculty are allowed to apply for patents. In assigning the patent to Drew, Scudder most likely was graciously acknowledging the fact that the invention was based on Drew's work.

34. To gain an understanding of Charles Drew and his research, I spoke at length with Dr. Cuthbert O. Simpkins, the founder of the biotech company Vivacelle Bio Inc. (vivacellebio.com) on January 20, 2020. I first met Simpkins when he was a staff sur-

geon doing general and trauma surgery at DC General Hospital and working as a clinical assistant professor in the Howard University Department of Surgery in the 1980s. Simpkins is an inventor who holds nine US patents and thirty-three patents in international jurisdictions. He retired in 2009 from his position as professor of surgery and chief of trauma and surgical critical care at Louisiana State University Health Sciences Center in Shreveport, Louisiana. Today he continues to deliver critical care as an intensivist at Lutheran Hospital in Fort Wayne, Indiana.

35. See https://www.nationalww2museum.org/sites/default/files/2017–07/blood-plasma-fact-sheet.pdf; and https://web.archive.org/web/20161218150653/http://history.amedd.army.mil/booksdocs/wwii/blood/chapter1.htm.

36. Stewart, *First Class,* 157.

37. Stewart, 157.

38. E. B. Henderson letter to the *Washington Post*, June 26, 1951.

39. Ashe and Rampersad, *A Hard Road to Glory*. See also Ashe and Rampersad, *Days of Grace.*

# 10

# RABBIT, BIG JOHN, AND DUKE

## From the Local to the Global

### Elgin Baylor, "the Rabbit"

Elgin Baylor is considered the best basketball player to ever come out of Washington, DC. He was born in 1934 in Southeast Washington. Baylor's father said his son was named after his watch, an Elgin, which he glanced at right after his son was born. Nicknamed "Rabbit" as a youngster because of his speed, leaping ability, and boundless energy, he describes the city in the early 1940s, when he was in elementary school in Southeast: "To get to Giddings, I walk past an all-white elementary school and then, if I want to save time, I cut through the park, the one on the left—the black park, which faces the white park. It's easy to tell them apart. The white park has a basketball court, baseball diamond, football field with goalposts, tennis courts, and swimming pool, as well as a playground with swings, slides, and a climbing structure, park benches, neatly trimmed grass, and freshly painted flowers. The black park has a sandbox and a swing. Nothing else."[1] He noted that "a lot of people who grew up in D.C. at the same time as I did feel the same way. They love the people; they don't love the city. Something about it makes you uneasy." He added "in all my years on Heckman Street" where he lived as a kid "I never [did] see one black police officer" adding without comment "I hear of a guy that gets picked up by the cops and disappears."[2]

Baylor's first games were not at the YMCA but at "a place called Southeast Settlement House where kids could go." He recalls, "We could only go on the playground when it was closed, and the only thing you could do was try and shoot baskets."[3] Southeast House had been founded by Dorothy Bolding Ferebee as part of the Settlement House movement in the 1920s, to foster and promote the "health, happiness, welfare, intellectual, social and spiritual development" of people in communities of need.[4] Ferebee, a graduate of Tufts University Medical School, was the medical director of Howard University Health Services and a professor at Howard for twenty-seven years. She also worked at the Alpha Kappa

137

Elgin "Rabbit" Baylor, on the cover of a Los Angeles Lakers program, March 21, 1969. Baylor played at Spingarn High School and was the first African American named to the First Team All-Metro in 1954. He played several seasons of college basketball at Seattle University, winning All-American honors, and he was the first pick in the 1958 NBA draft, chosen by the Minneapolis Lakers (later the Los Angeles Lakers). A ten-time All-NBA First Team choice, in 1996 he was named one of the NBA's 50 Greatest Players and in 2021 he was named to the NBA's 75th Anniversary Team of 75 greatest players. A Naismith Hall of Fame Inductee (1977), Baylor served as head coach of the New Orleans Jazz and as vice president of operations for the Los Angeles Clippers. Wikimedia Commons.

Alpha Mississippi Health Project and was president of the National Council of Negro Women. Southeast Settlement house set up "sewing clubs, mothers' and fathers' clubs," and youth recreational opportunities for inner city youth like Baylor. It also allowed the Congress of Racial Equality to hold Freedom Schools there in 1964.[5] Just as Dr. Ferebee was influenced by Henderson, Baylor was the beneficiary of both.

Baylor's legendary status began at Phelps Vocational High School, which formed a quartet of Black segregated schools with Armstrong, Cardozo, and Dunbar High Schools. At one point Baylor dropped out of school but enrolled at Spingarn High School, the school that he made famous.[6] As John McNamara notes, the school "was the final all-Black segregated high school built within the

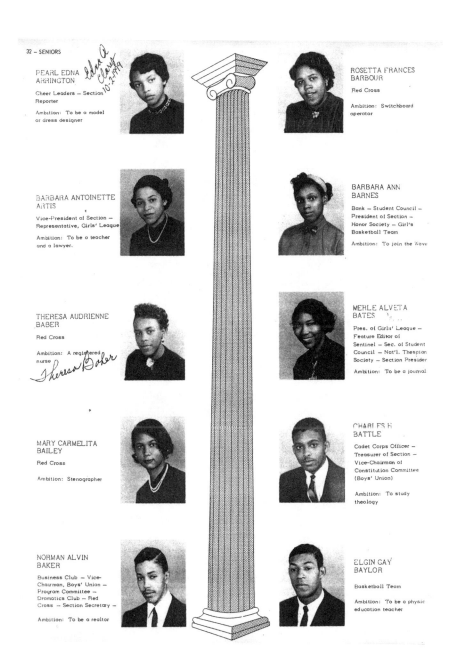

**PEARL EDNA ARRINGTON**

Cheer Leaders – Section Reporter

Ambition: To be a model or dress designer

**BARBARA ANTOINETTE ARTIS**

Vice-President of Section – Representative, Girls' League

Ambition: To be a teacher and a lawyer.

**THERESA AUDRIENNE BABER**

Red Cross

Ambition: A registered nurse

**MARY CARMELITA BAILEY**

Red Cross

Ambition: Stenographer

**NORMAN ALVIN BAKER**

Business Club – Vice-Chairman, Boys' Union – Program Committee – Dramatics Club – Red Cross – Section Secretary –

Ambition: To be a realtor

**ROSETTA FRANCES BARBOUR**

Red Cross

Ambition: Switchboard operator

**BARBARA ANN BARNES**

Bank – Student Council – President of Section – Honor Society – Girl's Basketball Team

Ambition: To join the Wave

**MERLE ALVETA BATES**

Pres. of Girls' League – Feature Editor of Sentinel – Sec. of Student Council – Nat'l. Thespian Society – Section Presider

Ambition: To be a journal

**CHARLES H BATTLE**

Cadet Corps Officer – Treasurer of Section – Vice-Chairman of Constitution Committee (Boys' Union)

Ambition: To study theology

**ELGIN GAY BAYLOR**

Basketball Team

Ambition: To be a physic education teacher

Elgin Baylor aspired to play basketball in the only way open to him in 1953: by becoming a physical education teacher. Courtesy District of Columbia Public School Records, Charles Sumner School Museum and Archives, Washington, DC.

city's boundaries."[7] Named after Joel Elias Spingarn, a founder of the NAACP, the school opened in 1952, a few short years before Washington schools were integrated. In his senior year Baylor was named to the First Team All-Metro, the first African American so named in the city. Still, his team came in second in polling to the all-white Washington-Lee High School in Virginia as the area's top team. Its second-place finish was still a first for a Black team.

Baylor left Washington to attend the College of Idaho before moving to Seattle University, then leading the Seattle team to the 1958 National Championship game against Adolph Rupp's all-white Kentucky Wildcats. The integrated Seattle team played in front of an all-white crowd of over eighteen thousand, losing 84–72. After coming in second to Oscar Robertson as the nation's top collegiate scorer, Baylor was the top pick in the 1958 NBA draft, taken by the Minneapolis Lakers and at the end of that first season was named NBA Rookie of the Year. He was called to military duty from 1961 to 1962, and he served in Washington as a reservist while playing weekends for the Lakers when possible. He retired in 1972 and was named to the Basketball Hall of Fame in 1977.[8] Baylor was named to the 50th NBA Anniversary Team in 1996 as one of the fifty greatest NBA basketball players of all time.[9] He was inducted into the College Basketball Hall of Fame in 2006. Baylor died on March 22, 2021. Five years before he died he wrote on the front page of his autobiography *Hang Time: My Life in Basketball.*

> I'm flying, heading home. I'm going to DC, where I grew up, to visit my family and retrace my roots, maybe for the last time in my life. I'm eighty-one, and I haven't been back in more than twenty years. I'm not sure I'll go back again. I hesitated to come on this trip, if you want to know the truth. I don't know if I want to dredge up a lot of memories, to relive my time in DC. Don't get me wrong: I have a lot of good memories—time with my family and friends, and mostly, of course, playing basketball. But the District was a different place back then. A hard place. A racist place. Segregated parks, schools, movie houses, lunch counters. I experienced ugly, uncomfortable things.

He continued: "I told myself that once I left DC, other than visit my family, I wouldn't be back. A lot of people who grew up in DC at the same time as I did feel the same way. They love the city, they don't love the place. Something about it makes you uneasy." He concludes in saying, "The only place I ever felt totally comfortable was on a basketball court. That was home."[10] It is not surprising that he felt differently about his hometown than Shirley Horn or Buck Hill felt about theirs. Perhaps coming from a more humble background made his experiences different. Perhaps a Black man with a ball was seen differently than one with a horn. Perhaps it was the "unforgettable things" he experienced. Perhaps it was that, as he wrote, "one event in particular changed my life. I told myself that once I left DC, other than to visit my family, I wouldn't go back."[11]

Not long after he died, on the 75th Anniversary of the NBA, he was honored as one of the Top 75 ever by a panel of current and former players, sportswriters, and team executives.[12] Many other DC-born athletes and musicians felt the same way.


## Big John Thompson

> I came as a shadow,
> I stand now a light;
> The depth of my darkness
> Transfigures your night.[13]

John Thompson Jr. was born in 1941 in Washington, DC, to devout Catholic parents. His "birth class included 'Good Trouble' John Lewis, Student Nonviolent Coordinating Committee leader Kwame Ture (born Stokely Carmichael), and Black Panthers cofounder Huey Newton."[14] His father, John Sr., came from St. Mary's County, Maryland, where the Jesuits, founders of Georgetown University, enslaved Black people. The senior Thompson worked at a marble and tile factory; though he could not read or write, he told his son to "study the white man" and "learn their system."[15]

John Jr.'s mother, Anna, was Washington-born and a graduate of Dunbar High School and Miner's Teachers College. "Despite the fact that my mother was a trained educator, she took what we called 'day work' to make ends meet. Day's work sounds better than 'cleaning white folks' houses, doesn't it?" he asked.[16] Like other Black women who could not find a teaching job, she daily crossed over to the western side of Rock Creek Park, "the city's forested dividing line, where black folks only ventured to go to work."[17] When he struggled to keep up with his studies, his sixth-grade teacher, Sametta Jackson, simply said, "You're not stupid. You just can't read," and she found him a reading specialist. "She saved my life . . . and had as much influence on my coaching as some of the greatest minds in basketball," teaching him that all Black kids needed was for someone to believe in them and, given the opportunity, they could succeed.[18]

"A lot of Washington was segregated at that time," he told WAMU (American University) radio host Kojo Nnamdi. The first time he spoke to a white person was as a teenager; even in church, he "had to wait for white parishioners to finish their prayers before he could approach the altar."[19] Neighborhood men told him to give up playing first base in baseball and take advantage of his size, so he gravitated to basketball. Whites could play in Jelleff's Boys Club League, but Blacks went to the Police Boys Club. Thompson gravitated to playgrounds and later to the First Street Northwest Police Boys Club No. 2.

Thompson attended Archbishop Carroll Catholic High School, one of three Black students to enter the school his freshman year. The Archdiocese of Washington integrated its school and the Catholic Athletic Conference in 1949, five years before Brown v. Board of Education. Yet, in what continued to be a mostly white league, his team was often hit with racial taunts from spectators.

*Washington Post* sportswriter Leonard Shapiro outlined the racist taunts Thompson and his two Black teammates endured while winning fifty-five straight games and league and tournament championships. As a junior Thompson was named to the Second Team All-Metro, and as a senior he was named First Team All-Metro, leading the Washington Catholic Athletic Conference in scoring.[20] The 1958–59 teams also featured Edward "Monk" Molloy, a First-Team All-Metro who was ordained a Catholic priest in 1960 and became president of the University of Notre Dame in 1987.

Two things stood out during Thompson's school years. McNamara describes "the six-foot-ten" teenager as "a shy and quiet young man with loads of potential at that point that needed polish." He adds that "it is rare to find a newspaper story from one year to the next that fails to mention Thompson's continuous improvement from one year to the next. He was simply too driven and too dedicated not to succeed . . . traits that would serve him well when he became a coach."[21]

Nnamdi interviewed Thompson on April 26, 2012, asking about his childhood and sports. Thompson said of his early years, "At the time, I was living at 1425 W St. NW. . . . And we used to walk, Kojo, to Griffith Stadium anytime the Cleveland Indians came in town because that was the team that had an African American—in fact the second African American who came into baseball several weeks after Jackie Robinson, Larry Doby, number 14, center fielder." Later, Blacks would turn to rooting for the Dallas Cowboys because the Washington "Redskins," like the Washington Senators, refused to hire African Americans. Thompson added: "My dad would be in the bleachers yelling and screaming for Doby and arguing with the guy behind him. We had a lot of fun. But that probably gave me the sports bug as much as anything."[22]

Thompson said basketball "started for me at U Street NW when I was 14 at Boys Club Number 13. When I was [living at] 1425 W St. NW. Then I moved out into far northeast. But the thing that drew me to the club was the fact that a lot of Washington was segregated at that time. And the players that played with me at John Carroll High School could play in the Jelleff's Boys Club League on Wisconsin Avenue. But the African Americans had to go to Police Boys Club. . . .

So, I got attached to Police Boys Club No. 2."[23] Years later sportswriter Leonard Shapiro wrote that, in response to "rising rates of juvenile delinquency in the city," the First Street Northwest Police Boys Club No. 2 was started.[24]

When asked about the inability of Blacks to play in the recreational leagues at the Chevy Chase playground located at Livingston Street and Western Avenue, Thompson said that "a lot of the guys in the inner city would come up. In my latter years, you'd come up to Chevy Chase Playground, where I think it's a library there now . . . you know, and we always said they built a library because too many African Americans were coming there. . . . But at one point where we would come up there, there was a painting, 'N—ers, go home.'"[25] He added, "During the summertime, the white players could only play west of the park . . . but that's how I got attached to Number 2 Sherwood . . . because we couldn't even play in summer league tournaments with the guys that we were winning championships with at a Catholic school. So, you had to adjust to that. You had to be able to digest that and deal with it and put it in a proper perspective as you grow up." Over time the Jelleff's Boys Club integrated, and by the late 1970s the twenty-two-team league became the most competitive in the area.[26] At the Jelleff's League, elementary, junior high, and senior high school kids from all over the city created the most integrated place in the city.[27]

Thompson was asked about Arnold "Red" Auerbach, the legendary former coach at St. Albans School for Boys, at George Washington University, and for the Boston Celtics, where he also became team president.[28] Auerbach maintained a home in Washington. Thompson said, "That is one of the reasons why I respected Red an awful lot—if you can imagine a guy winning as many championships as he won . . . but yet during his spare time, sitting out on a playground, giving instructions or talking to young people." Auerbach was known to roam the basketball courts and at the Jabbo Kenner Summer League games.

Thompson was recruited to play college ball at Providence College, earning a degree in economics while becoming a NCAA All-American his senior season.[29] Nnamdi asked Thompson, "You played college ball at Providence, but I was also intrigued by the story of who took you in when you first lived there. Who are Harold and Marty Furash?" Thompson responded by telling a story similar to Louis Armstrong's. Armstrong always wore a Star of David necklace to honor the Karnofskys, a Jewish family who aided him when he was a child in New Orleans. Armstrong recalled they treated him as someone "who [was] just like a relative."[30] He added that he "shared meals with them, even borrowed money to buy his first cornet from a pawnshop from them." As Armstrong said, "They were always warm and kind to me . . . just a kid who could use a word of kindness . . . and just starting out in the world."

Thompson told a similar story of the Furashes, a Jewish family who impacted him in New England:

> Yeah, well it was a family in Boston, and really, they took me in more so when I was with the Celtics. But they would come down and watch the games when I was at Providence. And I spent an awful lot of time and learned a lot [about] family. They're a Jewish family that was in Westwood, Massachusetts. And they treated me as if I were their son, you know what I mean, and really exposed me to a lot of things that I had not been exposed to. And I was away from home at the time. . . . And I enjoyed, most of all, in the evenings just sitting and talking with them, and particularly with Marty Furash. . . . But I had a great deal of time. And it's like everything else. . . . A lot of people contribute to your education, exposing you to things. I tell people, I went to college to play basketball. I didn't go to college to get an education. I went to play basketball. But after meeting people and being exposed to people, the value of being there for something else other than playing basketball connected itself to you. You know, certainly my mother and my father told me the importance of it. But sometimes, you listen to things more clearly when others say it than when your parents say it to you.[31]

He earned a degree, became an All-American, and was drafted by the Boston Celtics, winning two championships playing behind Bill Russell. He said that "Russ was the first person I knew who embraced his Blackness," leading him to embrace his own.[32] He also learned from Auerbach, perhaps seeing a bit of his father in Red, whose "work ethic" Thompson so admired.

When selected in the 1996 supplemental draft by the Chicago Bulls, Thompson decided to instead move back home to raise his family; he began by coaching at St. Anthony's Catholic High School. In 1972 he was recruited to coach at Georgetown, where he stayed for twenty-seven years. A few years after he was hired, the school president, Father Timothy Healy, a larger-than-life figure himself, said "After the 1968 riots it became obvious that the university's position wasn't very smart—We began making some changes, some statements to the local community that we were going to try to be at least more responsible and useful." He added: "I think it's fair to say that hiring John Thompson was one of those statements."[33]

Falsely, Coach Thompson was accused of recruiting only Black teens, although some thought that the school was an HBCU because of its famed crop of Black players. He counted as friends Black coaches like legends John McLendon and Clarence "Big House" Gaines, as well as his contemporaries John Chaney and George Raveling.

Thompson came to embody Du Bois's idea of double consciousness: he can see you but does not want you to see him. He commented that whites "preferred to say I was a bully rather than say that I was intelligent" and "some white people like to run around saying 'I don't see color.' That's ridiculous. I'm a large Black person. . . . When I meet a white person, I bring all my history and experiences. . . . I'm haunted by my past. Maybe my assumptions are wrong, but you better not blame me for having them, because they are based on real history."[34]

Thompson became, as in the words of Sterling Brown, a "strong man": a strong Black man accused of being an angry Black man. One of the men he admired most was Dean Smith, the white coach of the University of North Carolina, who voiced few opinions on race but spoke unequivocally for the equality of his players, including Michael Jordan and James Worthy. Smith impressed on him the importance of dressing nicely, of eating at places other than McDonald's, of never chastising a player's intelligence, "because you are telling the whole arena the boy is stupid." Thompson did not always take that advice: "Some of the things I said to [the players] was wrong. . . . I tried never to curse anyone out who didn't know I loved him."[35] He often said, "I tell everyone I speak two languages fluently— English and profanity."[36]

"Big John" used language and stories, just like Maya Angelou and James Baldwin did, always including a lesson. "Not only am I Black," he writes, "but I have dark skin. My feet are big, my body is big. Sometimes I'm loud . . . because I'm composed of big things."[37] In choosing *I Came as a Shadow* as the title of his autobiography—the same title of the poem "Nocturne Varial" by his uncle, Harlem Renaissance writer Lewis Grandison Alexander—Thompson shows that his mind is one of the big things that make "Big John."

When his greatest player Patrick Ewing was taunted by white Georgetown students, Thompson challenged the university. At opposing arenas signs went up, saying "Ewing Kan't Read Dis"; bananas were thrown. Ewing said, "Pulling us off the floor. Telling them they got to take these signs down . . . death threats . . . just the way he protected us, the way he stood up for us" was all that was needed.[38] Father Healy spoke up forcefully: "No one on the earth can tell me that if Patrick were a 7-foot high white man that people would carry those signs around. . . . This all strikes me as dreadful.[39]

Thompson said that "we didn't need racism to motivate us," although it was evident that he used the actions of bigoted students to motivate his team and himself, while at the same time trying to shield his players. In reality, Black athletes and musicians and Black people in general have long had to use such instances of societal racism to motivate, to organize, and to combat that racism. Thompson's words, however, do ring true when he writes that "our community tends to rally around Black people who are subjected to racist attacks. . . . People from coast to coast wore Georgetown jackets, caps and T-shirts. These items became a status symbol in Black neighborhoods."[40]

At a home game on February 5, 1975, just as the National Anthem was playing and "not far from a crucifix and an American flag," someone hung a "banner," more like a sheet, that read "Thompson the N——er Flop Must Go." Healey condemned the action, and Thompson said, "I still can't get used to" these type of actions. At every home game he arranged for inner city students from the public schools and the boys clubs to attend and sit in a section called Coach's Corner. Thompson said, after that game, what bothered him most were "those little kids that saw that—it'll be in their memory banks forever."[41]

Thompson's deep respect for women, including for his mother, his sisters, and Mrs. Sametta Wallace Jackson, was apparent. He wrote that "to whatever extent I helped women get ahead, I'm as proud of that as I am of what I may have done for Black people."[42] With Thompson's support, athletic trainer Lorry Michel became the first woman to be head athletic trainer at any men's basketball program; Mary Fenlon was both the academic coordinator and assistant coach. Thompson said, "she had a deep respect for Black kids but was not afraid to speak up to them." She sat on the bench with the coaches. Stressing academics, Thompson was often quoted as saying "Don't let eight pounds of air be the sum total of your existence."[43] Respect for the working man and woman was at his core. "My father never learned to read, never made anywhere near the kind of money I make, but he was a success. So was my mother."[44]

Thompson recruited from the communities where he grew up. He went to high school and playground games, just like his former coach Auerbach. He recruited local youngsters like Ed Spriggs, "who was working in the Post Office and playing in the rec league."[45] He visited the boys clubs; when he took Patrick Ewing with him, the same men who knew him as a high schooler said "he's still one of our kids."[46] Michael Graham, from Spingarn, became a city favorite. "He was a big, strong kid and he shaved his head a long time before it became fashionable," but he was scared to death of Mary Fenlon. Thompson spoke to his nephew Eddie, who also attended Spingarn, who told him, "Uncle John, Michael is not like people think he is." This image was what "he needed . . . in order to not be a target" where he lived, in early 1980s Washington, DC.[47]

In 1982, when in New Orleans, Thompson was asked how he felt about being the first Black coach to reach the Final Four. He answered: "I resent the hell out of that question. It implies that I'm the first Black coach *capable* of making the Final Four. That's not close to true. I'm just the first own who was given the opportunity to get here."[48]

In the 1982 NCAA Championship game against Michael Jordan's University of North Carolina, Georgetown guard Fred Brown accidently threw the ball to UNC's James Worthy, and the Tar Heels won the game, 63–62. When front page pictures showed Thompson hugging an inconsolable Brown, he said, "It was my natural reaction, based on what I was taught by my parents, by Sametta Wallace Jackson." His Hoyas defeated the University of Houston for the NCAA championship on April 2, 1984.[49] Coach Thompson said he "made a beeline for Fred Brown . . . this time our hug was joyful."[50] He was again asked about being the first Black coach to win the NCAA title. And again he was forceful in his reply: "I'm not interested in being the first or only black coach to do anything, because that implies that I'm also the first with the ability."[51]

The victory "touched off celebrations across the District. Georgetown students chanted 'Hoyas!,'" as they took to the streets following the game. The elation was far from limited to the university's predominantly white community. Throughout the city many Blacks also cheered on their hometown team, which included three players from local high schools, Gene Smith, Bill Martin, and Michael Graham.[52] Ewing was named the NCAA Final Four Most Outstanding Player in 1984. Michael Jordon won the National College Player of the Year that year and Ewing won the National College Player of the Year in 1985 and was inducted in the College Hall of Fame in 2012. Ewing was honored in 2008 and again in 2010 as part of the 1992 US Olympics Dream Team. The NBA Rookie of the year in 1986, he was also named to the NBA 50th and 75th Anniversary teams.[53]

Mayor Marion Barry hosted a rally for the Hoyas on April 7, 1984. He told the boisterous crowd, "The Hoyas are number one!" In call-and-response fashion the crowd refrained "The District is number one! The fans in the District of Columbia are number one!"[54] In a city so divided by racial distrust, "Hoya Paranoia" united areas and the twains met. President Reagan welcomed the team to the Rose Garden that same day, and on November 12 the world welcomed Thompson and Ewing's photo on the cover of *Sports Illustrated*.

Filmmaker Spike Lee was a regular whenever the Hoyas played at Madison Square Garden. Lee produced an episode featuring the 1995–96 Hoyas for the HBO series *Real Sports with Bryant Gumbel*. Lee's feelings reflected Black America's: "When they won, it was like Jackie [Robinson] or Joe Louis for us. The same type of feeling, this pride from within that went to such a different level than just basketball."[55] Indeed, in his film the character Mars Blackmon often wore a Georgetown shirt.

One man said of Thompson: "I don't think he owns Washington. But he's got a hell of a down payment."[56] Another commented that the coach "and his players were icons of black success and defiance during a period of racial regression." In "the 1980's, many African Americans suffered from deplorable inner-city conditions, exacerbated by a devasting crack cocaine epidemic."[57] Thompson was called a "miracle worker," but as *Sports Illustrated* noted some years after

Naismith Hall of Fame coach John Thompson with Naismith Hall of Fame player Patrick Ewing, Georgetown's greatest and one of the top 75 NBA players of all time , standing on the steps of Healy Hall at the Hoyas on-campus victory celebration. Courtesy Georgetown University Library.

the championship, "perhaps the only miracle is that, given their disparate backgrounds, Thompson and Georgetown found each other."[58]

One of Coach Thompson's most meaningful moments came when he combatted Proposition 42, an NCAA proposal that he said "set a minimum standard for athletes to compete as freshmen: a 2.0 high school GPA or 700 on the SAT. . . . Athletes who took the ACT needed a score of 15." He said it "made it harder for poor kids, most of them Black, to receive athletic scholarships."[59]

In his autobiography he explained that while many school districts, mainly white, "have more money, better facilities and more advanced classes" . . . "poor schools," mainly in Black areas, "don't even have proper equipment for science classes. Black kids are more likely to be poor."[60] He added that "in terms of basic fairness, we should provide the same educational opportunity to everyone. What Proposition 42 did was accept that inequality and compounded it. . . . The NCAA judged disadvantaged kids by the results of the privileged." Noting that the ruling would eliminate "over six hundred players, over 90 percent of them African American," he also declared that "none of my recruits would be affected, but that didn't change how I felt." Thompson made it clear that he was not for devaluing education, and that "he could live with" Proposition 48, an earlier ruling where players who may not have met NCAA "benchmarks" could still be the recipient of athletic scholarships but would have to sit out their freshman year until they got their grades up. Proposition 42 offered no such remedy.

In a painfully honest moment the coach said "I doubt if I got 700 on my SAT, but when I got to Providence I passed the same classes as everyone else," even when a "professor warned us athletes to get out." Citing his bachelor's degree in economics, a teaching certificate in social studies, and his master's degree in counseling and guidance, he said that "under Proposition 42 I might never even have attended college. There but for the grace of God, go I." "I've been accused of being a lot of things, but stupid is not one of them."[61] A descendant of enslaved Africans, he believed that "the root issue was that Black kids perform worse aca-

President Ronald Reagan with Patrick Ewing and John Thompson, posing for the cover of *Sports Illustrated* in the White House map room on November 12, 1984. Courtesy Ronald Reagan Presidential Library & Museum/White House. Wikimedia Commons.

demically due to the residual effect of slavery and segregation" and that "white people benefit from wealth that Blacks were prohibited from obtaining."[62]

When the NCAA passed Proposition 42 on January 11, 1989, Thompson set himself in motion. He called famed *New York Times* columnist William Rhoden. He met with Georgetown Athletic Direct Frank Reinzo and university president Father Healy, who "understood my principles and supported me publicly and privately." He met with John J. "Jack" DeGioia, who Thompson describes as the school's vice president and Healy's top assistant, who "had a comprehensive understanding of athletics, from both an educational and sociology perspective" and "did not characterize my point of view as militant, like a lot of other people did."[63] Some years later DeGioia, a former member of the Georgetown Football and Track Teams, became the first layperson to become president of the school, and in that capacity DeGioia served as the chair of the NCAA Board of Governors.

Thompson "boycotted" two games in protest of the NCAA's Proposition 42. His players wanted to join his protest but he insisted that they play. He did not want them to suffer for his decisions. On January 14, 1989, the Hoyas played Boston College at the old Capital Centre in Landover, Maryland. The coach traveled to the stadium with the team but after the warmups and the starters had been introduced, he passed his white towel (always worn draped over his shoulder, to honor his mother) to one of his assistant coaches, Mike Riley. The crowd gave him a standing ovation while chanting "Way to go, Way to go." Thompson left the arena without "any destination in mind," then "found myself driving through the neighborhoods I lived in as a child. Anacostia, W. Street, 19th Street and Benning Road. I looked at the Black faces on street corners and wondered, is this where athletes will end up if they don't qualify under Proposition 42?" When the Hoyas beat Boston College 86–60 that night, Thompson proudly noted, "The guys said they were playing for something bigger than themselves."[64] The next year the NCAA modified its rule according to many of Thompson's complaints and suggestions. Coaches like Temple's John Chaney, Thompson's close friend, supported his efforts. "He did that before anybody," said Syracuse coach Jim Boeheim, Georgetown's Big East rival. "Not just the Prop 42 stuff, that was one thing," Boeheim recounted, "just everyday things. And he was always outspoken and willing to put himself on the line. And he would do it today. You know, we need people like him today that are willing to do that and he set that example."[65]

Thompson came to know Raymond Medley, a man who had come upon hard times, whom the students called "Peebles." Medley had grown up with "Mr. Jabbo," who recalled their days playing sports in "Black Georgetown." He had gotten a job with the university Athletic Department years prior, and lived in rooms above the school's gym. Over time Medley became an alcoholic and at games students made fun of him, rubbed his head for "good luck," and gave him alcohol while posing for pictures. The coach at first felt "unsettled about Peebles," perhaps embarrassed, but "the more I thought about it the more I realized that he had to do what he did to survive." When Medley died in 1982 Thompson "named an award after him, the Raymond Medley Award for Citizenship. I made sure the name Peebles was nowhere to be found on that award."[66] The coach said that he came to be "ashamed at being angry at Peebles . . . his life wasn't easy. He did the best he could." Thompson kept a picture of Medley on his desk."[67] He restored the man's dignity, as he maintained his own. He knew "There but for the grace of God go I."[68] Medley's people had also come from Southern Maryland, just like Thompson's.

Patrick Ewing, named one of the fifty greatest NBA basketball players of all time in 1996 and a member of the NBA's 75th Anniversary Team of the seventy-five greatest players in 2021, served as the Hoyas' head basketball coach from 2017 to 2023. When Thompson died in 2020, the new coach said Thompson had "changed the world and helped shape the way we see it. He was a great coach but an even better person."[69] Tom Boswell, the *Washington Post* sport columnist and a Thompson friend for nearly fifty years, summed it up well: "Before anything else, he saw himself as, and truly was, a catalyst for change who used his national plat-

Saturday, January 14, 1989, during the Boston College–Georgetown University NCAA men's basketball game at the Capital Centre in Landover, Maryland. Coach John Thompson Jr. walks off the court in protest three days after Proposition 42, an NCAA academic eligibility rule, passed. Overturned one year later, Proposition 42 denied scholarships to student-athletes with lower than a 2.0 grade point average or a 700 SAT score. Courtesy Georgetown University Athletics.

form for social justice."[70] Thompson was inducted into the Naismith Basketball Hall of Fame in 1999 and the College Basketball Hall of Fame in 2016. He died on August 20, 2020.

## Dave "Duke" Bing

The second greatest player to come out of Washington after Elgin Baylor was Dave Bing, who also went on to be named one of the fifty greatest NBA players of all time. Sailing like a feather and with a jump shot "as smooth as silk," Bing, like Baylor, played high school ball for the Spingarn High School Green Wave. He was given the nickname "Duke" for his rec league reputation in Northeast DC at the Kelly Miller and Watts Branch playground and on YMCA courts. One of his early competitors was Marvin Gaye, who also ended up at the top his game in Detroit at Motown. By the time Bing was in high school, kids sometimes played

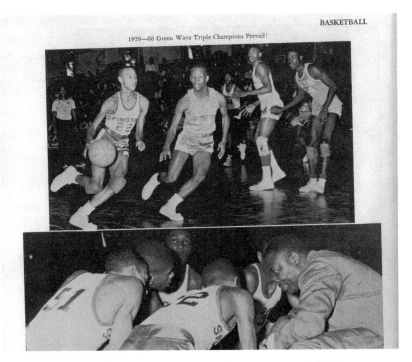

1959–60 Spingarn Green Wave yearbook captures Dave Bing (no. 22) dribbling past Eastern High. Courtesy District of Columbia Public School Records, Charles Sumner School Museum and Archives, Washington, DC.

interracial games, if not in the schools then on the playgrounds and rec centers—even at Chevy Chase in upper Northwest DC.

In the 1961 city title game, "Duke" Bing scored 21 points and led the Green Wave to a victory over the famed DeMatha team, coached by the legendary Morgan Wooten. Bing was named an All-Metro and *Parade* magazine All-American in 1962. He attended Syracuse University, where he became a First Team All-American and was selected second in the NBA draft in 1966. One of the most prolific shooters of his time, Bing missed much of one NBA season with a detached retina when he was poked in the eye accidentally in a preseason game. Many did not know that as a young child he had accidently injured an eye and most of his life he compensated for impaired vision.[71] With all his accolades, Bing once said that his southern-born "parents never wanted you to brag or toot your own horn."[72] After retirement from the game and induction into the Naismith Hall of Fame, he went on to work as a manufacturing magnate, leading the Bing

Dave Bing, while playing for the Detroit Pistons against the Washington Bullets in Baltimore, Maryland, ca. 1975. Bing played basketball at Spingarn High School, where he was named First Team All-Metro. He attended Syracuse University, where he was named an All-American. Drafted by the Detroit Pistons, in 1996 he was named one of the NBA's 50 Greatest Players and in 2021 he was named to the NBA's 75th Anniversary Team of 75 greatest players. A Naismith Hall of Fame Inductee (2006), Bing served as mayor of Detroit from 2009 to 2014. Wikimedia Commons.

Group and eventually elected mayor of Detroit, where his quiet temperament was not suited for big city urban politics.[73]

Bing was inducted into the Basketball Hall of Fame in 1990 and the College Basketball Hall of Fame in 2006. Like Rabbit Baylor, Duke Bing was named to the 50th NBA Anniversary Team in 1996.[74] Like Baylor, he was also named to the NBA 75th Anniversary Team in 2021.[75]

## Notes

1. Baylor with Eisenstock, *Hang Time*, 10. Baylor died on March 22, 2021. Columnist Colbert King, who saw him play as an eighth or ninth grader, wrote that Baylor got the nickname "Rabbit" because he seemed "to have eyes on both sides of his head, enabling him to see what was coming from either side" (*Washington Post*, March 23, 2021). Sportswriter Tom Boswell, who also grew up in the area, said the nickname was for "his leaping ability" (*Washington Post,* March 22, 2021).

2. Elgin Baylor, *Hang Time*, 2.

3. McNamara with Chamblee and Elfin, *The Capital of Basketball*, 33. McNamara was a sportswriter and award-winning journalist at the *Capital* newspaper in Annapolis, Maryland, for over thirty years. On June 28, 2018, he was gunned down in a mass killing at the paper.

4. Interview of Dorothy Boulding Ferebee, Black Women Oral History Project, Radcliffe College Schlesinger Library, Cambridge, Massachusetts, interviews 1976–1981, 44–50.

5. Valk, *Radical Sisters*, 29. For her dedication Ferebee was blacklisted by the HUAC.

6. Harrison Smith, "Elgin Baylor: All Star and Godfather of Hang Time," *Washington Post*, March 23, 2021, A1.

7. McNamara, *The Capital of Basketball*, 34.

8. He also served as head coach of the New Orleans Jazz and vice president of the Los Angeles Clippers.

9. NBA, "NBA at 50: Top 50 Players," nba.com, https://www.nba.com/history/nba-at -50/top-50-players.

10. Baylor, *Hang Time*, 2.

11. Baylor, 2.

12. Ben Goliver, "NBA Unveils 75th Anniversary All-Time Team," *Washington Post*, October 20, 2021.

13. Thompson with Washington, *I Came as a Shadow*, 43, 154.

14. Kevin B. Blackistone, "Among Black Basketball Royalty, Thompson Was Clearly the King," *Washington Post*, September 2, 2020, D1.

15. Thompson with Washington, *I Came as a Shadow*, 35.

16. Thompson with Washington, 8.

17. Shapiro, *Big Man on Campus*, 19. His star Georgetown recruit, Patrick Ewing, also endured these bigoted taunts.

18. Thompson with Washington, *I Came as a Shadow*, 25–26.

19. Liz Clarke, "Coach, Mentor, and Father Figure," *Washington Post*, September 1, 2020, 1.

20. McNamara, *The Capital of Basketball*, 52–55, 282.

21. McNamara, 52, 55.

22. Nnamdi interview of John Thompson, *The Kojo Nnamdi Show*, April 26, 2012.

23. My children, Lena and Miles, both played basketball at Jelleff's, which, to my opinion then and today, is the most interracial—multiracial—place in all of DC.

24. Shapiro, *Big Man on Campus*, 23.

25. Nnamdi interview.

26. Donald Huff, "Jelleff League: Heat's Still On," *Washington Post,* August 11, 1978.

27. Lena and Miles played in the Jelleff summer leagues in the mid- to late 1990s.

28. Red Auerbach drafted the first Black man, Chuck Cooper, to the NBA in 1950 and hired the first Black coach, Bill Russell, in 1966. Russell had led the team to eleven NBA championships in a thirteen-year career and was inducted into the NBA Hall of Fame. Auerbach was named to the Hall of Fame in 1969 and voted the greatest coach in NBA history. Auerbach attended and played basketball at GWU and coached at St. Albans and Roosevelt High.

29. Shapiro, *Big Man on Campus*, 23, 25, 27–28, 31, 47–49.

30. Teachout, *Pops*, 32.

31. Kojo Nnamdi interview of John Thompson Jr., WAMU, April 26, 2012. I thank Georgetown's Office of the President for providing the typed transcript. Nnamdi first asked Thompson about his childhood love of the Cleveland Indians (instead of the Washington Senators). Thompson explained that it was because "my dad would be in the bleachers yelling and screaming for Doby and arguing with the guy behind him. . . . You know, we used to walk to Griffith Stadium anytime the Cleveland Indians came in town because that was a team that had an African-American. In fact, the second African-American who came into baseball, several weeks after Jackie Robinson, was Larry Doby, number 14." See also Thompson with Washington, *I Came as a Shadow,* 72.

32. Thompson with Washington, *I Came as a Shadow,* 65.

33. Gilbert, "The Gospel According to John," 93.

34. Thompson with Washington, *I Came as a Shadow,* 52.

35. Thompson with Washington, 105.

36. Frank Ahrens, "John Thompson: Holding Court of Talk Radio," *Washington Post,* March 2, 1999.

37. Thompson with Washington, *I Came as a Shadow,* 154.

38. Gene Wang, "Patrick Ewing and John Thompson Were Georgetown Family Members for Life," *Washington Post,* September 4, 2020.

39. Gary Pomerantz, "Ewing Under Siege: Won't Continue to Ignore Use of Star, Says Thompson," *Washington Post,* February 9, 1983, D1.

40. Thompson with Washington, *I Came as a Shadow,* 113, 116, 117.

41. Thompson with Washington, 113, 116, 117, 113.

42. Thompson with Washington, 153.

43. Clarke, "Coach, Mentor and Father Figure."

44. Clarke, "Coach, Mentor and Father Figure."

45. Thompson recruited players from the communities he knew: Bill Marin and Gene Smith from McKinley Tech; Anthony Jones from Dunbar; Michael Graham from Spingarn; Michael Jackson from South Lakes in Reston; Reggie Williams and David Wingate from Dunbar in Baltimore; Ralph Dalton from Suitland; Ed Springs from Prince George's County (who he discovered while the young man was delivering mail—just like Buck Hill); Jon Smith and Merlin Wilson from St. Anthony; Mike Riley from Cardozo (who came to the Hilltop after a stint in the US Navy); Craig "Big Sky" Shelton from Dunbar; Lonnie Durren from Dunbar and Augusta Military School; John Durren from Dunbar; Eric Smith from Potomac; Terry Fenlon from McNamara; Tom Scates from St. Anthony; Mike Hancock from Roosevelt in Alexandria; and Jeff Bullis from Forest Hills in Alexandria.

46. Jane Leavy, "John Thompson's Winning Secret: Harsh Now, Hugs Later," *Washington Post,* November 17, 1982, F1.

47. Thompson with Washington, *I Came as a Shadow,* 168–69.

48. John Feinstein, "Thompson and I Argued Plenty of Times, But Very Few People Ever Taught Me More," *Washington Post,* September 1, 2020, D1.

49. John Feinstein, "Georgetown's Pressure Cooks," *Washington Post,* April 3, 1984, D1; Ken Denlinger, "Thompson Wants to Divvy Up the Pride," *Washington Post*, April 3, 1984, D1.

50. Thompson with Washington, *I Came as a Shadow,* 159, 179.

51. Denlinger, "Thompson Wants to Divvy Up."

52. Tupper, "Georgetown Basketball in Reagan's America," 279.

53. NBA, "NBA at 50"; Goliver, "NBA Unveils."

54. Eve Zibart and Mark Asher, "Hoyas Honored by City, White House," *Washington Post,* April 8, 1984, A1.

55. Mike Wise, "'Big John,' the Leader of Black America's Basketball Team," *Washington Post,* September 2, 2020. Lee appeared later on Thompson's radio program.

56. Jane Leavy, "Team Without Dissidents Is Team Without Dissension." *Washington Post,* November 16, 1982, F1.

57. Tupper, "Georgetown Basketball in Reagan's America," 268–69.

58. Gilbert, "The Gospel According to John."

59. Thompson with Washington, *I Came as a Shadow,* 166, 221.

60. Thompson with Washington, 234.

61. Thompson with Washington, 222–23.

62. Thompson with Washington, 227.

63. Thompson with Washington, 224.

64. Thompson with Washington, 225.

65. Stephen Borelli, "Georgetown's John Thompson: Coach Was a Civil Rights Giant to Team, Nation, World," *USA Today,* February 9, 2021.

66. Thompson with Washington, *I Came as a Shadow,* 96, 97.

67. Matthew Quallen, "The Life of Peebles," *The Hoya,* September 25, 2015.

68. Thompson with Washington, *I Came as a Shadow,* 215. This quote is a paraphrase of 1 Corinthians 15:9–10.

69. Richard Goldstein, *New York Times,* September 1, 2020, B10.

70. Thomas Boswell, "He Bent the World and Made It Better," *Washington Post,* September1, 2020, D1.

71. Bing went on to play college basketball at Syracuse University.

72. McNamara, *The Capital of Basketball,* 69.

73. Boyd, *Black Detroit,* 274–75, 319.

74. NBA, "NBA at 50."

75. Goliver, "NBA Unveils."

# 11

# SOCCER

### The "Beautiful Game" and the Howard Bisons

The fall 1971 issue of *Ebony Magazine* ran a feature story headlined "Bisons Kick Their Way to Top," complete with eight team pictures. The magazine told the story of the Howard University Soccer Team. The article began in recounting the hiring of Lincoln Phillips as part-time coach in 1969. Phillips was a twenty-nine-year-old goalkeeper from Trinidad and Tobago who had played on the Trinidadian National Soccer and Basketball Teams, including the team that played at the 1967 Pan American games in Winnipeg, Canada. At the time, cricket was perhaps more popular among Caribbean youth than soccer.[1] Before coming to Howard, Phillips had been player-coach of the Washington Darts of the American Soccer League, the first Black athlete to lead any professional soccer team in the United States. That year the Darts won the title. In the summertime Phillips was also the goalkeeper coach of the Baltimore Bays, a youth soccer team, at a time when most college and high school coaches needed other jobs to make ends meet.[2] While coaching at Howard, he also coached the Bowie State College Soccer Team. He had also been the goalkeepers coach of the US National Team.

Phillips was hired by James "Ted" Chambers, the founder of the Howard University Soccer Team in 1944. At that time no local white school would schedule a match against Howard, so the team played against teams out of foreign embassies based in the city. Chambers led the team to the third annual National Association of Intercollegiate Athletics (NAIA) Championship game in 1961.

By the time Phillips arrived at the school, Howard had not advanced to NCAA tournament play since 1963, when it suffered a first round 5–1 loss to the US Naval Academy. Phillips described the atmosphere at Howard in the late 1960s as a time when "civil rights leaders electrified the campus" and "Stokely Carmichael (Kwame Touré) easily pulled 3,000 to a talk at the gym."[3] It was a place where "Angela Davis, imprisoned on racist charges for murder and kidnapping, was named Homecoming Queen even as she languished in prison" and

Howard University Championship Soccer Team in 1971. Courtesy Trinidad and Tobago
Football Association.

where "women grew proud Naturals" like Davis. Howard students also gave her
the title of "Queenmother," which in some West African and Caribbean traditions signifies the highest honor. He adds: "Soon after she was acquitted Davis
made her way to campus to speak."

In 1970, after the team qualified for the NCAA Final Four, Phillips was hired
as its full-time coach. As part of his contract Phillips received full tuition benefits
toward completion of his undergraduate degree. Education was important to the
coach and he instilled in his players the need to do well in school. Often he and
his players were taking the same classes, where they were equals, but that fact
did not diminish his authority on the pitch. "It was a difficult time," Phillips said,
"because I was in a few classes with some of my players. It was a very humbling
experience, as all of them were A students while I was struggling sometimes with
C grades. As a result of such a unique experience, a very serious and lasting bond
developed between me and those players that continues today." He adds: "Our
graduation rate was among the highest in the nation."[4]

In his *How Soccer Explains the World: An Unlikely Theory of Globalization*,
Franklin Foer argues that one can use soccer "as a way of thinking about how people . . . identify themselves in this new era" of globalization.[5] The Howard University Soccer Teams of the early 1970s helped give Howard and the Washington,
DC, Black community this "way of thinking," as Pan-African concepts were

growing. The team came into its own soon after the 1968 riots, a time when the African American population was over 70 percent of the district's residents.[6]

When Phillips arrived at the Howard Hilltop, the University of Maryland was considered the best local team. Phillips said that "when I arrived at Howard, most of the top local universities avoided us. They just did not want to play a bunch of n——s and, due to the NCAA rules, they didn't have to." He adds: "the University of Maryland did its best to stay away from having to play on a substandard pitch, in the ghetto."[7] One line in an *Ebony* article read that "the possibility that Howard would become a national soccer threat seemed as far removed as the Redskins making it to the Super Bowl"[8]—something the Washington football team did three times in the 1980s and early 1990s. But soccer won a championship before football.

In 1970 the Howard team started the season 9-0. When they played the Naval Academy that season, Navy's coach told the *Washington Post*, "I hope the weather falls below 25 degrees so it can freeze the *you-know-whats off* those Jamaicans and Africans."[9] The Bisons qualified for the NCAA Final Four that same year but lost their semifinal game to UCLA, which then lost to St. Louis University in the championship game. At the time St. Louis University was the most dominate team in NCAA soccer history. St. Louis had won eight of the previous twelve Division I championships. St. Louis's all-white team was based in a city having a long history with soccer. The city of St. Louis had at least twenty-five thousand young people engaged in soccer, from kindergarten to high school. Washington had no such pipeline but Phillips was soon to change that.

By 1971 Phillips, using his soccer pedigree, connections, and Howard's reputation, molded the team into a disciplined, free-spirited, and offensively aggressive team. The 1971 team featured a squad of international students, a real united nation of young people. Of the eleven starters, seven hailed from Trinidad, two from Bermuda, and others from Guinea, Ghana, Nigeria, Eritrea, Ethiopia, and Jamaica. That year the school had enrolled students from seventy-two nations. Of a student body of 10,152, 1,700 were foreign students, and soccer brought them together and helped forge a unified cultural identity. Soccer is "a language, probably the most universal language on the planet. It is spoken more widely than English, Arabic or Chinese and practiced more widely than any religion," writes historian Laurent Dubois. At Howard, soccer became a language among students from the disparate Third World.[10]

Howard made it through an undefeated season going into the 1971 championship game at the Orange Bowl in Miami, ready to play the equally imposing reigning national champions from St. Louis University, which had won twenty-four straight matches. St. Louis employed the European paced game, and Howard was barely hanging in, with the game tied 2–2 at halftime. Howard's star player, Keith Aqui, who had scored twenty-five goals during the season, was sick with a high fever on the sidelines when he should have been home in bed. Phillips said that during the halftime break, "Aqui came to me, with tears in his eyes, and said he wanted to play. I knew he should not have played, but I just couldn't tell him no."[11] The coach said that when "the horn blew for the substitution, the band struck up a samba that the bandmaster had included especially" for the team, and when "Keith ran on he looked ten feet tall."[12] Once Aqui got on the field, Howard went on the attack, using pacing, skill, and aggression. Phillips said "they put two and three men to guard Aqui, which left two of our men free."[13] Alvin Henderson scored a goal and Howard won 3–2, becoming the first HBCU to win the NCAA National Championship and the only team to ever win both NCAA and NAIA titles in any sport.

Instead of returning home right away, the team, tired but enthusiastic, accepted an invitation to travel to Jamaica to play that nation's top teams. The entire team and the coach wore green and black African-styled dashikis and were greeted by future prime minister Michael Manley, who wore a Jamaican-style Kariba, adapted from the Kaunda suit made popular by Zambian president Kenneth Kaunda.

In the January 1972 edition of the student paper the *Hilltop*, its first-ever woman editor, Lena Williams, wrote a column headlined "NCAA Champions Return Home." She describes the atmosphere as the team came off the airplane at National Airport, looking surprised but weary, after their four-game playing tour of Jamaica. The NCAA Champions admitted that the ceremonies were more than they had excepted." The team bus then was escorted through the city by a police motorcade, as horns honked along the way. Howard's victory helped create social cohesion and bonding in the city not long after the 1968 riots. At Cramton Auditorium the team was met by Mayor-Commissioner Walter E. Washington, himself a Howard graduate. DC's leading deejay, Bob "Nighthawk" Terry from WHUR-FM, Howard's new radio station, emceed the program, which was joined by five hundred students inside and outside Cramton. Washington said that "It's not too often we get a winner here in the District, so that when we do, you have to be willing to share it a little . . . you know what I mean."[14] Howard's president, James Cheek, called it a victory for Black people everywhere.

The same *Hilltop* issue ran a feature entitled "Campus Speak Out," with nine students answering the question, "What do you think was the most significant event in 1971 to affect Black People?" Two of the students listed the murder of George Jackson and one listed "Attica." Two others named the national wage freeze, and one the campaign for president by New York congresswoman Shirley

Chisholm, the first Black woman to seek the office from a major party.[15] (In 1968 Charlene Michell, who ran on the Communist Party USA ticket, had been the first Black woman to run for the presidency.)[16]

A telegram from President Richard M. Nixon was also read at the celebratory event. The team was invited to the White House, "but the players declined, determined not to be used for Richard Nixon's political purposes during an election year."[17] Years later Mori Diane, one of the most outspoken members of the team, told the *Washington Post*: "I regret it now—we should have gone. But at the time, with Vietnam and everything else, we felt we had to make a statement."[18] Coach Phillips was "dying to go," he said. But the team chose not to, seeing the protest as "an opportunity to stand up against injustice."[19] The student body approved the team's decision.

Not long after HU won the championship, rumors began to spread that the NCAA was investigating the team for having too many "foreign" players, some of whom had played professional soccer. Rumors also spread that several players had grade point averages below the 1.6 required by the NCAA. Longtime Howard athletic director Leo Miles soon replied that the "lowest average" of any player was 2.35, and that "most of the members of the team have at least a 3.0 average." He added that "there was little evidence to prove that any of Howard's players had ever played professional soccer" and that "three of the leading players will finish their four-year requirements in three years and at least 90 percent of all past team members have gone to grad school."[20] Many of the players had part-time jobs.

Then, on January 26, 1972, three weeks after their Orange Bowl victory, someone sent the NCAA an "anonymous" message, questioning the team's victory and calling for an inquiry. Many suspected the Navy coach had sent the accusation, which questioned the players' eligibility, age, nationality, and intelligence. St. Louis coach Harry Krogh insisted that he did not send the letter, saying, "I don't know what happened. You have to trust me. I am a soccer coach. I am coming to beat you."[21] Phillips believed him. (Krough—while working at the Post Office—had been a defender on the 1950 US World Cup Team that beat England, a game considered one of the greatest upsets in sports history.)

Even with this cloud hanging over them, the 1972 Howard team, with new players from Jamaica, went on a thirty-game winning streak through the season and reached the championship title match against St. Louis that December. This time Howard lost 2–1 in overtime. At the NCAA-sponsored banquet following the loss, twenty-four Howard team members and Phillips and his staff were all dressed in colorful dashikis. Heads turned. Phillips opposed the idea: "I was a suit and tie man! My guys were revolutionaries. But after we'd debated it, I had approved. I felt proud of my African garb."[22]

Phillips spoke to the roomful of players, coaches, soccer officials, university administrators, and the media. After congratulating their opponent, he said, "We played against the entire wretched system of this society. I would say the NCAA is guilty of practicing racism. . . . Today, I just want to tell you *that* St. Louis did not beat Howard. They beat the remnants of Howard. Anytime a group of people get together to deprive another group of their rights, that is racism."[23] All four of the final teams stood and enthusiastically applauded the Howard coach. Phillips also said: "It's pretty evident that a Black school isn't supposed to win. Once we start winning, it's considered unfair, we're cheating somehow and things have to be righted."[24] Phillips continued: "There was a real sense of purpose and having something to prove was the tip of the proverbial arrow that drove not only the team but the entire Howard University community. There was a sense we were cheated out of a championship, and our situation fit in the social milieu at the time with the rise of black consciousness and the community's pride in producing a team that was considered among the best. We wanted to be the best at a sport largely identified and dominated by Europeans."[25]

The NCAA Committee on Infractions had already opened an investigation of the Howard team. Investigators had gone to campus to investigate Keith Aqui. He was twenty-five years old but had a 3.4 grade point average. He had never played professional soccer in Trinidad, never even had any cleats paid for, but the NCAA ruled that a foreign student would lose a year of NCAA eligibility for every year played in any organized sport back home. The NCAA ruled that Aqui's eligibility expired in 1970, a year before he led the championship team, and also alleged that Aqui and Rick Yallery-Arthur had played too many years of soccer back home before the age of nineteen, and also that Guinean forward Mori Diane had not taken either the ACT or the SAT entrance exams.

On January 9, 1973, a month or so after the banquet, the committee reported in its year-long investigation that Howard had violated three rules concerning player eligibility. The committee claimed that some freshmen had not achieved high enough scores on their entrance exams, although the reality was that all the freshman had passed higher entrance requirements based on their more rigorous British Commonwealth and French equivalents. The *Atlantic* later reported that "the violations that Howard was punished for were relatively minor, and Phillips hadn't made any real attempt to break or exploit the rules for Howard's favor. Some students were exempted from entrance exams to the university after having completed equivalent work abroad. Others had played in leagues that could at best be described as semi-professional in their home country. All of Howard's players, though, were studious. The team had a higher GPA than any of the school's other teams with some crediting Phillips, who at the time was still a student himself, with keeping his students on the straight and narrow."[26] Phillips had in fact instilled in the players the importance of an education that would last long past their playing careers.

The punishment was harsh. The team was stripped of its third-place finish in 1970 and championship title in1971. The NCAA also removed five players from the Howard team. It placed the team on probation for the 1973 season, including being banned from postseason play. The NCAA committee also heard a motion to limit the number of foreigners on a soccer team, despite the fact that Maryland had co-won (with Michigan State) the NCAA soccer championship in 1968 using all foreign players, as did San Francisco in 1975, 1976, and 1978, and Michigan State in 1967. "They were all *white* foreigners. They just want to pass rules to limit us," Phillips said.[27] The University of Maryland, the University of San Francisco, Michigan State, and Howard all had one thing in common: they showed the increasing globalization of the game and of the world even on "segregated" teams.

The normally reserved Howard president Cheek, himself a staunch member of the Republican Party, said in an official university statement: "It's pretty evident that a black school is not supposed to win." Phillips said the NCAA was "guilty of practicing racism." Cheek said that he intended to challenge the ruling, commenting that "we feel that it is simply because we are a black institution that the NCAA was requested to investigate the eligibility of our outstanding players."[28]

The team and the public reacted. Mori Diane said that "in my opinion, the Howard University team . . . stood knee-deep in the civil rights struggle. We played our little part, even unbeknown at the time. Our struggles were pebbles in the sandstorm that brought acceptance of blacks as equals."[29] Phillips said: "Each player on the team had to decide what the struggle meant to him. And the team acted as one."[30] Rock Newman, a member of the Howard Baseball Team who later became a prominent sports promoter, said. "These [NCAA] rules are so crazily written . . . I never accepted it—that's bull. . . . You win the fight in the ring, you're the winner."[31]

Howard appealed the NCAA decision. The NCAA denied the appeal but ruled that the "violations" were unintentional. When the NCAA offered the championship trophy to St. Louis, its legendary coach, Harry Keough, displayed soccer diplomacy: he refused to accept it.

Ian Bain, a member of 1971 team and captain of the 1973 and 1974 teams, who later was hired as soccer coach and Spanish teacher at Springbrook High School in suburban Maryland, declared after the 1973 season, "There will be no more losses like this next year."[32] Phillips and Howard kept at it and further globalized the school's team, adding goalkeeper Amde-Michael Debre-Selassie from

Eritrea, Sonny Izevbigie a Nigerian at midfield, and other players from Nigeria, Senegal, and Ghana.[33]

Before the 1974 season, Phillips felt it was "the moment" and invited his "close friend and one of our professors, Dom Basil Matthews, to address the team, when everything fell into place for the staff and players."[34] Matthews, a priest and devoted soccer fan, had been a principal at a secondary school in Trinidad before becoming a professor at the School of Social Work at Howard in the 1970s. Matthews said that little Howard University "sat at the centre of the Triangle of Blackness," which he described as "stretching from Africa to the Caribbean to North America." Phillips quoted Matthews as saying that "we are at the epicenter of a global civil rights struggle. It is our job to instill pride. We are ambassadors of our race. . . . On this field—African and Caribbean peoples, surrounded by their American brothers; the Triangle of Blackness condensed into a university stadium."[35] Reversing the image of the triangular slave trade, Matthews told the team "all of us whether we're from Africa, the Caribbean, North America, we were all taken away and had pieces of our culture stripped from us. The only line that was missing was a direct line back to Africa, that's where Howard is, in the middle of that triangle, brings us all together. You have an opportunity to go out and connect us all with your excellence on the field. Howard University is the custodial of that triangle of blackness."[36] When Mathews finished his talk the locker room fell silent. Phillips said: "It was some fairly heady stuff that blew everybody away."[37] Bain said, "That was the first time that all of us as a group related to the idea of race in the environment we were now living in. But it was beyond race. It was like [Nelson] Mandela speaking. . . . Matthews wanted the season to be not so much a blow against white America or the NCAA but to bring pride to all of the different African groups, so that people all over the black world would notice our team."[38]

Matthews's words fired up the souls and bodies of the players, and Phillips said that "we knew now that by winning a championship we would strike a blow against injustice."[39] French existentialist philosopher and football adherent Jean-Paul Sartre wrote, "In a football match everything is complicated by the presence of the opposite team."[40] Phillips's teams used that complication both in soccer and in 1970s life in the United States.

During the 1974 season, games at Greene Stadium were filled to capacity and resounded with the rhythms of African drums and reggae beats. Phillips said that Africans and West Indians have "cultural similarities . . . both have rhythm and love to dance; they also enjoy some of the same food, albeit prepared in different ways." In a reference to African religious practices, he said that some from the Caribbean "were skeptical of African mystical practices," just as goalkeeper Selassie, an Eritrean, was skeptical of Jamaicans who had adopted Rastafarian practices.[41]

Brazilian legend Pele came to Washington five months after the Howard team was stripped of its title, for a series of friendlies (exhibition games). Pele was known to the world after his Brazilian team's 1970 World Cup victory in Mexico and his country's three subsequent titles. Pele had even played against Phillips when his Santos Club team played against Phillips's Bays in a 1973 exhibition match in Washington.

Phillips invited Pele to Howard, using his many connections, including as the spokesperson for soccer at the DC Department of Parks and Recreation. He believed that "the problem we had in soccer at the time was that not many blacks were really involved in the game. And so at Howard we did a lot of work in the inner-city, we did a lot of promotions. . . . I thought it would be a good idea for him to bless Howard with his presence." The team took pictures with the star, who had on a white T-shirt and sweatpants, and delighted in his stories. Alvin Henderson said that "Pele was so adored by us and is still adored by many. He was not only a great athlete and a great person but he was a Black man at a time when it was so difficult to be the greatest of anything. Look at Muhammad Ali and the difficulties he had. To be a Black man and be the greatest in your sport was exceptional at a time when elsewhere people were fighting for human rights."[42]

Pele met the team, who had gathered on the pitch. Team captain Bain said that "he was just a kind and generous spirit. He told us we must always play the game passionately . . . he had heard that we were a good team and that we'd had success and he just told us to keep playing the game with passion. If you love something, do it with passion."[43]

Although the team had refused to visit Nixon's White House, Pele did go there in 1973. Nixon, still angry that the 1971 team had refused his invitation, told Pele, "Howard has our nation's finest soccer team but they had a little problem with eligibility."[44] Within a year Nixon was out of the White House, accused in the Watergate conspiracy with high crimes and misdemeanors against his country. Pele joined the New York Cosmos of the North American Soccer League in 1975, where he ended his career.

The Bisons reinvigorated the Howard Hilltop with an undefeated 1974 season, marked by a blistering 19-0 record with 63 goals scored and just 6 goals allowed. The team continued to deal with racism. Keith Tulloch, a midfielder on that squad, recollected, "When I came here, it was the first time someone had ever called me n——. The first time a player had ever spat on my face."[45] Phillips said that during road games, "They'd say, 'Go back, banana boat. Go back, monkey. Go back to the jungle.' I had to tell my players that anytime that it is done, it's fine to get angry, but you have to know how to get angry. Put the balls in the back of the net."[46] But the coach drew the line when a white player called his men "n——." He did not hold them back.

The team adopted the motto "Truth, crushed to earth shall rise again," paraphrasing the words of Martin Luther King Jr., who often quoted the nineteenth-century poets William Cullen Bryant and James Russell Lowell.[47] At the NCAA tournament that year, Howard beat George Washington, Philadelphia Textile, and Hartwick, setting up a match against St. Louis, the two-time defending champion that had won nine of the previous fifteen NCAA Division I men's soccer titles. St. Louis played "Barcelona-style soccer—very possessive with lots of close passing" that "probed constantly until they found a gap to exploit," Phillips recalled. But, he said, "we were deadly on the counter-attack—pass, pass, off to the races."[48] In the midst of the game a large sign appeared. It was unclear as to whether it was on the electronic scoreboard or carried by a St. Louis fan. Whatever the case, he recalls that it said "'The monkeys are here' or 'See the monkeys dance' or something about gorillas playing soccer. No one seems to remember clearly. Maybe we just had more important things to do that day than fret about bigotry."[49]

The game went to a fourth overtime when Kenneth Ilodigwe "banged in a beautiful cross from Richard Davy for a pulsating end to a perfect season: a Jamaican to a Nigerian, a multiethnic connection that encapsulated what Phillips had created."[50] Howard scored first in the last overtime and won the game, defeating the Billikens 2–1 at Busch Stadium in St. Louis. Phillips wrote that "for the second time we'd become the first African American college to win a NCAA championship." Adapting the team motto, he said, "Truth, I tell you. Truth. Nothing but the truth."[51] Perhaps he and the team preferred to defeat bigotry more than fret about it.

Filmmaker Spike Lee, himself a product of HBCU Morehouse College, produced the film *Redemption Song,* directed by Kenan K. Holley. The film chronicled the team's 1971 championship year, showing how the Bison kept their determination to win back the trophy they felt was unfairly taken. The tittle was taken from Bob Marley and the Wailers' "Redemption Song" album *Uprising,* Marley's twelfth and final studio album before his death in 1981. It was one of Marley's few solo recordings, singing and playing the acoustic guitar. Some of the words were taken from a Marcus Garvey 1937 speech titled "The Work Has Been Done," which includes these words:

> We are going to emancipate ourselves from mental slavery because whilst others might free the body, none but ourselves can free the mind. Mind is your only

ruler, sovereign. The man who is not able to develop and use his mind is bound to be the slave of the other man who uses his mind.[52]

The documentary was part of Lee's "Lil' Joints" four-part series on sports that premiered in the United States on ESPN. A crowd flocked to Howard's Cramton Auditorium in June 2016 to watch the world premiere of *Redemption Song*. Keith "Barnaby" Tulloch, one of the seven Jamaicans on Howard's roster that year, was featured in the film and said that playing for Howard was more difficult than playing on teams in Jamaica because of the racism, where some games were refereed "one-sided" and the "N-word" was directed at the players. The other Jamaicans featured in the film were Richard Davey, Michael Davey, Vertram Beckett, Mario "Zero" McLennan, Lincoln Peddie, and Paul "Pep-Up" Pringle. Howard athletic director Kery Davis said *Redemption Song* showed that "the soccer team at that time galvanized the university. It was a source of pride; everyone came out. The seats were filled."[53] In a promotion for the film, Rock Newman said, "This wasn't just about a soccer championship. This was black excellence." Ian Bain said that "every time we took the soccer field we had to represent a group of people in a country who needed a voice . . . we grew because of the struggle." Tulloch said that "in Trinidad we had [social] divisions, but they were based more on class than on race."[54] Newman paid tribute to the social impact the team had on the campus and in the Washington community. Newman noted that Howard students could be cliquish and clannish, with those from Senegal or Ghana or Nigeria or the United States just "hanging" with their countrymen only.[55] But the Howard soccer team transcended nation, class, and caste and brought the campus and much of the Black community together. Most Howard professors even allowed students to miss class for 2:00 p.m. games. Green Stadium became an entertainment center and a place where students watched the game as a combination of sport, entertainment, and a temporary escape from life's challenges. In 2023 one of the members of the 1971 team, Mark W. Wright, produced a three-part podcast titled "The Bison Project" in coordination with Meadowlark Media's "Sports Explains the World," to document the achievements of the 1971 team. In addition to team members and Coach Phillips, the podcast featured Lena Williams, the *Hilltop* editor and later a *New York Times* reporter.[56]

Both the *Washington Post* and the *Baltimore Sun* reported that entertainer Common, along with former US National Team players Jozy Altidore, DeMarcus Beasley, Mo Edu, Oguchi Onyewu, and Charlie Davis, were producing a film entitled *Rising Above*, about Howard University soccer teams and based on Phillips's book.[57] Phillips said, "So, I believe Howard had a role in the impact of black footballers on the game in this country" among Black, white, and Latino boys and girls, young women and young men.[58]

Phillips said, "We weren't just playing soccer. We were representing the game, our school and blackness. We felt black people needed to tell themselves they could succeed just like anybody else. So we had to be good."[59] Historian Laurent Dubois writes that soccer is a "dialectic, never-ending struggle between two teams."[60] He adds that "soccer is most of all human" and "probably the most widely shared form of culture on the planet." It teaches us "about being human."[61] The Howard University soccer team certainly did that in Washington, DC.

## Notes

1. James, *Beyond a Boundary*; Manley, *History of West Indian Cricket*.

2. Phillips, *Rising Above and Beyond*.

3. Phillips, 33.

4. Tom Dunmore, "Q. and A. with Lincoln Phillips," *New York Times*, January 4, 2013.

5. Foer, *How Soccer Explains the World*, 5.

6. In 1971 the Black population was 71.1 percent. Lawrence Feinberg, "D.C. Population Rate of Whites, Blacks Is Stable," *Washington Post*, February 28, 1981.

7. Phillips, *Rising Above and Beyond*, 69.

8. "Bisons Kick Their Way to Top," 42.

9. Phillips, *Rising Above and Beyond*, 70.

10. Dubois, *The Language of the Game*, 5.

11. "Bisons Kick Their Way to Top," 43.

12. Phillips, *Rising Above and Beyond*, 74.

13. "Bisons Kick Their Way to Top," 43.

14. Lena Williams, "NCAA Champions Return Home," *The Hilltop*, January 28, 1972.

15. "Campus Speak Out," *The Hilltop*, January 28, 1972.

16. Clay Risen, "Charlene Michell, 92 Dies; First Black Woman to Run for President," *New York Times*, December, 23, 2022.

17. Mike Wise, "Howard University, 1974 NCAA Soccer Champions, Brought World Together," *Washington Post*, July 12, 2014.

18. Wise, "Howard University."

19. Phillips, *Rising Above and Beyond*, 77.

20. "Bisons Kick Their Way to Top," 52.

21. Phillips, *Rising Above and Beyond*, 99.

22. Phillips, 72.

23. Phillips, 82; "Howard's History-Making Men's Soccer Champions Needed to Be Twice as Good," *Guardian* (sportsblog), December 6, 2016.

24. Scott Allen, "Bisons 1971 Soccer Team Tells Its Story," *Washington Post*, November 23, 2023.

25. Dunmore, "Q. and A. with Lincoln Phillips."

26. Maurer, "When Pele Visited Howard."

27. "Bisons Kick Their Way to Top," 52. The NCAA stripped the University of San Francisco of the 1978 National Championship for what it said was using ineligible foreign players.

28. *Sports Illustrated,* Vault online archive, January 24, 1997. Cheek demurred student activism and once threatened to expel students who protested against the polices of Ronald Reagan and a visit by Vice Present George Bush. He resigned in 1989 after a student protest against the appointment of Lee Atwater to the Howard board of trustees.

29. "Howard's History-Making," *Guardian* (sportsblog).

30. Phillips, *Rising Above and Beyond*, 34.

31. Phillips, 83.

32. Grant Wahl, "Men on a Mission: The 1973 Howard University Soccer Team Wanted to Win More Than an NCAA Title," *Sports Illustrated,* February 24, 1997.

33. See https://eri-internationalsports.blogspot.com/2008/06/eritreans-and-college-soccer-untold.html.

34. Dunmore, "Q. and A. with Lincoln Phillips."

35. Phillips, *Rising Above and Beyond*, 72.

36. Wise, "Howard University."

37. Dunmore, "Q. and A. with Lincoln Phillips."

38. Wahl, "Men on a Mission."

39. Phillips, *Rising Above and Beyond*, 72.

40. Sartre, *Critique of Dialectical Reason*, 473.

41. Phillips, *Rising Above and Beyond*, 89.

42. Maurer, "When Pele Visited Howard."

43. Maurer, "When Pele Visited Howard."

44. Maurer, "When Pele Visited Howard."

45. Wahl, "Men on a Mission."

46. Wahl, "Men on a Mission.".

47. Phillips, *Rising Above and Beyond*, 98.

48. Phillips, 102.

49. Phillips, 103.

50. Wise, "Howard University."

51. Phillips, *Rising Above and Beyond*, 103.

52. Hill and Bair, *The Marcus Garvey Papers*, 791.

53. Stephanie Cornish, *Afro News,* May 4, 2016.

54. Wahl, "Men on a Mission."

55. Wise, "Howard University."

56. Allen, "Bison's 1971 Soccer Team." The film was done in conjunction with ESPN.

57. Angelique Jackson, "Common and Steel Springs Productions to Produce 'Rising Above' about Howard University's 1971 Soccer Team and Coach Lincoln 'Tiger' Phillips," *Variety,* July 9, 2021; Allana Haynes, "The Story of Columbia Resident and Legendary

Soccer Coach Lincoln Phillips Will Head to the Big Screen," *Baltimore Sun*, September 1, 2021.

   58. Dunmore, "Q. and A. with Lincoln Phillips."

   59. Wahl, "Men on a Mission."

   60. Dubois, *The Language of the Game,* 5.

   61. Dubois, 22.

# 12

# MOMENTS OF LORE

## You Could Either Play or You Couldn't

### New York's Power Memorial vs. Hyattsville's DeMatha Catholic High School

One of the city's biggest days of racial solidarity, if that is the correct term, is comparable to the one that drew crowds who had gathered when the Washington football team won the Super Bowl in 1983, 1988, and 1992, came on January 30, 1965. It was a basketball game between the 1964 national high school basketball champion, Power Memorial of New York, led by Lew Alcindor (now Kareem Abdul Jabbar), and the 1963 national champion, DeMatha Catholic High School of Hyattsville, Maryland. Demand for tickets exceeded the pregame hype and the game was subsequently moved from the DeMatha gym to the University of Maryland's Cole Field House. The game was the gym's first sellout crowd, even though it had hosted Atlantic Coast Conference (ACC) championship games since the mid-1950s.[1] Jabbar scored 35 points and grabbed 17 rebounds, and his team won 65–62, boasting a forty-eight-game winning streak and tying the New York City record for consecutive wins at that time.

The rematch on January 30, 1965, broadcast on WOL AM-Radio, was also played at Cole Field House, and dominated talk among the Washington area's devout sports fans. Power Memorial came into the field house having won its previous seventy-one games. Anticipation reigned as both teams were integrated—as was the standing room only crowd of 12,500. The rematch came in what Naismith Memorial Basketball Hall of Fame coach Morgan Wooten, one of the few high school coaches to be so inducted, called "the greatest high school basketball game ever." The *Washington Daily News* hyped the game as the "Nation's Best Clash Tonight."[2] The DC team came into the gym having won twenty-three games straight. Helping to double-team Alcindor, the 7-foot-2 center, was Sid Catlett, the youngest player on the floor, a 6-foot-8 sophomore who was later called by sportscaster (and teammate) James Brown, "physically what LeBron is today."[3] DeMatha won the game 46–43.[4]

Wooten also spoke of the character of the Power Memorial team, which came to the DeMatha locker room following its victory in the first game to congratulate their opponent. DeMatha wanted to return the favor when they won the next year, but the New York team beat them to the locker room, bringing congratulations to DeMatha on its victory. Such was the power of basketball to build the character of young people and bring the cities together. Wooten was ultimately named Outstanding Male Prep Coach of the 20th Century. He was introduced by James Brown and was presented the honor by Red Auerbach.

Wooten's Hall of Fame page notes that he won more than twelve hundred games with at least twenty wins every season for more than forty consecutive seasons. His teams were ranked number one in the Washington Metro area more than twenty times; they won thirty conference titles and national championships in 1962, 1965, 1968, 1978, and 1984. Wooten always put academics first, and more than 150 of his players went on to play at the collegiate level while over twenty went on to coach at the prep, collegiate, and professional levels. One of his greatest players, Adrian Dantley, was inducted into the Naismith Hall of Fame in 2008.[5]

In the late 1960s the Washington Post reported that "when college coaches begin their annual (recruiting) search, Washington is their very first stop."[6] As Sports Illustrated reporter Rick Telander noted, "One would not be far wrong in saying that in the cities, environment and black potential have merged to form unusually fertile ground."[7] Coincidentally, the 1966 NCAA National Championship game between Adolph Rupp's all-white University of Kentucky team and the all-Black team from Texas Western University was also played at Cole Field House. Called "the racial statement" championship game, it was won by Texas Western.[8]

Jazz and basketball met in the relationship between the star of the DeMatha team, Sid Catlett, and Jabbar. Catlett was the youngest player on the floor and scored 13 points to Jabbar's 16. James Brown went on to play college ball at Harvard University before becoming a nationally renowned sportscaster, and Catlett had a stellar career at Notre Dame University in Indiana. Jabbar was well known as a collector of jazz recordings and author of a best-selling book on his college coach, John Wooden.[9] Catlett's father was the stellar drummer known as "Big Sid Catlett," who for years was Louis Armstrong's drummer of choice in his big bands and when recording. Known as one of the early "be-bop" drummers, the senior Catlett died of a heart attack at forty-one years old. Jabbar, on a visit to Washington years later, tracked down Catlett and gave him a rare recording of his father speaking and playing. The younger Catlett said in an interview that he didn't remember ever hearing his father speak, and expressed gratitude to Jabbar. Without the DeMatha–Power Memorial game of 1965, he would not have been able to say, "Here I was, a guy in his 50s, hearing his dad talk for the first time. It was an incredibly private, emotional moment."[10] Morgan Wooten later told the same story on a news program, complimenting Jabbar and noting that the elder Catlett died when his son was only three or four years old. During the same program Jabbar told of another recording of Big Sid playing with Charlie Parker and Dizzy Gillespie at Carnegie Hall. Jabbar had his own personal connection with jazz and history. At the death of his own father, Ferdinand L. Alcindor, his *New York Times* obituary on December 13, 2005, revealed that, while his main occupation was as a member of the New York City Police Department, he also was a gifted musician who had attended Juilliard School of Music before serving in the US Army for four years during World War Two. While on the police force he played trombone with the New York Transit Authority Police Band. The obituary read: "His musical talents led to his involvement in one of the most famous events in U.S. history, as Mr. Alcindor was in attendance as a band member when Marilyn Monroe serenaded John F. Kennedy with 'Happy Birthday' on May 19, 1952, an event that according to his son he never forgot."[11] The event occurred at Madison Square Garden.

**Mister Pollin**

Two men—Abe Pollin, a Jewish American, and James W. "Jabbo" Kenner—made Washington a better city. Before the Washington football team's Super Bowl wins in 1983, 1988, and 1992, before the Georgetown Hoyas' 1984 NCAA Championship, and before the University of Maryland's national win in 2002, the Washington Bullets brought a professional basketball team championship to the city in 1978. The team was founded as the Chicago Packers in 1961 and became the Zephyrs in 1962. In 1963, through the efforts of Abe Pollin, the team moved to Baltimore and became the Baltimore Bullets. Born in Philadelphia in 1923 and moving with his family to Washington when he was about eight years old, Pollin was dedicated to the city where he had grown up, living just seven blocks from Griffith Stadium. Graduating from Roosevelt High School and George Washington University, he was simply called "Mister Pollin" throughout his entire professional career. He renamed the team the Capital Bullets and moved the franchise to the Capital Centre in Landover, Maryland, in 1973, then again renamed the team the Washington Bullets in 1974. They had reached the NBA Finals two other times in the 1970s. In the 1971 Championship series, Earl "the Pearl" Monroe's Baltimore Bullets lost to Kareem Abdul-Jabbar's Milwaukee Bucks. They again lost in the 1975 Championship series to the Golden State Warriors, even after adding the power forward Elvin Hayes. The team was led by Wes Unseld, the undersized center and one of the game's greatest passers and rebounders, who in 1969 became the only NBA player to win both the Rookie of the Year Award and the MVP in the same year. Monroe, the NCAA Division II Player of the Year in 1967, was the NBA Rookie of the Year in 1968. Monroe was traded to the New York Knickerbockers after the season. The Bullets added Bobby Dandridge, the Richmond-born star of Maggie Walker High School and Norfolk State College, in 1977. Dandrige had played on the Milwaukee Bucks team that defeated the Bullets 4–0 for the 1971 NBA championship. Monroe, Hayes, and Dandridge (2021) have been inducted into the NBA Hall of Fame. Hayes and Unseld were named to the College Basketball Hall of Fame in 2006 and both were named among the 50 Greatest NBA Players of All Time in 1996 and to the NBA 75th Anniversary Team in 2021. (Monroe, the former Bullet, also received that honor.) When Unseld retired in 1981 he was hired as the team vice president. Although he had little coaching experience, he had become a close confidant of Pollin, who named him the head coach in 1988. In 1994 he resigned and became the team's general manager. In later years Unseld could be seen at the Cap Center escorting underprivileged kids to games. He brought youngsters from the school that his wife, Connie, had founded in 1979 in Baltimore and where he served as office manager and head basketball coach. He also brought kids with disabilities and treated them with the same respect as he did season ticketholders. One of the real beauties of the old Cap Center was the mixing of attendees, before the bifurcation that set in with the rise of ticket prices, luxury seats, and corporate box offices. Like at the old RFK, the rich and the poor, Black and white, often sat next to each other and spoke to each other.

Originally the Bullets' name was derived from Superman's mantle, "Faster than a speeding bullet." But with a spate of violence, much of it became associated with the crack cocaine epidemic, so Pollin, with community support, changed the name to the Wizards in 1995. Pollin built a new arena in 1997 in DC's Chinatown, financing the arena himself rather than asking city taxpayers to do so.

This leading philanthropist once said that he'd like to be remembered "for feeding hungry children, for taking care of the homeless." A few years before his 2009 death, he visited Uganda as the Washington chairman of UNICEF. Upon his return, he said, "To allow children to starve to death when there is food to go around is simply inexcusable. Nobody knows about them. But they're human."[12] Becoming one of the city's largest commercial developers and builders, he and his wife, Irene, built the Irene Pollin Memorial Housing Project in southeast Washington, where three- and four-bedroom apartments rented for sixty dollars a month and where fifteen hundred children eventually lived. Pollin was the son

Washington Bullets championship banner and retired numbers in the rafters of Verizon Center, Washington, DC. Flickr.

of immigrant Jewish parents from Russia; his father, first a plumber and then a construction magnate, along with his mother instilled in him the notion of giving back. He once said: "Those of us who are fortunate enough to be on the giving end, rather than the receiving end, are very lucky. Because the more we give, the more we get back. . . . In America, the richest country the world has even seen, there are almost 5 million children who go to bed hungry every night. That's a disgrace. So I believe that for people who are in a position to give, it is incumbent upon us to help."[13] He served as a board member of UNICEF, the Red Cross, the American Israel Public Affairs Committee, and the American Foundation for Autistic Children. Pollin believed that building the MCI Center downtown would spur the type of development that would provide job opportunities and affordable housing. He could have bought the entire area but chose not to. He hoped that other community-minded developers would follow his lead. Few did. He was one of the first wealthy men or women to go into a public school, pledging to finance the education of fifty-nine elementary school children in 1988 at Seat Peasant Elementary School in Maryland. Of those, forty-nine "graduated from high school and 39 went to a trade school or college on the owner's dime. As of 2007, 17 had received at least a college degree."[14] Polin and Unseld played a role in ensuring the induction of Alexandria, Virginia–born Earl Lloyd into the Naismith Hall of Fame in 2003. He joined the old Washington Capitols in 1950, becoming the first Black player in the NBA.

## Marvin Gaye

One of the great days uniting Blacks through sports and music, in the city and in the nation, was presented by a DC native on February 13, 1983. It took place at the NBA All-Star Game at the Forum in Inglewood, California. Marvin Gaye, whose ancestors were enslaved, sang the "Star-Spangled Banner" by Francis Scott Key, an early American who spent much of his adult life in Washington and was himself a slaveowner. Gaye had sung the National Anthem before, in 1968 in game four of the 1968 Baseball World Series matchup up between the Detroit Tigers and the St. Louis Cardinals.

The year 1968 was a rough one for Black Americans, beginning with the assassinations of Martin Luther King Jr. in April, just as he was embarking on the Poor Peoples Campaign, and Bobby Kennedy in June, as he was campaigning for US president in Los Angeles. Then came the tumultuous Democratic Party Convention in Chicago in August. During the World Series in September, when Gaye had sung the anthem, nothing seemed special about the performance. At the next game, however, Puerto Rican singer Jose Feliciano, famous for his song "Light My Fire," lit up his version of the anthem. For his spicy rendition he was criticized by the mainstream but hailed by young people, who were so desperate for change during those Vietnam War years. Two weeks after the end of the World Series the sports world was turned on its head at the Summer Olympics held in Mexico City in October, when two African American sprinters, Tommie Smith and John Carlos, who had won the gold (Smith) and medaled in the 200-meter dash, protested the condition of Black Americans by raising their clenched fists clad in black gloves as they stood on the podium where the medals were being presented.

Gaye had released one of the highest-selling albums in history, *What's Going On*, in May 1971. The album ranks among the top musical recordings of social protest. He was moved by the letters his brother had sent him from Vietnam. One of the album's songs, "Inner City Blues (Makes Me Wanna Holler)," reflects the violence, inequality, and denial of democratic rights and poverty felt by "inner city" youth, who took the song as their own. The song begins, "Rockets, moon shots / Spend it on the have nots," and, as Michael Eric Dyson writes, takes "the government to task for probing outer space while leaving the poor to fend for themselves."[15] Gaye said: "What mattered was the message. For the first time I felt like I had something to say."[16]

By the early 1980s Gaye had gone into a cycle of depression and drugs. The organizers of the finals had wanted Lionel Richie, but for some reason the office of the NBA commissioner vetoed Ritchie who, as it turned out, would have three

Marvin Gaye's rendition of the "Star-Spangled Banner" at the 1983 NBA All-Star Game
forever linked the importance of sports and music to Black people and to the nation. Gaye
was featured on a US postage stamp as part of the USPS's Music Icon Series, in a tribute
to the Washington-born entertainer's eightieth birthday on April 1, 2019. Courtesy Rob
Corder, Flickr.

songs in the Billboard Top 100 song chart by year's end. Gaye was the second
choice, plan B.

Gaye's song "Sexual Healing," recorded in late 1982, propelled him back to a
better reality and back to the charts. When he sang the "Star-Spangled Banner"
at the 1983 All-Star Game something sparked inside him and he delivered what
must be considered the most soulful rendition of the song ever performed. He
took a song that was meant for the freedom of whites and made it truly a song for
the nation. DC native and sportswriter David Aldridge and Marcus Thompson
II, recaptured the moment forty years later: "He was resplendent in a steel-blue
suit, set off by a light-blue bankers' shirt and a blue gingham tie; a dangling
white handkerchief added a bit of flair."[17] As they relate it, Gaye had practiced
the song before the Sunday prime time game accompanied only with a drum
machine. The Forum producers complained to him that his six-minute version
of the anthem was too long and needed to be cut to two and a half minutes. And
though they wanted him to go over the song again before the game, he agreed.
"Okay, I'll come back tomorrow with a shorter version." But on gameday he had
not shown up by noon, even though he was expected at the Forum a good while
earlier. The producer was so nervous that he had a backup high school chorus at
the ready. Then suddenly, as Aldridge and Thompson recall, Gaye came "walking
down center aisle of the Forum dressed to the nines, with a cassette tape in hand.
It was the drum track that had been laid down Saturday by Gaye and his longtime collaborator, guitarist Gordan Banks." As Gaye sang the song—to the drum
beats—his voice steadily but calmly going up the register, the volume slowly esca-
lating, the beat pulsating—the crowd went mad. Those watching at home could

not contain themselves either. Their hearts were full of sorrow and joy. The NBA All-Stars could no longer stand at attention. Among them were future NBA Hall of Famers Kareem Abdul-Jabbar, Alex English, George Gervin, Magic Johnson, Artis Gilmore, David Thompson, Jamal Wilkes, Larry Bird, Julius Irving, Moses Malone, and Isiah Thomas. Among the All-Stars were future members of the 1992 Olympic Dream Team, Bird and Johnson. Hall of Famer and two-time NBA champion Thomas said: "I will never forget it as long as I live. . . . It was the most amazing feeling in the world. . . . We all loved Marvin Gaye. We knew how cool he was. But you've got to put yourself in our place as players. For the anthem, you stand straight, at full attention. Hands by your side, or you put you hand over your heart. The place is silent, except for the person who's singing."[18] Marques Johnson, who grew up in Los Angeles and played on the UCLA championship team in 1965 and later for the Lakers on the 1983 All-Star team, four decades later said that "I listened to it again" (the previous month)" "and I still got chills."[19] It was that way for the millions who watched the show on Sunday afternoon in their homes and the millions who have watched the broadcast since. It was especially true for Gaye's hometown fans in Washington, DC. The listeners knew that Gaye "had something to say." For many, quite simply it may have been the first time they felt that they were truly Americans or that this land *was* their land, that they should, could, and would be heard.

### Mister "Jabbo"

James W. "Jabbo" Kenner was born in 1915 and raised in Georgetown. As many young Blacks, he had to walk across town to attend school at Armstrong. There he became inspired by E. B. Henderson to work with Black youths in the city. His "initial involvement came when Dr. E. B. Henderson and some prominent Negroes got together and went to talk to the district commission about their desire to create a club for Negro kids. After some discussion, they were awarded a building on 12th and U Streets NW. They told me 'to set up the boxing ring and that's how the club got started.'"[20] That was in 1934, when Kenner helped form what is now the Metropolitan Police and Boys Club of Washington, DC. He told the *Washington Post* that all the other clubs at the time were for whites only.

John Thompson Jr., who was one of "Mr. Jabbo's kids" at the No. 2 Boys Club, said that "Jabbo is one of the most unusual people you will ever meet. He is so sincere and so consoling. Whenever you had a problem, he was there and seemed to have a way of finding a solution."[21] Basketball was played at courts all over town, from Turkey Thicket in Brookland near Catholic University to the Chevy

Chase Recreation Center in Upper Northwest. Intense pickup games—especially when collegiate or professional players were willing to face all comers—inspired young ballers.[22] The Kenner League was the product of inner-city basketball that in the 1950s and 1960s was played at Turkey Thicket, Kelly Miller, River Terrace, Sherwood, and other mainly outdoor courts. Started in the early 1970s, the DC Urban Coalition League eventually ended up at Dunbar High (although games had also been held at American University and the University of the District of Columbia). By most accounts Thompson played a major role in bringing some local coaches together in 1982 to start the Jabbo Kenner League. The league allowed players from schools in Georgetown and other places to play in a safe and structured environment and gave high school and college players the opportunity to showcase their abilities under the watchful eye of college scouts and coaches. Thompson often spoke of Kenner and of becoming one of "Mr. Jabbo's Kids" at the boys club. Others attending "Mr. Jabbo's training school" were Marvin Gaye and Sugar Ray Leonard.

The Kenner League soon found a home at McDonough Gym at Georgetown University. It allowed for Thompson and other area college coaches to keep an eye on players over the summers.[23] At the 1981 Georgetown graduation ceremony, the university's 182nd, Kenner was awarded an honorary degree. Kenner was a big man at 6-foot-3-inches and weighing 295 pounds. Thompson, at 6-foot-10, recommended Kenner for the award, saying, "I didn't have to argue with anybody once his resume was submitted." He added, "He's the most Christ-like person I've ever met. A lot of people preach the gospel. He lives it—all the time."[24] At another time Thompson said of Kenner, "He's one of the finest men I've ever met. It's very difficult to describe him. Everybody felt close to him. I know he supplied me with a great deal of psychological security.'"[25] Others who went through Mr. Jabbo's training school were future congressman Walter Fauntroy, former Green Bay Packer All-Pro Willie Wood (also Armstrong and the University of Southern California), Marvin Gaye, and legions of basketball players. Sugar Ray Leonard, from nearby Palmer Park, Maryland, and perhaps the greatest athlete the Metro region has produced—Golden Glove winner, Olympic gold medalist, and professional boxing champion in five weight divisions—said that "Mr. Jabbo didn't just teach me how to box, he taught me to be a man."[26] Kenner and his wife, Beatrice, adopted or fostered at least nine children, including Woodrow Wilson Kenner, who they took in at age twenty-two months.[27]

Although Kenner died in 1983, the Kenner League continued at Georgetown University. One of the biggest and most anticipated nights in Washington basketball history occurred at a Kenner League game on August 4, 1994. The *Washington*

Allen Iverson during a game against DePaul University before 10,107 fans at USAir Arena in Landover, Maryland, December 3, 1994. The Hoyas won 74–68, behind the freshman's season-high 31 points. Iverson made his 1994 Georgetown University debut at the Jabbo Kenner League. Among those in attendance were Georgetown history professors Jim Collins and Marcus Rediker, both former collegiate basketball players. Courtesy Georgetown University Library.

*Post* reported, "In his first organized game in more than a year, Georgetown basketball recruit Allen Iverson scored 40 points, 30 in the first half, in a summer league playoff game."[28]

Then on August 6, 1994, the "the standing room only crowd was treated to a breathtaking display from Iverson, a 6'1" guard, who scored on dunks, mid-range jumpers and National Basketball Association–length three-pointers." He scored 33 points to lead his team "the Tombs," named after the famed restaurant and student hangout near the Georgetown campus. Iverson had already made history as a young man from Hampton Roads (Newport News and Hampton) and top basketball and football prospect in Virginia, as well as one of the nation's top players in both sports. Iverson had "missed his high school senior season because of an arrest stemming from his involvement in a brawl at a bowling alley in his hometown of Hampton, Va."[29] Because of this, many potential scholarship offers were rescinded and his mother called John Thompson, pleading for her son. Thompson recruited him to Georgetown, adding aura to both the school and the Jabbo Kenner League.[30] Over three games Iverson scored 99 points. With that showing Iverson, just nineteen years old and fresh out of both high school and prison, added to the allure of basketball in Washington, the power of the game, and its possibilities.[31] Iverson would go on to have a seventeen-year career, mainly with the Philadelphia 76ers, where he was named Rookie of the Year in 1996–97, Player of the Year in 2001, and a four-time NBA scoring champion.[32] In his induction speech at the Naismith Hall of Fame in 2016, Iverson credited his mother, who first called Thompson, and Thompson, for believing in him and "saving my life," just as Thompson had said about Sametta Jackson.[33] Iverson was named to the NBA 75th Anniversary Team in 2021.

Thompson ended his book with a description of driving through his father's southern Maryland home base, where he had spent youthful summer days.

"The same Jesuits who founded Georgetown owned my father's ancestors." . . . "Georgetown is not one of those deniers. I was proud of how the school, and especially President Jack DeGioia, faced it head-on."[34] Frederick Douglass died in Anacostia. Thompson "came as a shadow" and spent his first ten years in the Frederick Douglass Housing Projects in Anacostia. And, like Douglass, he left as the North Star.[35]

## Notes

1. Carlson, "The Greatest Ever," 132.

2. *Washington Daily News,* January 30, 1965, 17.

3. Matt Schudel, "Sid Catlett, Basketball Star in 'Greatest High School Game Ever,' Dies at 69," *Washington Post,* November 8, 2017.

4. Catlett went on to play at Notre Dame for three years. He was drafted in 1971 by the NBA's Cincinnati Royals but was cut from the team at the start of the season and never again played in the NBA. In a 2011 interview with the *Washington City Paper* he was asked about the Power Memorial vs. DeMatha game; he replied, "Nothing I was involved in was bigger." He was the son of the legendary tenor sax man Big Sid Catlett, who died in 1951 shortly before his son's third birthday.

5. Wooten had many sayings, but perhaps the most well-known is "Don't let basketball use you. You use basketball to become the best all-around human being you can become." He often added "That's the beauty of basketball. Basketball can make you a better person. A better student, a better player, everything. Because all the fundamentals of basketball are the fundamentals of life." Noah Frank, *WTOP News,* April 1, 2019.

6. "Proving Ground for Stars of Tomorrow," *Washington Post,* January 14, 1966.

7. Kuska, *Hot Potato,* ix.

8. Carlson, "The Greatest Ever," 130.

9. Abdul-Jabbar, *Coach Wooden and Me.*

10. Schudel, "Sid Catlett, Basketball Star." Catlett's mother told the *New York Times* that Kareem Abdul-Jabbar called her son one day forty years after the high school game and told him he was sending him a DVS of his father speaking during a jazz performance, "a sound his son had never heard." Catlett died in November 2017. Richard Sandomir, "Sid Catlett, 69, High School Basketball Star," *New York Times,* November 17, 2017.

11. Ferdinand L. Alcindor obituary, *New York Times,* December 13, 2005. The obit also noted that he had played with jazz greats Dizzy Gillespie, Benny Carter, and Tito Puente. Alcindor attended New York's Franklin Lane High School and was on the school's championship team captained by Red Holzman, the New York Knicks' legendary coach. The full story of the event was told to me by the legendary pianist Hank Jones who played Happy Birthday as Monroe sang and personally instructed him at the piano.

12. Richard Goldstein, "Abe Pollin, Team Owner and Philanthropist, Dies at 85," *New York Times,* November 4, 2009.

13. See "The Wizards of Washington" at https://aish.com/48880787/.

14. Dave McKenna, *Washington City Paper*, November 24, 2009.

15. Dyson, *Mercy, Mercy Me*, 66.

16. Marvin Gaye, *The Very Best of Motown* (UTV, 2001), liner notes by David Ritz.

17. David Aldridge and Marcus Thompson II, "Marvin Gaye's Iconic NBA All-Star Game National Anthem: 'He Turned That Thing into His Own,'" *The Athletic*, February 16, 2023.

18. Aldridge and Thompson, "Marvin Gaye's Iconic."

19. Aldridge and Thompson, "Marvin Gaye's Iconic."

20. Gene Wang, "Iverson Connects for 33 in Kenner League Win," *Washington Post*, August 7, 1994.

21. Edward Hill Jr., "Jabbo Kenner: One Man Evangel for Good Will," *Washington Post*, December 10, 1981.

22. "Proving Ground for Stars of Tomorrow," *Washington Post*, January 14, 1966.

23. Georgetown Basketball History Project, accessed January 24, 2020, hoyabasketball.com.

24. Diane Granat, "Georgetown Honors Mr. Jabbo," *Washington Post*, May 28, 1981.

25. Donald Huff, "Mr. Jabbo," *Washington Post,* June 3, 1979.

26. Granat, "Georgetown Honors."

27. Beatrice Kenner, a career government employee, also was an inventor; she patented several items that were beneficial to Black women's health. I first met her when our family moved to near her home in Sixteenth Streets Heights.

28. David Nakamura, "Hoyas' Recruit Iverson Hits 40 in His Summer League Debut," *Washington Post*, August 4, 1994.

29. Wang, "Iverson Connects."

30. David Nakamura and Gene Wang, *Washington Post*, August 9, 1994: "Iverson's academic progress has been set back in part because of his conviction in July 1993 on three felony counts of maiming by mob for his involvement in a chair-throwing bowling alley brawl in his hometown of Hampton, Va., in February of that year. Iverson was sentenced in September 1993 to five years in prison, but in December, four months into his sentence, he was granted conditional clemency from then-Virginia Gov. L. Douglass Wilder, who felt that conflicting trial testimony shed some doubt on Iverson's guilt."

31. At the time of the Kenner League games I was in graduate school, studying with Jim Collins and Marcus Rediker, both of whom had played basketball in college. Iverson came from the same projects in Newport News that I had grown up in two decades earlier. My older brother knew Iverson's mother. During summers when I went to Newport News and visited with my mother and friend Aaron Brooks, who coached Little League baseball and was later a University of Virginia and Oakland Raiders quarterback, I learned "Bubachuk," as Iverson was called, played on his team. In separate emails Collins, still at Georgetown, and Rediker, now at the University of Pittsburgh, described the excitement of seeing Iverson in the Kenner League games. Wrote Rediker on January 27, 2020: "At the game's opening jump ball GU center Don Reid tapped the ball to Allen Iverson, who

took off like a rocket toward the basket, exploding upward at the rim and throwing down a thunderous tomahawk dunk—all in his first three seconds as a Hoya. The overflow crowd lost its collective mind and nearly brought down the old rafters at McDonough. Amid the din the normally laconic Professor James Collins turned to me and, with eyes popping out of his head, said, 'Did we really just see that?' It must have been the most electrifying start ever for a college player's career." On January 25, 2020, Collins had written: "In that Kenner first game, the crowd was substantial but not overflowing; a few seats were empty, as I recall. No one knew if he was going to play because he had not played in any of the regular season Kenner games; it was the first game of the playoffs. Marcus somehow knew and said we had to go . . . on the Tombs' first possession, AI brings the ball up the court, suddenly blows by his defender (like he was invisible) and heads into the lane. Big guy for the other team, about 6′8″ . . . moves into the lane to draw a charge. AI jumps OVER him and dunks. Crowd went absolutely nuts, never seen anything like it. Next possession, he comes down, the defender lays way off of him: he stops and takes a 3 from about 30 feet. Swish. At this point, the crowd is so raucous, so convinced that JT Jr is on his way to another national championship, that I thought the building would collapse." He added: "The next day, Marcus and I show up about 20 minutes before tip-off. The crowd was three-deep OUTSIDE the building. The place was full already and everyone was waiting, hoping someone would leave and they might get in. The crowd stayed even though they could not see the game."

32. Dyson, "For the Culture."

33. Allen Iverson's Hall of Fame Enshrinement speech, September 10, 2016, quoted in Mike Wise, "Iverson Has a Night for the Ages," Andscape, September 11, 2016, https://andscape.com/features/iversons-hall-of-fame-speech-adds-to-his-legend/. Thompson was inducted in 1999, Patrick Ewing inducted in 2008 and again in 2010 as part of the 1992 Dream Team, Alonzo Mourning in 2014, and Dikembe Mutombo in 2015.

34. Thompson with Washington, *I Came as a Shadow*, 322.

35. Thompson died on August 30, 2020. In a posthumous opinion piece in the *New York Times* titled "Drop the Charade: Pay College Athletes" (November 15, 2020), with quotes taken from his autobiography, Thompson explained why he thought players ought to be compensated.

# EPILOGUE

Community, fellowship, and the quest for "the dream" have so clearly reflected the sense of kinship displayed by Black people who played and listened to music and played or watched sports in Washington, DC. One organization, the Capital Pool Checkers Club, has met for decades in the Shaw neighborhood to play the game of checkers. Common to the members is a sense of shared interest, experiences, mutual support, and comradeship. The club's members come from all walks of life: cab drivers and physicists, barbers, university professors and musicians, landscapers and artists. From their stories it is clear that they have always been "people of distinction." When the club was forced to move from its Shaw home of forty-two years, as the inaugural chair of the DC Commission on African American Affairs, appointed by the Mayor, I worked with city officials to find a new location in Adams Morgan where the club could meet. As I told the *Washington Post*, "As you move African Americans out, you lose the culture, you lose the flavor, your dreams are deferred."[1]

The Listening Group was founded in the early 1980s by Dr. Reed Tuckson, then the medical director of the District of Columbia; Dr. Cuthbert Simpkins, who worked in the emergency room at DC General Hospital; poet Gaston Neal; former DC election official Norval Perkins; and others, including musicians, university professors, city officials, and civic leaders. The club has met once a month for years, to listen to and discuss jazz music, along with enjoying good food and conversation. They discuss the music of Washington-born jazz musicians Shirley Horn, Buck Hill, Duke Ellington, and Geri Allen, one of the first to graduate with a degree from Howard's jazz studies program. They discuss younger Washington area artists like Ben Williams, Corcoran Holt, Kush Abadey, Elijah Jamal Balbed, and Janelle Gill. They discuss the work of musicians like Jason Moran, who succeeded Billy Taylor as head of jazz programming at the Kennedy Center in New York. As with the Capital Pool Checkers Club, Listening Group members check their egos and professional identities at the door. It never matters whether one

Inside the Capital
Pool Checkers Club
at 9th and S Streets
NW, Washington,
DC, August 29, 2009.
Courtesy Peggy Fleming.

has a PhD or no D, a Maserati or a Mazda, a Buick or a Bronco. Regardless of whether the groups are discussing checker board moves or Charlie Parker riffs, what is common to both is a sense of shared interests, experiences, mutual support, and comradeship.[2]

When the Bohemian Caverns Club was forced to close because of a high rent prices brought on by gentrification, Listening Group members helped lead the protests against the forced move.[3] When the Twins Jazz Lounge closed, the club's members registered their disapproval. Sisters Kelly and Maze Tesfaye, who owned the club, sent a letter addressed to "Friends, Patrons, Musicians and Community," on August 27, 2020. It read, "It is with profound sadness and sincere regrets for the impacts on all of you that we must announce that, owing to the harsh economic circumstances brought on by the ongoing pandemic, Twins Jazz has been forced to close its physical location at 1344 U Street NW Washington, DC."

On the west side of town, west of Rock Creek Park, after a few years hiatus, sports games as part of the Kenner League still exist, albeit as part of the national Nike Pro Circuit. Kenner League games are still played at the McDonough Gym at Georgetown University. In the cramped, old gym, folks from all over the city and region continue to gather. In Georgetown, Jelleff Community Center remains one of the most integrated places in the city. The Jelleff Boys & Girls Club of Washington, based there, was established in 1886 as the Newsboys and Children's Aid Society and became the Working Boys Home and Aid Society in the first decade of the 1900s. In 1953 it became known simply as the Boys Club of Washington, with the support of local businessman Frank R. Jelleff. Twenty years later, in 1973, it accepted girls as full members as part of the Boys and Girls Clubs of Greater Washington. At first the Boys Club was as segregated as any other institution in the city. But along the way the center became one of the very few

The Listening Group stands outside Ben's Chili Bowl, located at 1213 U Street NW. (*Front row, left to right*): John Whitmore, Keith Jawara Hunter, Aminifu Harvey, Fred Foss, Gaston Neal, Sam Turner, Joe Selmon, Howard McCree, Michael Wallace, and David Truly. (*Middle row, left to right*): Phil Roane, Lew Marshall, Ron Clark, Medaris Banks, Wilmer Leon, Bill Brower, Maurice Jackson, Muneer Nassar, Barry Carpenter, James Early. (*Back row, left to right*): Bill Shields, Tariq Tucker, Askia Muhammad, Elijah Smith, and Willard Jenkins. Photo by Marvin Tupper Jones. Author's collection.

meeting places for youngsters of all economic and social backgrounds, colors, and nationalities. They took swimming lessons, attended after-school programs and summer camps. The Jelleff Basketball Leagues for elementary, junior, and senior high school kids from all over the city became perhaps the most racially and economically diverse organization in the city, bar none.[4] Youngsters who may not have made the cut on their school teams, in basketball, soccer, and volleyball, could find a team at Jellefs.[5]

On the east side of town, east of Rock Creek Park, the Kingman's Boys and Girls Clubs still exist. Two years after the 1968 riots, Washington businessman Richard L. Peters and fellow members of the Rotary Club, plus longtime Boys and Girls Club supporter John R. Thompson Jr., joined to form the Kingman's center.[6] It is not far from where Big John first developed his craft and gained his confidence. Many played in the youth basketball leagues in summer and winter.

Georgetown University (Doha campus) and the US Embassy in Doha, Qatar present *An Evening of Jazz*, featuring Nasar Abadey and SUPERNOVA in tribute to Duke Ellington's 125th birthday, April 21, 2004. Band members (*left to right*): Charles Covington (piano), Justin Mendez (saxophones), Herman Burney (bass), Kenny Rittenhouse (bass), and Nasar Abadey (drums and percussion). Courtesy of Maurice Jackson.

And many who did make their school teams came back for pickup games and summer leagues. Decades later, in the midst of a rapidly gentrifying Shaw area near U Street NW, one of directors said that the Kingman "has been both educator and athletic director to thousands of children." Though the center still serves mostly Black youth, he remarked that young people of all backgrounds, "black, white, Hispanic and Ethiopian," now come to the center.[7]

Black people in the city often rallied in the sports arenas and the jazz venues. When his Georgetown teams were on top, Thompson proclaimed that "we didn't need racism to motivate us." Sad to say, that has not always been true for others. Black athletes and musicians, and Black people in general, have indeed used examples of societal racism to combat societal racism. Thompson's words do ring true, especially when he writes that "our community tends to rally around Black people who are subjected to racists attacks."[8]

There have been times when people new to the city have not been respectful of past traditions that have brought Black people together. An example is the Drum

Tony Gittens with his grandson, Niko Gittens, at the Malcolm X Drum Circle. The Drum Circle was started more than fifty years ago and meets on Sunday afternoons in Malcolm X Park at 16th and V Streets NW. All are welcome. Gittens is director of the Washington, DC, International Film Festival and former executive director of the DC Commission on the Arts & Humanities. Courtesy Tony Gittens.

Circle at Malcolm X Park, in the heavily gentrified area between Adams Morgan and Columbia Heights. The park was established as Meridian Hill Park by an Act of Congress on June 25, 1910.[9] The Drum Circle's name and origins went back to February 12, 1965, the day Malcolm X was assassinated. Drummers gathered at the park and collectively started making music, and the place was eventually renamed Malcolm X Park. In 1972 the first African Liberation Day was held there on the weekend closest to the slain leader's May 19 birthday, bringing together Black activists from all over the city and nation.[10] Participants were self-styled Marxist, Pan-Africanist, and other types of radicals.[11] Over the years, competing ideologies created disunity and the celebrations ended—but the Drum Circle remained. At one point some people new to the area wanted to take the name back to Meridian Hill Park. But when young whites joined in the Drum Circle they were welcomed, as long as they knew they were at Malcom X Park and accepted the Drum Circle's basic parameters. The values of the drummers were best expressed by a young white educator and writer, who posted: "You come to make music and dance, meditate, collaborate, converse and you come in peace."[12]

In recent years the CapitalBop Music Festival has been held at Malcolm X Park. CapitalBop was created in 2013 by young Black and white cultural organiz-

Nic Ojeda and his son, Caetano, with the Malcolm X Drum Circle. Courtesy Nic Ojeda.

ers and artists to promote, present, and preserve jazz in Washington. Along with its musical programs, the festival hosted seminars on all aspects of Washington history and began to build new audiences to bolster the larger community around jazz, which has been so important to the city's historic identity and the continued vibrancy of its culture. CapitalBop sought to make sure that jazz and creative improvised music continued to have a home in the radical, off-the-beaten-path spaces and unmediated, noncommercial venues, where creativity has always thrived the best. In recent years CapitalBop has worked to present the Jazz and Freedom Festival around MLK weekend and Malcolm X Day loft-style shows, which bring together big names from all over the world to play with the best players based in DC.[13] Starting in the early 2020s, the Home Rule Music Festival has held annual June events, featuring Jazz, GO GO and World Music at the Great Lawn at the Parks at Walter Reed (former grounds of the Walter Reed Army Hospital.) In the summer of 2024, the DC Jazz Festival held its 20th anniversary event. The festival was first started by Charles Fishman and his wife Stephanie Peters in 2004 as the Duke Ellington Jazz Festival. It has now served almost 2 million listeners, and presented hundreds of internationally acclaimed artists, including many National Endowment of the Arts (NEA) Jazz Masters as well as over 150 DC-based musicians at venues all around DC.

This book has attempted to show how Washington's African Americans have come together to advance society through music and sports. It has shown how, in the nation's capital, African Americans have used their natural born talents, their creative genius, and their determination to learn and develop their crafts in music and sports to improve their lot, to cope with day-to-day racism, and to be a credit to and bring joy to their communities. Nothing could be finer.

## Notes

1. Paul Schwartzman, "We're Losing a Piece of Our History: The Checkers Club Is Closing After Nearly 40 Years," *Washington Post,* March 19, 2021. As a member of the Listening Group I was appointed the inaugural chair of the commission (2013–17).

2. Jackson, *Crown Me!,* 2–3.

3. Michael J. West, "Last of the Bohemian: Legendary U Street Jazz Club Bohemian Caverns Will Close at the End of March," *Washington City Paper,* March 18, 2016.

4. In 2019 the Maret School, a private school in Northwest DC, signed a partnership with the city's Department of Parks and Recreation. Maret financially supported the renovation of the Jelleff Rec Center soccer field and in exchange uses the field for several hours after school for team practice. But the field remains under DPR supervision and is used by youth teams citywide.

5. Peggy Sands, "Jelleff Rec Center Schedule Sees New Complex in 2025," *Georgetowner,* November 14, 2022.

6. Learn more about Kingman Boys and Girls Clubs at http://kingmanbgc.org/.

7. Hamil Harris, "Boys and Girls Club Started After 1968 Riots Continues to Guide in Athletics, Academics," *Washington Post,* June 8, 2016.

8. Thompson with Washington, *I Came as a Shadow,* 113, 116–17. He adds, "People from coast to coast wore Georgetown jackets, caps and T-shirts. These items became a status symbol in Black neighborhoods."

9. US Statutes-At-Large, 676 Stat. 36. 1910.

10. Joseph, *Stokely,* 295–97.

11. See Black Power in Washington D.C., https://experience.arcgis.com/experience /5e17e7d1c4a8406b9eaf26a4eae77103/

12. Kristin Doherty, "The Awesomeness of a Drum Circle: Malcolm X Park, Washington DC, accessed August 23, 2023, https://medium.com/@kristindoherty9/the-awesomeness -of-a-drum-circle-malcolm-x-park-washington-dc-5163d12cc3de.

13. CapitalBop also runs a web magazine and newsletter, keeping a record of DC's musical happenings and giving fans the resources they need to engage with and support jazz and the African American culture. Its 2023 festival was held at the old Walter Reed Hospital site.

# ACKNOWLEDGMENTS

I owe a great deal to my late mother, Zee, and my late stepdad, Pete, from Newport News, Virginia. As a kid I remember how they and their music-loving friends Juanita, Grant, Jesse Powers, and Albert "Junior" McIver Jr. loved listening to Ruth Brown, Rudy Keys, Nancy Wilson, and Count Basie. I remember all of them grieving when John Coltrane died. Thank you, Los Aficionados. Ma Pearl. If God truly made man and woman in his own image, he threw out the mold after he made you. You struggled to read and write, but you were the greatest teacher anyone could have ever had, and your lessons remain with me—and will forever.

Music and sports were a vital part of our household as the children grew to adulthood. Daughter Lena had great high school coaches: Jim Ehrinhaft and Douglass "Bos" Boswell in track and Jonathon Scribner in basketball, at National Cathedral School for Girls. (Scribner later became a championship coach at St. John's High School.) The legendary Boston Celtics great Sam Jones, a childhood hero of mine, once showed up at one of Lena's games and we chatted.

Son Miles was first coached in soccer when he was five or six years old, by Bob Pinkard, the father of a schoolmate at Beauvoir School. On their Jelleff Community Center youth teams both Lena and Miles were coached by Christy McCaulie. Lena was later coached by Shelia Roberts. Kevin McShane and Hart Roper coached Miles in varsity soccer at St. Albans School for Boys. Coach Dave coached him with the Legends in the Bethesda Soccer League; other coaches of his were Len Oliver, a member of the National Soccer Hall of Fame, and Zaki Hamzoui, of the Stoddert Soccer League. Both kids competed at the varsity level for their respective universities: Lena ran track at Georgetown and Miles played soccer at the University of Michigan. Thank you, coaches, one and all.

Both children also played in the DC Youth Orchestra, conducted by Lyn McLain, and the National Cathedral Orchestra under Scott Woods, the latter of whom also gave Lena individual trumpet lessons. Miles took contrabass lessons from

Lena Jackson, age 4, and Miles Jackson, age 18 months, listening to DC native Duke Ellington's *Sophisticated Ladies*, at the Jackson family's first home in Columbia Heights. Author's collection.

Lena anticipating a rebound during a basketball game for her school, the National Cathedral School for Girls. Lena also ran track at NCS and for the Georgetown University Track and Field Team. Author's collection.

Miles, no. 21 (*top row, third from left*), with the 2008–9 University of Michigan Men's Soccer Team. Author's collection.

Miles in New York City at a 2014 photo shoot for the company he founded and directs, Cuba Skate Inc. Author's collection.

local legend Pepe Gonzalez, who I had known since my first days in the city and who became his Tio Pepe. My wife, Laura, and I am grateful to all those who inspired Lena and Miles in music. Thank you Maestros Woods, McLain, and Gonzalez.

My thanks to Johnny Wilson, Dave Clark, and Anne Holloway, for the occasional free ticket to see the Washington Redskins, and to Jerry "Wash" Washington, a.k.a. "the Bama," for comp tickets to see the Washington Wizards. Thank you, Professors Marcus Rediker, Jim Collins, and Hisham Sharabi, for helping me learn about Georgetown basketball and how to develop the craft of becoming a historian. GU basketball players Patrick Ewing Jr., Jeff Greene, and Kevin Braswell were among the many Georgetown student athletes in my classes. Patrick was the best "big fella" I have ever seen on the dance floor. Often during the first class of the week, he would come in and show the young ladies and young men the newest dance steps. I often interspersed my class instruction using jazz lyrics or sports talk. In an interview after one Saturday game, Jeff said, "The cats were jelling." I realized he had been listening in class to those jazz stories. He wrote a paper on the Harlem Rens basketball team. When Jeff was a member of the Boston Celtics, at one point he needed lifesaving cardiac surgery. While sitting out the year, he came to campus a few times during the semester or we spoke by email or phone during the tutorial he took with me, one of the last classes he needed to graduate.

Dave Ogden was also in class with Jeff and Patrick. He wrote a fine paper, which I still have, on the Negro Leagues. He followed his father into the US Secret Service. One night, as I was flipping the channels, I came upon Jerry Seinfeld's show *Comedians in Cars Getting Coffee*, with President Barack Obama as the guest. "The Beast," the presidential limousine, appeared on screen being driven by Dave. In one class was Alex Buzbee, the first Georgetown graduate to be drafted into the NFL in many years. Faith Woodard, a star on the Georgetown women's basketball team, went on to earn a graduate degree from the Columbia School of Journalism and is now an evening news anchor in Little Rock, Arkansas. Rebekkah Brunson, the Hoyas' all-time leading rebounder and winner of five WNBA Championships, was in one of my classes. Also Sugar Rodgers, who wrote the autobiography *They Better Call Me Sugar* (2021). We spoke of our backgrounds in Tidewater, Virginia, which were similar to Allen Iverson's and Alonzo Mourning's. (Mourning's son, Trey, often came to visit me in my office, and Dikembe Mutombo's son, Ryan, studied with me as well.) I did not teach Allen Iverson; he left Georgetown after three semesters. But whenever I saw him on campus, we spoke of my buddy Hank Hucles, who coached him in baseball at the Newport News Shipyard Recreation Leagues. Thank you, Hoya athletes.

Along the way I have met many Georgetown coaches. John Thompson Jr., JT 3, Craig Esherick, and Coach Ed Colley. In soccer, former Georgetown coach Keith Tabatznik coached our kids in summer camp, as did Tommy Hunter, the men's golf coach. Soccer coach Brian Wiese, whose team won the 2019 NCAA Championship, has always emphasized to his players the need to excel in schoolwork. He is a model for others to follow. The same is true of Alton McKenzie, director of track and field and cross-country. Special thanks to the academic counselors at Georgetown, who make sure the athletes stay on course, especially Dr. Shelly Habel, associate director of student athletics, and Debra Martin. Thanks to Mary Fenlon, who served as the basketball team's academic coordinator. She sat on the bench near Coach Thompson under the moniker "assistant coach," demonstrating Coach's commitment to academics. She would be proud of the work of the academic counselors across all team sports, just as Coach Thompson would be. Thank you, Big John Thompson. Your strength, courage, and dignity have served as a lodestar to so many. Miles still remembers when he and his buddy Robbie took naps in your office one summer, while attending your basketball camp as young kids. And they remember the deflated basketball you kept there.

Athletic Director Lee Reed has always answered my calls and shared his knowledge. From him I have learned the complexities of keeping an athletic program on track. Paul "Tags" Tagliabue, former GU basketball player, NFL commissioner, and chair of the Georgetown board of directors, has shown me that compassion and making hard decisions are not always in opposition. Pat McArdle in the Athletic Department was always generous is helping me obtain photographs of various Hoyas. Father Ray Kemp has always given me a boost when I needed it most. Kemp, a legend among generations of Blacks in DC and a godsend to countless Georgetown athletes who took his "Church and the Poor" and other classes, freely shares his deep knowledge of the city and wisdom, and his kindness knows no bounds. Over the years, he has witnessed marriage vows for many and christened their children, no doubt future Hoyas.

I joined the Listening Group, a gathering of jazz-loving African American men, during its first year. Through it I have met some fine and remarkable Black men and their families. Two photographs and the names of many members appear in this volume. Thank you, gentlemen, for the jazz, the talk, and the food. I am especially thankful to the beloved departed brothers of the Listening Group: Norval Perkins, Alden Lawson, Gaston Neal, Joe Selman, Frank Smith, Askia Muhammad, academic advisor Dr. Jim Miller, Harold "Foodhead" Finley, and Ron Clark. A debt of gratitude goes to the late Dr. Lew Marshall, who kept us as healthy as he possibly could.

One of my most memorable nights came through an invitation from Anne Abramson, who was taking one of my classes at Georgetown. A Washington Performing Arts Society patron, she invited Laura and me to the Kennedy Center to see Sonny Rollins, whose music I grew up with. We were invited backstage to meet Rollins. I have traveled to many parts of this nation and the world and met many people—some important, but few as important as they thought they were—but seldom have I been greeted with such warmth by a person I had never met. That warmth was extended to Laura as well. Not all great musicians are kind human beings, nor are all great athletes. But having read about the great saxophonist and listened to his music all my life, I learned that some can be both good in their soul and in their craft. When Laura worked at the AFL-CIO, she got tickets to basketball and hockey games. Seeing hockey on TV is one thing; seeing a game in person, with the puck flying and the skaters banging each other, gave the kids and us great joy. On more than one occasion we chatted with NBA legend Wes Unseld, then a general manager for the Washington Bullets and Wizards, who attended the hockey games with underprivileged kids. Like Rollins, Unseld's talent, humility, and public service reveal great beauty. Thank you, gentle giants.

My closest friends in life and in the movement for social justice have for decades been Hank Hucles in Capahosic, Virginia, and Jim Steele in Brooklyn, New York (where Hank grew up). In the last decade or so, along with our wives, Brenda (Jim) and Ande (Hank), we have formed Hank's "posse," gathering each fall at the Cape May Jazz Festival in New Jersey, joined by Listening Group cofounder Cuthbert "Tuffy" Simpkins and his wife, Diane, Jill Furillo and her husband Tomas Gargano, and others. Thank you, Hank's posse.

Programmers at WPFW past and present—Jerry Washington, Miyuki Williams, Don Williams, Trina Borras, Rusty Hassan, Willard Jenkins, Tom Porter, Miles Willis, Ellen Carter, Bobby Hill, Rusty Hassan, Donny McKethen, "Nap, Don't Forget the Blues" Turner, Larry Applebaum, James Pope, and Andrea "the Hat Lady" Bray—have made my life richer. Reuben Jackson went to the ancestors as I write these words. His knowledge of jazz, poetry, and Washington, DC, as well as his willingness to share freely of that knowledge, was infectious and he will be missed.

A special word of gratitude goes to those who worked with me on the book *DC Jazz*, especially coeditor Blair Ruble, along with Judith Korey, John Hasse, Rusty Hassan, Lauren Sinclair, Bill Brower (whom I had known from our days at Antioch College), Bridget Arnwine, Willard Jenkins, Anna Harwell Celenza, E. Ethelbert Miller, and Michael Fitzgerald. Blair, who has many passions, including jazz music, the DC theater, and baseball, offered insights on music and base-ball. Judith, who spearheads the Felix Grant Archives at the University of the District of Columbia (UDC), offered critical information on jazz at Lorton Prison. John has always answered all my queries, and I have had many long talks with Lauren Bradley, and attended many jazz concerts with Rusty Hassan.

Jennifer Lawson and Tony Gittens have been reliable sounding boards for various projects. Their friendship has meant the world to my family, as have the friendships of Drs. Tony Rankin and Frances Epsy Rankin, Judge Mike Rankin, Judge Zinora Mitchell Rankin, and former Smithsonian undersecretary James Early and his spouse, Miriam Early. Edward P. Jones, dear family friend and awe-inspiring writer: You make a difficult craft look effortless. Special appreciation goes to three friends who recently have gone to the ancestors: artist Lou Stovall, Howard Croft, and James "Bennett" Bennett.

My students at Georgetown University have often aided this technologi-cally challenged professor. Among them have been Amy Beyers, Lena Jackson, Sarah Vasquez, Chessa Gross, Isabella Brewster, and Gabrielle Barruso at the Washington campus. In Doha, Qatar, student helpers include Fariha Iqbal, Anjali Singh, Hana Elshehaby, and Mohammed Al-Kuwari. The students at the Georgetown Day School have been especially generous in helping me find resources. I thank all of them, especially my man Jacob Weitzner. They are so very lucky to have Georgetown University grad Lisa Rauschart as their teacher. And I am too.

I thank Pastor Brian Hamilton of the Westminster Presbyterian Church, Dick Smith and all the people at Westminster's jazz session, Harry Sniper of Blues Alley, and Omrao Brown, former owner of the Bohemian Caverns. Many great local musicians in and from or with strong ties to the DC area have enriched my life. These include Buck Hill and Shirley Horn, Keter Betts, James King, Nasar Abadey, Kush Abadey, Allyn Johnson, Butch Warren, Rueben Brown, Elijah Jamal Balbed, Brian Settles, Antonio Parker, Pepe Gonzalez, my former neighbor Miss June Norton, Nap Turner, Charles Woods, Peter Edelman, Rahmat Shabazz, Bruce Williams, Billy Hart, Corcoran Holt, Ben Williams, Rahsaan Carter, Peter Anderson, Will Anderson, Muneer Nassar, Kris Funn, Andrew White, Bill Harris, Janelle Gill, Steve Novosel, Fred Foss, Billy Taylor, Roberta Flack, Charlie Rouse, Byron Morris, Michael Thomas, Sharon Clark, Paul Carr, Russell Carter, George V. Johnson Jr., Aaron Myers, Herb Scott, Webster Young, Fred Irby, Eva Cassidy, James Zimmerman, Calvin Jones, Michael Bowie, Davey Yarborough, Amy Bormet, Luke Stewart, Reginald Cyntje, Frederic Yonnet, Lennie Cuje, Stanley Cowell, Pearl Bailey, Elijah Easton, Lawrence Wheatley, Lenny Robinson,

Richie Cole, Marc Cary, Sunny Sumter, Dick Morgan, Tarus Mateen, Lena Seikaly, John Malachi, Wade Beech, Sonny Stitt, Meshell Ndegeocello, and many many more.

Special thanks go to Clarence Lusane and E. Ethelbert Miller for their extensive and thoughtful suggestions throughout this project, and to my son-in-law, Rowan Moore Gerety, who read and offered ideas on the sections on sports with the eye of a masterful journalist.

The late Mica Ertegun helped fund a special issue of *Washington History* on jazz in Washington, DC. Lincoln McCurdy of the Turkish Coalition of America and the late Detroit congressman John Conyers helped me find a way to visit Turkey and explore its jazz scene and give a few lectures. Ricky Ricardi, Louis Armstrong biographer and director of research collections for the Louis Armstrong House in Queens, New York, provided useful information on Armstrong and his performances at Lorton and in Washington, DC. I have enjoyed hearing Adele Alexander talk about the role that her father, Arthur Logan, played as personal physician in New York to Washington-born Duke Ellington, whose music he adored. Lonnie and Maria Bunch have offered encouraging words as they have with countless scholars and artists.

In the Georgetown University History Department I could always talk sports with Amy Leonard and Jim Collins. Chandra Manning, a true baseball expert, read the section on baseball and offered ideas. I have spoken about music with many colleagues at Georgetown, especially Bryan McCann, Jordan Sand, and Father David Collins, SJ. Some years ago Angelyn Mitchell of the Georgetown English Department organized a two-day forum called "Let Freedom Ring": Art and Democracy in the King Years, 1954–1968. I was honored to work with her when some of America's literary giants and scholars, among them Sonia Sanchez, Amiri Baraka, E. Ethelbert Miller, Jayne Cortez, and Eleanor Traylor, joined in the dialogue. Music was always in the air. Thank you, Angie, for including me.

I will always be indebted to the late Richard Stites, a Russian and Soviet-era specialist and a teacher beyond compare. In the hallways of the History Department we used to sing or scat a few lines from the American Songbook. I still miss him. At Georgetown in Doha, anthropologist Rogaia Abusharaf and I have had many talks about the influence of music in the United States and among the Sufi Muslims in her native Sudan. Her uncle Abdel Khaliq Mahjub, the assassinated Sudanese Marxist freedom fighter, and my godfather, James E. "Jack" Jackson Jr., a leader of the Communist Party USA who was imprisoned during the infamous McCarthy era, knew each other decades ago as each roamed the world seeking social change. Jack's wife and my godmother, Esther Cooper Jackson, a 1934 Dunbar High School graduate and founder, with W. E. B. Du Bois and Paul

Robeson, of *Freedomways Magazine* in 1961, where she served as its longtime editor, would, I think, be proud of my efforts. She died at 105 years old in 2022, but her role as a key transmitter of the beautiful culture of Black people inspired me to explore all aspects of Black life and culture in Washington and beyond. For over twenty-five years *Freedomways* opened it pages to artistic and anticolonial leaders like Kwame Nkrumah and Jomo Kenyatta, authors like James Baldwin, Alice Walker, and Audre Lorde; poets Pablo Neruda, Amiri Baraka, and Langston Hughes; and towering figures such as Martin Luther King Jr. *Freedomways* published countless articles on sports, jazz, and folk music and opened its pages to their practitioners, such as Max Roach and Archie Shepp, some who performed benefit concerts to raise funds to support the magazine's publication.

Special appreciation goes to Rosemary E. Kilkenny, Georgetown's vice president for institutional diversity, equity & inclusion, and Charlene Brown McKenzie, Georgetown's director of the Center for Multicultural Equity & Access. Both have been key in making sure that the school adheres to its commitment to diversity, as has Dr. John Wright at the Doha campus. Thanks to Djuana Shields, Jan Liverance, Kathy Buc, and Nicole Gerber, the capable History Department administrators who have been so helpful to me over the years.

Many good people at libraries and archives have helped lead me to the "mother lode," perhaps without realizing it. Lynn Conway, Keith Gorman, Mary Beth Corrigan, Jeff Popovich, and Beth Marhanka at Lauinger Library at Georgetown University, where the Maurice Jackson Papers on the 1919 and 1968 riots and the Jackson Family Collection of Radical Pamphlets are located. Jamillah Scott-Branch Robert Laws, Pascalia Terzi, Arwa El-Kahlout, Murta Lendic, and Maria Sol Marra and others at the Georgetown Qatar library have helped me find materials and navigate search engines far away from home. Judith Korey and the late Reuben Jackson at the UDC Felix Grant Archives always answered my call. I was delighted to donate to those archives my collections of rare and original Cuban jazz albums. Paul Gardullo and Mary Elliot, senior curators at the Smithsonian Institution Museum of African American History and Culture, to which I donated my own *Black Radical* pamphlet collection, have always answered my requests, as have Damion L. Thomas, sports curator, and Dwandalyn R. Reece, curator of music and performing arts. Samir Meghelli, senior curator, Asantewa Boakyewa, associate director of collections and exhibits, and Alcione M. Amos shared illuminating insights and pointed to resources.

DC archivist Bill Branch has been a keeper of the faith and the records. The staffs at the Martin Luther King Public Library and the Georgetown Public Library, the Research Library of the Historical Society of Washington, the Sumner School, the Schomburg Center and Library in New York, ably led by Joy L. Bivens, and the Moorland-Spingarn Research Center at Howard University, have been essential. Dr. Carole Sargent, head of the Georgetown Office of Scholarly Publications, has always been a wonderful resource for struggling scholars like me. Thank you, Carole.

I thank Larry Applebaum at the Library of Congress, who led me to amazing finds, and Kim Connor and all the people at the Woodrow Wilson Center for International Scholars, as well as everyone at the Woodrow Wilson House, the Meridian House, Dumbarton Oaks, Busboys and Poets, and Politics and Prose, where I have given recent talks on the music of Washington, DC. Andras Goldindger at Politics and Prose has kept me abreast of the latest releases of CDs and records, as I remain "old school." Saxophonist Joe Lovano offered insight into Buck Hill just as Hill's mural was being painted near 14th and U Streets NW.

Laura and I have enjoyed attending Burnett Thompson's Piano DC jazz sessions and performances by Angel Gil-Ordonez and his PostClassical Ensemble. My walks with dear friends have always been invaluable to our health and our learning. Weekend morning walks with Lonnie Bunch, talking not about work but about history, about our children and grandchildren, and about sports, have enriched me. On walks with Omrao Brown we talk about music; graduate student Luke Frederick and I talk about the progress of his dissertation on the nineteenth-century carceral system in the District of Columbia, and about sports, especially his love of golf.

I owe a debt of gratitude to Georgetown University president John "Jack" DeGioia, who has lived in Washington for nearly five decades and sought to make the university an important hub in making life better for the people, government, and business communities in the city. When Charlie Haden and Hank Jones performed Negro spirituals from their CD *Steal Away* at Georgetown's Gaston Hall, DeGioia's office was the primary sponsor, just as it was when Kenny Barron replaced Jones a few years later and when Charlie came back to play songs from the CD *Come Sunday*. Not long ago DeGioia said to me, "I am asking ten professors to give me ten names of people who are on the cutting edge of scholarship and society to invite to visit the campus and give a talk. Take your time and think about it." I said, "I don't need any time. You will be getting many names from many peers. I can give you one right now: Jason Moran." For two years his office, under the guidance of Vice President and Chief of Staff Joe Ferrara, supported an appointment for Moran, the MacArthur Genius Award winner and head of jazz programing at the John F. Kennedy Center for the Performing Arts, as Distinguished Artist in Residence. Jason led workshops and invited creative innovators like Connaitre Miller and AFRO BLUE from Howard University; Elizabeth Alexander, president of the Andrew W. Mellon Foundation; and Alicia

Hall Moran. Jason worked with the artist and skateboarder Ben Ashworth, who curated "Finding a Line: Skateboarding, Music and the Media," and skateboarder Miles Jackson, founder of Cuba Skate. The Kennedy Center in New York built a skatepark and had jazz musicians and skateboarders in performance in 2015, accentuating the relationship between music and sports. Jason also offered valuable knowledge on James Reese Europe as part of his multimedia work titled "James Reese Europe and the Absence of Ruin." In 2019 Georgetown University hosted and cosponsored, with the Vatican's Pontifical Council for Culture, "Sports at the Service of Humanity." Miles was invited to participate as representative of the sport of skateboarding. Other notable sports figures who participated were Val Ackerman, commissioner of the Big East; Hall of Fame basketball player, Georgetown legend, and Hoyas' coach Patrick Ewing; Paul Tagliabue; and Cathy Engelbert, WNBA commissioner.

Thank you, Pat Metheny, innovator, creator, and great friend. I remember the day we first met at Charlie Haden's memorial at the Los Angeles home of Jack Black and Tanya Haden (who, along with her triplet sisters, Rachel and Petra, sings so beautifully). We talked into the night with Flea of the Red Hot Chili Peppers, Geri Allen, and the recently departed comedian Richard Lewis of *Curb Your Enthusiasm*. We have been talking ever since.

I am especially grateful to the director of Georgetown University Press, Al Bertrand. His judgment and encouragement have been awe-inspiring. Jenna Galberg, the press's publishing assistant, has worked with me diligently and patiently to assemble the many photos and documentary evidence included here. I also thank Francys Reed, the press's marketing coordinator.

As Duke Ellington would say to all the people mentioned in these acknowledgments: "You are too kind."

# BIBLIOGRAPHY

Abdul-Jabbar, Kareem. *Coach Wooden and Me: Our 50-Year Friendship On and Off the Court*. New York: Grand Central, 2017.

Adam, Peter. *Art of the Third Reich*. New York: Harry N. Abrams, 1995.

Anderson, Monroe. "The Young Black Man." *Ebony*, August 1972, 128–33.

Anonymous. "Louis Armstrong: The Reluctant Millionaire." *Ebony*, November 1964, 136–46.

Arnwine, Bridget. "The Beautiful Struggle: A Look at Women Who Have Helped Shape the DC Jazz Scene." In *DC Jazz: Stories of Jazz Music in Washington, DC*, edited by Maurice Jackson and Blair A. Ruble, 117–28. Washington, DC: Georgetown University Press, 2018.

Arsenault, Raymond. *Arthur Ashe: A Life*. New York: Simon & Schuster, 2018.

———. *The Sound of Freedom: Marian Anderson, the Lincoln Memorial, and the Concert that Awakened America*. New York: Bloomsbury, 2009.

Ashe, Arthur, and Arnold Rampersad. *Days of Grace: A Memoir*. New York: Ballantine, 1994.

———. *A Hard Road to Glory: A History of the African American Athlete*. 3 vols, vol. 1: 1619–1918; vol. 2: 1919–1945; vol. 3: 1946–Present. New York: Amistad, 1993.

Badger, Reid. *A Life in Ragtime: A Biography of James Reese Europe*. New York: Oxford University Press, 1995.

Baldwin, Kate. *Beyond the Color Line and the Iron Curtain: Reading Encounters Between Black and Red, 1922–1963*. Durham, NC: Duke University Press, 2002.

Baraka, Amiri (Leroi Jones). *Blues People: Negro Music in White America*. New York: Harper Perennial, 2002.

Barlow, William. *Looking Up at Down: The Emergence of Blues Culture*. Philadelphia: Temple University Press, 1989.

Baylor, Elgin, with Alan Eisenstock. *Hang Time: My Life in Basketball*. New York: Houghton Mifflin, 2018.

Benson, Michael. *Ballparks of North America: A Comprehensive Historical Reference to Baseball Grounds, Yards, and Stadiums, 1845–Present*. Jefferson, NC: McFarland, 1989.

"Bisons Kick Their Way to Top." *Ebony*, December 1971, 141–52.

Blackburn, Julia. *With Billie: A New Look at the Unforgettable Lady Day*. New York: Vintage, 2005.

Blackman, Arthur, Ken Freidus, David Robinson, and Florence Shelton. "An Interview with Topper Carew." *Harvard Educational Review* 39, no. 4 (December 1969): 98–115.

Blight, David W. *Frederick Douglass: Prophet of Freedom*, New York: Simon & Schuster, 2018.

Boyd, Herb. *Black Detroit: A People's History of Self-Determination*. New York: Amistad, 2017.

Brothers, Thomas. *Louis Armstrong's New Orleans*. New York: W. W. Norton, 2006.

Brown, Ashley. *Serving Herself: The Life and Times of Althea Gibson*. New York: Oxford University Press, 2023.

Buckley, Gail. *American Patriots: The Story of Blacks in the Military from the Revolution to Desert Storm*. Foreword by David Halberstam. New York: Random House, 2001.

Burgos, Adrian, Jr. *Cuban Star: How One Negro-League Owner Changed the Face of Baseball*. New York: Hill and Wang, 2011.

Carlson, Chad. "'The Greatest High School Basketball Game Ever Played': DeMatha vs. Power Memorial, 1965." In *DC Sports: The Nation's Capital at Play*, edited by Chris Elzey and David K. Wiggins, 129–46. Fayetteville: University of Arkansas Press, 2015.

Carter, Arthur. "Black Baseball in Washington." In *Rounding Third: Professional Baseball in Washington*, edited by Brian Price et al., 25–30. Washington DC: National Trust for Historic Preservation, 1979.

Carter, Marva Griffin. *Swing Along: The Musical Life of Will Marion Cook*. New York: Oxford University Press, 2008.

Celenza, Anna Harwell. "Legislating Jazz." In *DC Jazz: Stories of Jazz Music in Washington, DC*, edited by Maurice Jackson and Blair Ruble, 107–16. Washington, DC: Georgetown University Press, 2018.

Clarke, Catherine K. "Conversations with William (Billy) Taylor." *Black Perspective in Music* 10, no. 2 (1982).

Cohen, Harvey G. "Duke Ellington and *Black, Brown and Beige*: The Composer as Historian at Carnegie Hall." *American Quarterly* 56, no. 4 (Winter 2004): 1003–34.

———. *Duke Ellington's America*. Chicago: University of Chicago Press, 2010.

Collier, James Lincoln. *Duke Ellington*. New York: Oxford University Press, 1987.

Collins, Ann V. *All Hell Broke Loose: American Race Riots from the Progressive Eras through World War II*. Santa Barbara, CA: Praeger, 2012.

Conover, Willis. "Willis Conover." *Music USA Newsletter* 4, no. 3 (1968).

Coursey, Leon. "The Life of Edwin Bancroft Henderson and His Professional Contribution to Physical Education." PhD diss., Ohio State University, 1971.

Dabney, Ford. "Ford Dabney." In *Harlem Renaissance Lives from the African National Biography*, edited by Henry Louis Gates and Evelyn Higginbotham. New York: Oxford University Press, 2009.

Dance, Stanley. *The World of Duke Ellington*. New York: Scribner's, 1970.

Davenport, Lisa. *Jazz Diplomacy: Promoting America in the Cold War Era*. Jackson: University Press of Mississippi, 2009.

De Ferrari, John. *Historic Restaurants of Washington, D.C.* Charleston: History Press, 201.

Douglass, Frederick. *The Life and Times of Frederick Douglass*. Mineola, NY: Dover, 2003 [1881].

———. *The Life and Writings of Frederick Douglas, Volume 3, The Civil War*. Edited by Phillip S. Foner. New York: International, 2021.

———. *Narrative of the Life of Frederick Douglass, An American Slave, Written by Himself*. Edited and with an introduction by Houston A. Baker Jr. New York: Penguin, 1982.

Dubois, Laurent. *The Language of the Game: How to Understand Soccer*. New York: Basic, 2018.

Du Bois, W. E. B. *Darkwater: Voices from Within the Veil*. New York: Schocken, 1969.

———. *Dusk of Dawn: An Essay Toward An Autobiography of a Race Concept*. New York: Harper Brace and World, 1940.

———. "Returning Soldiers." *The Crisis* 18 (May 1919): 13–14.

———. *The Souls of Black Folk*. Greenwich, CT: Fawcett, 1961.

Dyson, Michael Eric. "For the Culture." *Slam Magazine*, July 13, 2016.

———. "Howard University, the Capstone of Negro Education: A History, 1867–1940." PhD diss., Howard University, 1941.

———. *Mercy, Mercy Me: The Art, Loves and Demons of Marvin Gaye*. New York: Basic Civitas, 2004.

Ellington, Duke. "The Duke Steps Out." In *The Duke Ellington Reader*, edited by Mark Tucker, 46–49. New York: Oxford University Press, 1993. The 1965 recording is cited.

———. *Music Is My Mistress*. New York: Da Capo, 1973.

———. "The Race for Space." In *The Duke Ellington Reader*, edited by Mark Tucker, 293–96. New York: Oxford University Press, 1993.

Ellington, Mercer, with Stanley Dance. *Duke Ellington in Person: An Intimate Memoir*. New York: Da Capo, 1979 [1978].

Elzey, Chris, and David K. Wiggins, eds. *DC Sports: The Nation's Capital at Play*. Fayetteville: University of Arkansas Press, 2015.

Ertegun, Ahmet, with Greil Marcus, Nat Hentoff, Lenny Kaye, Robert Gordon, Robert Christgau, Vince Aletti, Will Friedwald, David Fricke, and Barney Hoskyns. *"What'd I Say": The Atlantic Story, 50 Years of Music*. New York: Welcome Rain, 2001.

Europe, James Reese. "A Negro Explains Jazz." In *Readings in Black American Music*, 2nd ed., edited by Eileen Southern, 28–29. New York. W. W. Norton, 1983. Originally published in *Literary Digest*, April 26, 1919.

Faine, Edward Allan. *Duke Ellington at the White House 1969*. Takoma Park, MD: IM, 2013.

Ferguson, Blanche E. *Countee Cullen and the Negro Renaissance*. New York: Apollo, 1966.

Fitzgerald, Michael. "Researching Jazz History in Washington, DC." In *DC Jazz: Stories of Jazz Music in Washington, DC*, edited by Maurice Jackson and Blair Ruble, 170–82. Washington, DC: Georgetown University Press, 2018.

Fleming, Peggy, ed. *Crown Me!* Foreword by Maurice Jackson. Washington, DC: Three Sisters, 2010.

Floyd, Samuel A., Jr., ed. *Black Music in the Harlem Renaissance: A Collection of Essays*. Knoxville: University of Tennessee Press, 1990.

Foer, Franklin. *How Soccer Explains the World: An Unlikely Theory of Globalization*. New York: Harper Collins, 2004.

Frommer, Frederic J. *The Washington Nationals 1859 to Today*. Lanham, MD: Taylor, 2006.

Gardner, Bettye, and Betty Thomas. "The Cultural Impact of the Howard Theatre on the Black Community." *Journal of Negro History* 55 (1970): 253–55.

Gates, Henry Louis, Jr., and Evelyn Brooks Higginbotham, eds. *African American Lives*. Oxford: Oxford University Press, 2004.

Gates, Henry Louis, Jr., and Valerie A. Smith, gen. eds. *The Norton Anthology of African American* Literature. Vol. 2. 3rd ed. New York: W. W. Norton, 2014.

Gatewood, Willard B. *Aristocrats of Color: The Black Elite, 1880–1920*. Bloomington: Indiana University Press, 1993.

Giddings, Gary. *Bing Crosby: A Pocketful of Dreams—The Early Years, 1903–1940*. New York: Back Bay, 2002.

———. *Satchmo*. New York: Doubleday, 1988.

Gilbert, Bil. "The Gospel According to John." *Sports Illustrated*, December 1, 1980.

Gillespie, Dizzy, with Al Fraser. *To Be or Not to Bop: The Autobiography of Dizzy Gillespie*. New York: Doubleday, 1979.

Godshalk, David Fort. *Veiled Visions: The 1906 Atlanta Race Riot and the Reshaping of American Race Relations*. Chapel Hill: University of North Carolina Press, 2005.

Green, Constance McLaughlin. *The Secret City: A History of Race Relations in the Nation's Capital*. Princeton, NJ: Princeton University Press, 1993.

Green, Edward, ed. *The Cambridge Companion to Duke Ellington*. Cambridge: Cambridge University Press, 2015.

Greenfield, Robert. *The Last Sultan: The Life and Times of Ahmet Ertegun*. New York: Simon & Schuster, 2011.

Greenidge, Kerri K. *Black Radical: The Life and Times of William Monroe*. New York: Liveright, 2020.

Griffith (Marshall), Corinne. *My Life with the Redskins*. New York: Legare Street, 2022 [1947].

Harris, Stephen L. *Harlem's Hell Fighters: The African-American 369th Infantry in World War I*. Washington: Brassey's, 2003.

Hartley, James R. "Washington Baseball Fans: Losers No More." In *DC Sports: The Nation's Capital at Play*, edited by Chris Elzey and David K. Wiggins, 285–302. Fayetteville: University of Arkansas Press, 2015.

Hassan, Rusty. "Jazz Radio in Washington: A Personal Retrospective." *Washington History* 26 (2014): 74–87.

———. "Jazz Radio in Washington, DC." In *DC Jazz: Stories of Jazz Music in Washington, DC*, edited by Maurice Jackson and Blair Ruble, 91–106. Washington, DC: Georgetown University Press, 2018.

Hasse, John Edward. *Beyond Category: The Life and Genius of Duke Ellington*. New York: Simon & Schuster, 1993.

———. "David Baker and the Smithsonian: A Personal Perspective." In *David Baker: A Legacy in Music*, edited by Monika Herzig, 230–87. Bloomington: Indiana University Press, 2011.

———. "The Swinging Scions: How the Turkish Ambassador's Sons Jazzed Washington and the Nation." In *The Turkish Ambassador's Residence and the Cultural History of Washington, DC*, edited by Skip Moskey, Caroline Mesrobian Hickman, and John Edward Hasse, 94–130. Istanbul, Turkey: Istanbul Kültür University, 2013.

———. "Washington's Duke Ellington." In *DC Jazz: Stories of Jazz Music in Washington, DC*, edited by Maurice Jackson and Blair A. Ruble, 47–74. Washington, DC: Georgetown University Press, 2018.

Henderson, Edwin B., II. *The Grandfather of Black Basketball: The Life and Times of Dr. E. B. Henderson*. Lanham, MD: Rowman & Littlefield, 2024.

———. *The Negro in Sports*. 3rd ed. Edited by Daryl Michael Scott. Washington, DC: ASALH Press, 2014 [1939].

Henderson, Edwin B., and William A. Joiner, eds. *Spaulding Handbook History of Inter-Scholastic Athletic Association of Middle Atlantic States*. New York: American Sports Publishing, 1910.

Herzig, Monika, ed. *David Baker: A Legacy in Music*. Bloomington: Indiana University Press, 2011.

Hill, Robert, and Barbara Bair, eds. *The Marcus Garvey and Universal Negro Improvement Association Papers, Vol. 7, November 1927–August 1940*. Berkeley: University of California Press, 1990.

"History of the Treble Clef Club, Founded 1897." Gregoria A. Goins Collection, Moorland Spingarn, Howard University, box 36-15, folder 149.

Holmes, T. "Sweet Sounds of Success: The Department of Music Celebrates 100 Years of Musical Genius." *Howard Magazine* 22, no. 3 (Summer 2014): 12–17.

Howe, S. W. *Women Music Educators in the United States: A History*. Lanham, MD: Scarecrow, 2014 [1938].

Hubler, David E., and Joshua H. Drazen. *The Nats and the Grays: How Baseball in the Nation's Capital Survived WWII and Changed the Game Forever*. Lanham, MD: Rowman & Littlefield, 2015.

Hughes, Langston. "Our Wonderful Society: Washington." *Opportunity* 5 (August 1927): 226–27.

———. "Trouble with Angels: National Theater (1935)." In *D.C. Noir 2: The Classics,* edited by George Pelecanos, 45–52. Washington, DC: Akahashic, 2008.

Hundley, Mary G. *The Dunbar Story, 1870–1955.* New York: Vantage, 1965.

Jackson, Maurice. Foreword. In *Crown Me! Capital Pool Checkers Club.* Washington, DC: Three Sisters, 2010.

———. "No Man Could Hinder Him": Remembering Toussaint L'Ouverture and the Haitian Revolution." In *African Americans and the Haitian Revolution,* edited by Maurice Jackson and Jacqueline Bacon, 141–64. New York: Routledge, 2010.

Jackson, Maurice, and Jacqueline Bacon, eds. *African Americans and the Haitian Revolution: Selected Essays and Historical Documents.* New York: Routledge, 2010.

Jackson, Maurice, and Blair Ruble, eds. *DC Jazz: Stories of Jazz Music in Washington, DC.* Washington, DC: Georgetown University Press, 2018.

Jacobs, Sally H. *Althea: The Life and Times of Tennis Champion Althea Gibson.* New York: St. Martin's, 2023.

James, C. L. R. *Beyond a Boundary.* Durham, NC: Duke University Press, 2013.

Jenkins, Willard. "Bill Brower: Notes from a Keen Observer and Scene Maker." In *DC Jazz: Stories of Jazz Music in Washington, DC,* edited by Maurice Jackson and Blair Ruble, 75–90. Washington, DC: Georgetown University Press, 2018.

Johnson, Claude. *The Black Fives: The Epic Story of Basketball's Forgotten Era.* New York: Abrams, 2021.

Johnson, James Weldon. "The Washington Rits: An N.A.A.C.P. Investigation." *The Crisis* (1919).

Johnson, Thomas R. "The City on a Hill: Race Relations in Washington D.C., 1865–1885." PhD diss., University of Maryland, 1975.

Jones, Quincy. *Q: The Autobiography of Quincy Jones.* New York: Random House, 2001.

Joseph, Peniel E. *Stokely: A Life.* New York: Basic Civitas, 2014.

Kerlin, Tobert Thomas. *The Voice of the Negro: 1919.* Whitefish, MT: Kessinger, 2010.

Kimball, Robert, and William Bolcom. *Reminiscing with Sissle and Black.* New York: Viking, 1973.

King, Gilbert. "What Paul Robeson Said." *Smithsonian Magazine,* September 13, 2011 https://www.smithsonianmag.com/history/what-paul-robeson-said-77742433/.

Kirk, Elsie K. *Musical Highlights from the White House.* Malabar, FL: Krieger, 1992.

Kirshenbaum, Jerry. "Paul Robeson, Remaking a Fallen Hero." *Sports Illustrated,* March 27, 1972.

Korey, Judith. "From Federal City College to UDC: A Retrospective on Washington's Jazz University." In *DC Jazz: Stories of Jazz Music in Washington, DC,* edited by Maurice Jackson and Blair Ruble, 145–70. Washington, DC: Georgetown University Press, 2018.

Krugler, David. F. *1919, The Year of Racial Violence: How African Americans Fought Back.* Illus. ed. Cambridge: Cambridge University Press, 2014.

Kuska, Bob. *Hot Potato: How Washington and New York Gave Birth to Black Basketball and Changed America's Game Forever.* Charlottesville: University of Virginia Press, 2004.

Lacy, Sam. "Campy, Jackie as Dodgers." In *The Unlevel Playing Field: A Documentary History of African American Experience in Sport,* edited by David K. Wiggins and Patrick B. Miller. Chicago: University of Illinois Press, 2003.

Laverno, Thom. *Hail Victory: An Oral History of the Washington Redskins.* Hoboken, NJ: John Wiley & Sons, 2006.

Lees, Gene. *Friends Along the Way: A Journey through Jazz.* New Haven, CT: Yale University Press, 2003.

Lesko, Kathleen Menzie, Valerie M. Babb, and Carroll R. Gibbs, eds. *Black Georgetown Remembered: A History of Its Black Community from the Founding of "The Town of George" in 1775 to the Present Day.* 25th Anniv. ed. Washington, DC: Georgetown University Press, 2016.

Levine, Lawrence W. *Black Culture and Black Consciousness.* New York: Oxford University Press, 1977.

Lewis, David Levering. *W. E. B. Du Bois: Biography of a Race, 1868–1919.* New York: Henry Holt, 1993.

———. *When Harlem Was in Vogue.* New York: Penguin, 1979.

Lewis, George E. *A Power Stronger Than Itself: The AACM and American Experimental Music.* Chicago: University of Chicago Press, 2008.

Lightman, Marjorie, and William Zeisel. *Since 1851: 160 Years of Scholarship and Achievement in the Nation's Capital.* Washington, DC: University of the District of Columbia Press, 2011.

Locke, Alain, ed. *The New Negro: An Interpretation.* New York: Albert & Charles Bonni, 1925.

Logan, Rayford Whittingham. *The Diplomatic Relations of the United States with Haiti, 1778–1841.* Chapel Hill: University of North Carolina Press, 1941.

Lomax, Alan. *Mister Jelly Roll: The Fortunes of Jelly Roll Morton, New Orleans Creole and "Inventor of Jazz."* New York: Pantheon, 1950.

Luker, Ralph E. "Missions, Institutional Churches, and Settlement Houses: The Black Experience, 1885–1910." *Journal of African American History* 69, no. 3–4 (Summer–Fall 1984): 101–13.

Luxenberg, Steve. *Separate: The Story of "Plessey v. Ferguson," and America's Journey from Slavery to Segregation.* New York: W. W. Norton, 2019.

"The Lynching Industry, 1919." *The Crisis* 19, no. 4 (February 1920): 183–86.

Lyons, Shante J. "The Making of a Black Community Educator: Doxie A. Wilkerson, 1922–1943." *Vitae Scholasticae* 32, no. 2 (2015): 19–31.

Mack, Kenneth. *Representing the Race: The Creation of the Civil Rights Lawyer.* Cambridge, MA: Harvard University Press, 2013.

Manley, Michael. *History of West Indian Cricket.* Rev. ed. London: Carlton, 1988.

Margolick, David. *Strange Fruit: Café Society and the Early Cry for Civil Rights.* Philadelphia: Running Press, 2000.

Maurer, Pablo. "When Pele Visited Howard University's Soccer Team: 'He Transcended Everything.'" *Atlantic*, February 16, 2023.

McDonald, Scott. "Washington Redskins Urged to Lose Name, Pour Millions in Sponsorship." *Newsweek*, July 1, 2022. https://www.newsweek.com/washington -redskins-urged-lose-name-millions-sponsorships-1514894.

McGinty, Doris E. "The Black Presence in the Music of Washington, D.C.: 1843–1904." In *More than Dancing: Essays on Afro-American Music and Musicians*, edited by Irene V. Jackson, 81–106. Westport, CT: Praeger, 1985.

———. "Gifted Minds and Pure Hearts: Mary L. Europe and Estelle Pinckney Webster." *Journal of Negro Education* 51, no. 3 (1982): 266–77.

———. "'That You Came So Far to See Us': Coleridge-Taylor in America." *Black Music Research Journal* 21 (2001): 197–234.

———. "The Washington Conservatory of Music and School of Expression." *The Black Perspective in Music* 7 (1979): 59–74.

McKay, Claude. "If We Must Die." *Liberator* 2 (July 1919): 21.

———. "Soviet Russia and the Negro." *The Crisis* 26, no. 8 (December 1923): 61–65.

———. "The Void." *The Crisis* 27, no. 5 (June 1924): 116–18.

McNamara, John, with Andrea Chamblee and David Elfin. *The Capital of Basketball: A History of DC Area High School Hoops*. Washington, DC: Georgetown University Press, 2019.

McQuirter, Marya Annette. "Claiming the City: African Americans, Urbanization, and Leisure in Washington, D.C., 1902–1957." PhD diss., University of Michigan, 2000.

Miller, Carroll L. L., and Anne S. Pruit-Logan. *The Life of Lucy Diggs Slowe: Faithful to the Tasks at Hand*. Albany: State University of New York Press, 2012.

Miller, E. Ethelbert. "Sterling Brown and the Browning of My Life." *Black Renaissance Noire*, April 30, 2014.

Miller, Leta. *Union Divided: Black Musicians Fight for Labor Equality*. Urbana: University of Illinois Press, 2024.

Miller, Patrick B., and David K. Wiggins. *Sport and the Color Line: Black Athletes and Race Relations in Twentieth-Century America*. New York: Routledge, 2004.

Moore, Jacqueline Moore. *Leading the Race: The Transformation of the Black Elite in the Nation's Capital, 1880–1920*. Charlottesville: University of Virginia Press, 1999.

Moran, Jason. Foreword. In *DC Jazz: Stories of Jazz Music in Washington, DC*, edited by Maurice Jackson and Blair Ruble, xi–xiii. Washington, DC: Georgetown University Press, 2018.

Moskey, Skip, Caroline Mesrobian Hickman, and John Edward Hasse. *The Turkish Ambassador's Residence and the Cultural History of Washington, DC*. Istanbul, Turkey: Istanbul Kültür University, 2013.

Munson, Ingrid. *Freedom Sounds: Civil Rights Call Out to Jazz and Africa*. New York: Harvard University Press, 2007.

Murphy, Mary-Elizabeth B. *Jim Crow Capital: Women and Black Freedom Struggles in Washington, D.C., 1920–1945*. Durham: University of North Carolina Press, 2018.

Nolan, Tom. *Artie Shaw, King of the Clarinet: His Life and Times.* New York: W. W. Norton, 2011.

O'Toole, Andrew. *Fight for Old DC: George Preston Marshall, the Integration of the Washington Redskins, and the Rise of the New NFL.* Lincoln: University of Nebraska Press, 2016.

Pelecanos, George, ed. *D.C. Noir 2: The Classics.* Washington, DC: Akahashic, 2008.

Peress, Maurice. *Dvořák to Duke Ellington: A Conductor Explores America's Music and Its African American Roots.* New York: Oxford University Press, 2004.

Peretti, Burton W. *Lift Every Voice: The History of African American Music.* Lanham, MD: Rowman & Littlefield, 2009.

Peterson, Robert. *Only the Ball Was White: A History of Legendary Black Players and All-Black Professional Teams.* Oxford: Oxford University Press, 1970.

Phillips, Lincoln A. *Rising Above and Beyond the Crossbar: The Life Story of Lincoln "Tiger" Phillips.* Bloomington, IN: Author House, 2014.

Porter, Thomas J. "The Social Roots of African American Music." *Freedomways* (3rd quarter 1971).

Povich, Shirley. *The Washington Senators.* New York: G. P. Putnam's Sons, 1954.

Price, Brian, George W. Hilton, Gregory Kallen, and Arthur Carter, eds. *Rounding Third: Professional Baseball in Washington.* Washington DC: National Trust for Historic Preservation, 1979.

Rediker, Marcus. *The Amistad Rebellion: An Atlantic Odyssey of Slavery and Freedom.* New York: Viking, 2012.

Ribowsky, Mark. *A Complete History of the Negro Leagues: 1884 to 1955.* New York: Birch Lane, 1995.

Robinson, Randall. *The Reckoning.* New York: Plume, 2002.

Rojas, Aurelio. "The Private Funeral for Soul Singer Marvin Gaye Today." UPI Archives, April 5, 1984.

Rolf, Julia, ed. *The Definitive Illustrated Encyclopedia of Jazz and Blues.* London: Star Fire, 2007.

Ross, Charles K. *Outside the Lines: African Americans and the Integration of the National Football League.* New York: New York University Press, 1999.

Rubio, Philip F. *There's Always Work at the Post Office.* Chapel Hill: University of North Carolina Press, 2010.

Ruble, Blair A. *Washington's U Street: A Biography.* Washington: Woodrow Wilson Center Press and Johns Hopkins University Press, 2010.

Sandage, Scott. "A Marble House Divided: The Lincoln Memorial, the Civil Rights Movement, and the Politics of Memory." *Journal of American History* 80, no. 1 (June 1993): 135–67.

Sartre, Jean-Paul. *Critique of Dialectical Reason.* Vol. 1. Translated by Alan Sheridan-Smith. London: Verso, 2004.

"Satch Blasts Echoed by Top Performers: Nixes Tour, Raps Ike and Faubus." *Chicago Defender* 53 (September 28, 1957).

Schmalenberger, S. "The Washington Conservatory of Music and African-American Musical Experience, 1903–1941." PhD diss., University of Minnesota, 2004.

Schweninger, Loren. *Black Property Owners in the South, 1790–1915.* Urbana: University of Illinois Press, 1990.

Scott, Emmett J. *Official History of the American Negro in the World War.* New York: Arno, 1969 [1919].

Scott-Heron, Gil. *The Last Holiday: A Memoir.* New York: Grove, 2012.

Shapiro, Leonard. *Big Man on Campus: John Thompson and the Georgetown Hoyas.* New York: Henry Holt, 1991.

Sims, M. "Benny Golson." *Howard Magazine* 22, no. 3 (Summer 2014).

Sinclair, Lauren. "No Church Without a Choir." In *DC Jazz: Stories of Jazz Music in Washington, DC,* edited by Maurice Jackson and Blair Ruble, 129–43. Washington, DC: Georgetown University Press, 2018.

Smith, Eric Ledell. "Lillian Evanti: Washington's African-American Diva." *Washington History* 11, no. 1 (Spring–Summer, 1999): 24–43.

Smith, Thomas G. "Civil Rights on the Gridiron: The Kennedy Administration and the Desegregation of the Washington Redskins." *Journal of Sport History* 14, no. 2 (Summer 1987): 1–90.

———. *Showdown: JFK and the Integration of the Washington Redskins.* New York: Beacon, 2011.

Snyder, Brad. *Beyond the Shadow of the Senators: The Untold Story of the Homestead Grays and the Integration of Baseball.* Chicago: Contemporary, 2003.

Southern, Eileen. *The Music of Black Americans: A History.* 3rd ed. New York: W. W. Norton, 1997.

———, ed. *Readings in Black American Music.* New York: W. W. Norton, 1983.

Spellman, A. B. *Four Jazz Lives.* With a new introduction by the author. New York: Random House, 1966. Originally published as *Four Lives in the Bebop Business.*

Stewart, Alison. *First Class: The Legacy of Dunbar, America's First Black Public High School.* New York: Lawrence Hill, 2013.

Stokes, W. Royal. *Growing Up with Jazz: Twenty-Four Musicians Talk about Their Lives and Careers.* New York: Oxford University Press, 2005.

Swanson, Ryan A. "Less Than Monumental: The Sad History of Sports Venues in Washington, DC." In *DC Sports: The Nation's Capital at Play,* edited by Chris Elzey and David K. Wiggins, 19–36. Fayetteville: University of Arkansas Press, 2015.

———. *When Baseball Went White: Reconstruction, Reconciliation, and Dreams of a National Pastime.* Lincoln: University of Nebraska Press, 2014.

Szwed, John. *Alan Lomax: The Man Who Recorded the World.* New York: Penguin, 2010.

Taylor, Billy, with Teresa L. Reed. *The Jazz Life of Dr. Billy Taylor.* Bloomington: Indiana University Press, 2013.

Teachout, Terry. *Duke: The Life of Duke Ellington.* New York: Gotham, 2013.

———. *Pops: A Life of Louis Armstrong.* New York: Houghton Mifflin Harcourt, 2009.

Terrell, Mary Church. "History of High School for Negroes in Washington." *Journal of Negro History* 2, no. 3 (1917): 252–57.

Thompson, John, with Jesse Washington. *I Came as a Shadow: An Autobiography*. New York: Henry Holt, 2020.

Timner, W. E. *Ellingtonia: The Recorded Music of Duke Ellington and His Sidemen*. 5th ed. Lanham, MD: Scarecrow, 2000.

Trotter, James M. *Music and Some Highly Musical People*. New York: Johnson, 1968 [1878].

Tucker, Mark. *Ellington: The Early Years*. Urbana: University of Illinois Press, 1995.

———. "The Renaissance Education of Duke Ellington." In *Black Music in the Harlem Renaissance: A Collection of Essays*, edited by Samuel A. Floyd Jr., chap. 7. Knoxville: University of Tennessee Press, 1990.

Tupper, Zack. "Georgetown Basketball in Reagan's America." In *DC Sports: The Nation's Capital at Play*, edited by Chris Elzey and David K. Wiggins, 267–84. Fayetteville: University of Arkansas Press, 2015.

Tygiel, Jules, ed. "Jackie Robinson: 'A Lone Negro' in Major League Baseball." In *Sport and the Color Line: Black Athletes and Race Relations in Twentieth Century America*, edited by David K. Wiggins and Patrick B. Miller, 167–89. New York: Routledge, 2004.

———. *The Jackie Robinson Reader: Perspectives on An American Hero*. New York: Dutton, 1997.

Ulanov, Barry. *Duke Ellington*. New York: Da Capo, 1975 [1946].

Vail, Ken. *Duke's Diary: The Life of Duke Ellington, 1927–1950*. 2 vols. Lanham, MD: Scarecrow, 2002.

Valk, Anne M. *Radical Sisters: Second-Wave Feminism and Black Liberation in Washington, D.C.* Urbana: University of Illinois Press, 2008.

Von Eschen, Penny M. *Satchmo Blows Up the World: Jazz Ambassadors Play the Cold War*. Cambridge, MA: Harvard University Press, 2004.

Wade, Dorothy, and Justine Picardie. *Music Man: Ahmet Ertegun, Atlantic Records, and the Triumph of Rock'N'Roll*. New York: W. W. Norton, 1990.

Walker, George. *Reminiscences of an American Composer and Pianist*. Lanham, MD: Scarecrow, 2009.

Walker, Stephen J. "Uniting a Divided City: The 1969 Washington Senators." In *DC Sports: The Nation's Capital at Play*, edited by Chris Elzey and David K. Wiggins, 165–84. Fayetteville: University of Arkansas Press, 2015.

Ward, Geoffrey C. *Unforgivable Blackness, The Rise and Fall of Jack Johnson*. New York: Alfred C. Knopf, 2004.

Ward, Geoffrey C., and Ken Burns. *Jazz: A History of America's Music*. New York: Alfred A. Knopf, 2000.

Wiggins, David K., and Patrick B. Miller. *The Unlevel Playing Field: A Documentary History of the African American Experience in Sport*. Chicago: University of Illinois Press, 2003.

Williams, Edward Christopher. *When Washington Was in Vogue: A Lost Novel of the Harlem Renaissance*. Introduction by Adam McKibble. New York: Amistad, 2004.

# INDEX

Note: Illustrations are indicated by page numbers in *italics*.

# ABOUT THE AUTHOR

Maurice Jackson teaches in the History and African American Studies departments and is an affiliated professor of music (jazz) at Georgetown University. Before coming to academe, Jackson worked as a longshoreman, shipyard rigger, construction worker, and community organizer. He is author of *Let This Voice Be Heard: Anthony Benezet, Father of Atlantic Abolitionism* and *DC Jazz: Stories of Jazz Music in Washington, DC* (with Blair Ruble) and is the coeditor of *African-Americans and the Haitian Revolution* and *Quakers and Their Allies in the Abolitionist Cause, 1754–1808*. Jackson wrote the liner notes to Charlie Haden and Hank Jones's jazz CDs *Steal Away: Spirituals, Hymns, and Folk Songs* and *Come Sunday*. He has recently lectured in Egypt, France, Turkey, Italy, Puerto Rico, the Dominican Republic, and Qatar. He served on the Georgetown University Slavery Working Group. An inductee into the Washington, DC, Hall of Fame, he was appointed by the mayor and the city council as inaugural chair of the DC Commission on African American Affairs and presented a comprehensive report to city leaders titled "An Analysis: African American Employment, Population and Housing Trends in Washington, D.C." Jackson is also on the faculty of the Georgetown Qatar campus, where he is currently working with scholars on a volume on slavery in the Indian Ocean. Jackson is currently working on completion of *Halfway to Freedom: The Struggles and Strivings of Black Folk in Washington, DC.*